The WHICH KIT? GUIDE TO
KIT CAR BUILDING

First published as *How To Build A Kit Car* in 1993
Second Edition 1995
Third Edition comprehensively revised and re-titled in 1996, published by
Blueprint Books Ltd, 1 Howard Road, Reigate, Surrey RH2 7JE

ISBN 1-899814-15-9

Editor: Ian Stent
Computer graphics: Apec Graphics, Reigate
Printed by: Grapevine Print and Marketing Ltd
COVER: Dax Rush V8 with Domino Pimlico in background
Photograph by Ian Stent

About the Authors...

Monty Watkins is one of the great individuals amongst motoring journalists, a man blessed with cutting wit and a sharp ability for technical assessment. Initiated into auto writing on *Which Kit?* magazine, where he became editor, he moved on to be editor with *Fast Ford* magazine before moving to take the helm at *Mini World* magazine.

Longstanding editor of *Which Kit?* magazine, Ian Stent has driven and written about almost every kit car produced over the last six years or so. Builder of a Sylva Striker, he has also spent some three years constructing a Transformer HF2000 Lancia Stratos replica and has kept a close watch on all the *Which Kit?* in-house builds.

CONTENTS

INTRODUCTION

THOSE OF YOU TAKING THE plunge and buying yourself a copy of *The Which Kit? Guide To Kit Car Building* have obviously moved on from the initial inquisitiveness that brings many into the kit car scene. The chances are you've already got a pretty good knowledge of the cars on offer and the models that really take your fancy. But the step from innocent onlooker to hardened kit car builder is a big one that few people take lightly. Not only is such a move going to require no small amount of money, but it's also going to stretch your technical skills too. Maintaining an old and decrepit classic is one thing, building a car from the ground up quite another.

The Which Kit? Guide To Kit Car Building aims to not only show you how to build the kit you want, but also choose the right project and make sure you have the correct tools and facilities to do the job properly. After reading some of this book you may even decide that kit building isn't for you, or that you'll delay building a project until you have more suitable premises in which to put it together. You may even decide that getting someone else to do the dirty work for you is a better

route to take or that buying a project second-hand may be a more affordable path to kit car ownership.

We make no apologies if this book puts you off building a kit car. There's no black satanic art to kit car building, but neither is it something you should tackle without some idea of what you're getting into. A lack of anywhere suitable to build a kit, just not quite enough cash to complete your project or simply poor motivation are all quite justifiable reasons for knocking the idea on the head and saving yourself loads of agro and heartache. Dedication is perhaps the best weapon you have in your armoury and there will be many times when you need to draw heavily on it, sometimes even with the most simple of projects.

But let's not terrify you before you even get into the first chapter! The rewards for putting together a complete car, or even a certain part of that car, can be enormous. As a particular section of the build falls into place, the feeling a satisfaction is immense and, for some, even more rewarding than driving the finished article! But for most of us, it's the thrill of taking your car, the car you've spent perhaps a

Above: Throughout a kit car build project, and indeed once your car is on the road, the relevant kit car owners' club will prove invaluable. Especially if you are tackling something like this Countach replica (below)!

year putting together, out onto the road that fills us with the greatest joy. Kit building is still an exclusive club and only once you've joined its members can you fully appreciate the thrill.

In setting out this book, one obviously has to set certain limitations. *The Which Kit? Guide To Kit Car Building* doesn't try to cover any work outlined in excellent technical tomes such as the typical *Haynes Workshop Manuals* many of you will be familiar with. In fact, such is the vast array of skills you'll require during a typical kit car build (from stripping down a donor car to trimming a dashboard with leather) that we can only give the broadest of guidelines to certain areas. However, what we can impart is the experience and technical tips gained from no less than fifteen in-house build-up projects featured within the pages of *Which Kit?* magazine.

Whether it's

the basics of working out what your chosen kit is going to cost you or where you can find a certain widget to fix a particular problem, this book should be able to point you in the right direction. We've started pretty much at the beginning and taken you on through what should be a

typical build format – starting with the donor and ending with final suspension adjustments and other on-road tweaks to get the best from your completed project.

In setting a standard, we've always headed for the ideal, so you may well find that in some areas we may have gone slightly OTT with the tools you'll require in the garage or the levels to which you should go in finishing a particular job. Don't be too put off and do the best you can.

Before your project is even on its wheels, one of the most valuable contacts you can make is with a relevant owners' club. These are invariably filled with like-minded enthusiasts who

Company open days are proving increasingly popular these days. A few owners' cars are usually on show as well as the manufacturer's demonstrator, so it makes for a great opportunity to really get a feel for the company and its cars.

Kit cars come in all shapes and sizes and with vastly different build-up times. Most will recognise this Caterham. It was build by the Which Kit? team in just seven days!

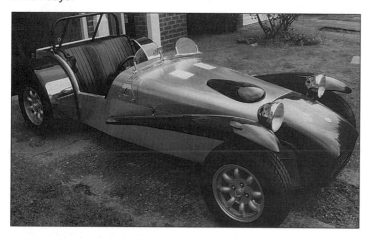

little operations run on a shoestring and, on occasion, they may provide just as good a service as the big boys. In other cases they can fall well short, so be very careful if you find yourself heading in this direction.

But clearly the mainstream section of the kit car biz is a very much more professional organisation than we've ever seen before. Organisations such as STATUS have helped move things in this positive direction while manufacturer organised groups such as the ASCM (Association of Specialist Car Manufacturers) continue the theme and promise ever increasing standards for their customers. It's no small wonder that the mainstream motoring press is taking an increasingly interested view of this previously unknown scene.

The other area where *Which Kit?* has managed to keep up with developments has been in

the area of registration and other legal aspects of kit car ownership. The way in which a completed kit car is registered is in the process of changing as this book goes to press and we've tried to summarise the new changes as best we can with the limited information currently available. Keep an eye on *Which Kit?* monthly for any further developments in this area.

The Which Kit? Guide To Kit Car Building is the latest version of Monty Watkins original book, *How To Build A Kit Car*, and whilst we've been through his original written copy and updated it where necessary, it is still very much his careful and meticulous writing skills and knowledge that endow this latest version with its real hands-on feel. Our thanks go to him for his excellent work and also to all the various companies who supplied information included within it.

We hope you find it as useful as the several thousand readers who have already bought copies before you. We hope it inspires you to build the car of your dreams, without overshooting your budget and in the comparative comfort of a well laid out and safe garage!

Ian Stent

have come across the problems you may face and will certainly have overcome them. Almost without question, the owners' club is the fount of all knowledge when it comes to your particular car and they will happily put you in touch with someone in your area who already has a car. When the head-scratching begins, and believe me it will, turning to a local enthusiast with another car can be a life-saver. Joining the owners' club should be your first port of call, almost before you even order your kit.

It's always pleasing to be able to report that the quality of cars we come across is ever increasing. *Which Kit?* magazine is at the very heart of the British kit car industry and as such we not only keep up with all the latest models but also see old established names updating their

products to keep pace with newer competition.

Which Kit? tends to concentrate on the mainstream of the kit car industry – these are the companies who actively promote their products, respond to customer feedback and generally present themselves in a professional manner. It's these companies that we can feel confident in recommending and it's these companies who sell 98% of the industry's cars. The final 2% are usually obscure

Whilst some project cam be completed in a relatively short period, this Transformer Stratos replica took Ian Stent some three years of steady construction. It looked totally amazing but perhaps it's not the ideal first time build project.

Chapter 1
DEFINITIONS

Section 1
What's the difference

BY THE TIME YOU'VE GOT this far, you'll probably have a pretty good idea that kit car building is no longer the exclusive territory of a tiny minority of gifted mechanics and racers. Thousands of amateur mechanics and car enthusiasts have already taken advantage of the numerous kits available in the UK which, in general terms, allow you to make a vehicle for yourself using parts from production cars along with specially produced bodies, chassis and peripherals.

The key requirements these days, apart from the budget, include enthusiasm, patience, diligence and the ability to understand and use the technical maintenance manuals (such as *Haynes*) dedicated to your kit car's donor vehicle (the production car on which many of the mechanical parts are based). Skills such as welding, turning,

milling and laminating are no longer needed to build the vast majority of kits.

This historic practice of amateur home car building has been catered for by the law in that builders of kit cars may register, MoT and insure such vehicles quite legally and with a minimum of fuss. In this way, several famous production car marques have emerged from an idea. Try TVR, Lotus and Ginetta for starters.

At the time of going to press (see Chapter 10), there is something called the 'amateur build exemption' which gives the home mechanic the legal right to construct a car, on an amateur basis, without having to undertake the expensive Type Approval process for that car. Type Approval, as some will know, is the rigorous testing procedure whereby commercial vehicle producers must prove that their products attain set standards. It's very expensive and is aimed primarily at the big

corporations who can easily afford it.

Amateur-built kit cars need not be crashed into blocks of concrete at 30mph, nor do all their components have to be given systematic part numbers etc. As long as the constructor is not building the car as his or her main business, for commercial gain, then the vehicle must comply with the requirements of the standard MoT test and any Construction and Use Regulations relevant to that vehicle's registration plate year.

In Chapter Ten, we'll be taking a look at the finer points of C&U, the forthomcing introduction of Single Vehicle Approval and we'll be explaining which kit cars have to comply with which laws. Generally speaking, the Construction and Use Regulations detail such things as design and safety considerations, position of car lights, emissions and general roadworthiness. They apply to all road vehicles but to a varying extent,

depending upon age and intended use. The ways in which they relate to kit cars are simple enough to grasp and to comply with.

Well over a hundred different kit car manufacturers, with premises ranging from large industrial units to small, dusty garages, offer specialist kits which will allow you to escape the dull homogeneity of modern motoring – on a favourable budget. Whether you're after outright performance, a replica of a classic, rugged all-weather reliability or other totally original designs, there's probably something to catch your eye.

Section 2
The most options

SO WHY WOULD SOMEONE buy a kit car? What are they for? What kinds of kit exist? The only broad generalisation about kit car types that is correct is that they can generally offer you what the

Kits come in all shapes and sizes. Something like this Fiesta based Quantum might prove an ideal first project for the budding kit car constructor. It's available as an open-top or coupe.

Supercars such as this amazing Ferrari P4 replica from NF Auto Development may be sensational performers but they use parts from all sorts of sources and are far more complex to build.

production car manufacturers either can't or won't without an amazing price tag. There are even exceptions to that rule, as kits such as the Ford-based front-wheel-drive Quantum and rear-drive Rickman Ranger are thoroughly practical modes of transport on a year-round basis.

down into sub-categories such as the superfast sprinters like the Caterham Seven, Westfield SE and SEi and a good number of similar 'Seven clones.'

There are also the replicas such as the Cobra 427 and 289 lookalikes from companies like DJ Sportscars, Pilgrim GRP,

THE WHICH KIT? TIP

Although an exotic mid-engined GT car may be your dream machine and you have the funds to undertake such a project, building a much more simple project, such as Lotus Seven replica, may be the wiser option. It'll give you some practice and show you whether you have the aptitude, patience etc for something far more complex

Probably the best-selling category of kit cars comes under the general heading of performance two-seater convertibles. This group splits

Hawk Cars, Gardner Douglas and Southern Roadcraft. It must be said that the word 'replica' very rarely denotes a car made from the actual jigs,

Top right: Caterham is a top quality kit with a straightforward build and lightning performance. Above: Marlin Cabrio provides a little more sedate travel while Grinnall is mid-engined motorbike mayhem.

patterns and moulds used for the original. In the kit car world, it is used to describe a lookalike car. The last sub-category includes the original designs from companies such as the Ronart Cars, Marlin Engineering, JBA Engineering etc.

Next on the popularity agenda come the usually-not-so-fast open roadsters, tourers and replicas. Some of the above-named companies produce these, as well as many other specialists. Try Teal Cars, Douglas Car Company, SP Motors, NG Cars etc. Many of these kits feature two-seater and 2+2 models, the latter allowing you to fit the kids/pets/extra luggage in the back seats.

Another general group involves a number of exotically styled coupes and convertibles, replicas and otherwise, which quite often combine high performance with streamlined bodies, high-tech chassis and usually a higher budget. Such cars as the GTM Coupe and Rossa, Midas, Minari etc. all have their places in the market.

Utility vehicles remain strong sellers as many first-time and experienced kit builders need to have a car that will pay for its keep by working year-round as reliable commuter transport. These can be Jeep-like vehicles such as the Jago Sandero and White Rose Husky or more modern designs like the Quantum hatchback or the Rickman Ranger which is inspired by the

Suzuki Jeeps. Don't forget the Eagle RV, the NCF Diamond and various Mini Moke clones.

Added to this lot is a whole selection of really specialised kit cars designed for the off-roader, the keen circuit racer or the lover of general oddities. You can still get beach buggies and a few other VW floorpan-based machines but these are quickly losing out as the Beetle gains in value. There are three-wheelers based on anything from the Renault 5 to the Citroen 2CV, Mini and even the Honda CX500 and 650 motorcycles.

Because the buyer does all or most of the construction work, kit cars, if treated as an amateur's hobby, cost you only their value in parts and any specialised services you might use, such as paint spraying or engine preparation. Latching onto the evergreen demand for more performance, many kit car companies set out to offer outrageously quick roadburners at a fraction of the price you'd pay for a production car of equivalent stature.

What the kit car trade (with a few exceptions) has not been good at is the manufacture of cars that approach production car standards of comfort and interior equipment. There are too many good second-hand production cars available if you're after a saloon or estate car. Without the design budget and facilities of a multi-national corporation, it's difficult to reach the standards of Toyota and Ford. Buyers shouldn't expect the kit car trade, in most cases, to compete in the 'normal car' stakes.

Although some very capable all-season kits are appearing, most kit cars set out to offer the customer a chance to indulge in open-top motoring with the accent on anything from simple nostalgia to pure rubber-burning muscle. Some have detachable hardtops, some are coupes and others also have integral hardtops but the convertible is what most people want. There's a wide choice of these.

Many people are hardly aware of the existence of this huge choice of kit cars and either dismiss the notion as mere rumour or identify the kit car concept with some of the awful stuff produced in the seventies and early eighties. Sadder still, there are car enthusiasts out there who yearn for the chance to build their own creation but feel that they lack the ability to do so.

Above: Sylva Clubmans can be a great weekend racer as well as road rocket. Below: The industry's come a long way since the beach buggy.

Check out *Which Kit?* magazine. It may be a minority pastime but there's certainly a large amount of interest. Due to the relatively low cost of designing a car for the amateur builder, new companies often appear. However, because of the relatively small market share that most manufacturers have, it's not uncommon to hear of a liquidation every now and then.

Needless to say, the buyer must be aware of this when choosing between companies. We'll be dealing with some of the criteria for choosing kits of different kinds in the next two sections. In the first section of Chapter Two, we'll also discuss the art of interpreting brochures and vetting companies.

Section 3
Horses for courses

ALTHOUGH IT'S VERY difficult to make generalised remarks which apply to all kit cars, we can say that just about every kit car builder has the option of making his or her creation into something that drives and performs like a true sports car. Good power-to-weight ratios often enable excellent performance characteristics from kit cars with engines as small as a 1300 or 1600cc unit. The beefier sports kit cars and replicas allow you use the big V8

engines, often from the USA, to achieve outrageous performance matched only by the world's top dream cars.

So, apart from having a vehicle that drives superbly and looks dead cool, what are the arguments for and against building and owning a kit car? Most kit car builders will invest an average of £6500 in their project and the resale price of a vehicle in very good condition will often only reflect its cost in parts. High-budget replicas and a few cult originals will sometimes make a profit for their creators but usually you'd expect to break even.

That means that you're giving

Above: Pilgrim Cars' Sumo shows what can be done with a standardised kit car trim and carpet set. Below: You'll be hard pushed to match the trim standards of a production car such as this Toyota.

away a large amount of labour hours for nothing - or are you? After all, building a kit car should not be taken merely as a profit-making pastime. What it really amounts to is a hobby. It's something that you will gladly spend time on.

Among the habitual kit car builders, you'll find a hard core of creators who simply lose interest in a car once it's built. They'll sell it at a fair price and then start again with another meticulous project. In essence, this reflects a pretty widely felt consensus that the fun really is in the preparation and in the reward felt when completing a task or stage, no

matter how small or large.

It could well be true to say that the successful kit car builder is the one who looks to the build-up, and not the finished car, as an end in itself. Woe betide the builder who wants to quickly dash through the construction stage and get driving as soon as possible. Things don't often work that way. In every sense, your finished kit car is a reflection of the care and consideration invested in it.

You will reap the rewards for starting out with the attitude that every job can be overcome, it's just a question of how to do it and who to ask for advice when

necessary. During the build-up, the car builder might, at some stage or other, have to stop and consider a dwindling selection of options. The sort of problem that is covered neither by the donor vehicle's Haynes Workshop Manual nor by the manual supplied with the kit. This kind of glitch shouldn't be the cause of major setbacks or even a complete retreat.

Quite often, there's a friend or group of friends with some considerable mechanical expertise. There's the manufacturer at the end of the phone or, better still, the owners club relating to the model of kit in question. These OCs are very often the fount of all car building knowledge and even the manufacturers themselves sometimes get information from them.

If there is no specific club for the make of kit you're building, then the manufacturer should have a list of past customers who are willing to help out others. It really is a very friendly network of enthusiasts in most cases and experts often like to impart selected gems of wisdom to learners. Why try to reinvent the wheel when someone else is happy to tell you how?

With this incredible network of back-up, coupled with your own enthusiasm and patience, there are few reasons why a project might have to fail outright and be sold part-completed. One of the usual reasons for a complete change of heart is a budget shortcoming. If you haven't priced up the whole thing effectively, then you may well find yourself short of a few bob and unable to go on for the foreseeable future.

In the next chapter, we'll be looking at prices but at this stage it's worth saying a bit more about build times. We would certainly

Above and below: As you read through this book you'll soon realise just what an important source of knowledge and enjoyment kit car clubs can be. There's always someone who can help you.

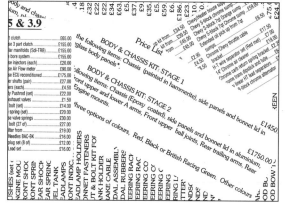

Above: Sifting through manufacturers, price lists is a tricky task, but it's important to work out reasonably accurate build costs. If not, you might find your car appearing in the classifieds.

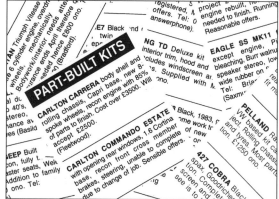

Chassis come in all shapes and sizes. This White Rose Vehicles Locust chassis is a very simple ladderframe affair which gains further strength from the fitment of its tough bodywork.

This Midas Gold Convertible has no separate chassis and gains all its strength from its fibreglass monocoque construction. It works extremely well and takes rust prevention to the limit.

agree with the assertion that five consecutive days spent building a car are more productive than five days each separated by a week. If you're going to spend just one day every weekend building your kit car, then you can expect it to take longer (in terms of total hours spent) than the same car built using four consecutive days each month.

Manufacturers often quote guideline build-up times for their kits. These are usually an underestimate as most kit builders will want to invest greater effort in their project than is strictly necessary for a 'standard' build-up. A good rule of thumb is to avoid any estimated build-up deadlines for as long as possible.

Experience shows that inaccurate timing leads to rush jobs or total failure. Only when the car is at least half complete can you start to accurately estimate your time scale for the project. This is a particularly important point if you've rented or borrowed a garage and have to move out of it by a certain date or have to find extra money to keep it on.

If you are sufficiently successful in coping with technical, budgetary and timing problems, then the undescribable pleasure of driving your personal creation is something worth experiencing. Something that goes beyond the satisfaction of driving a mere production car that you have fixed-up, or something

that you have simply purchased at extreme cost. You'll be intimately familiar with every last nut, bolt and washer and the pride derived from operating a machine that combines all of those widely varied tasks is immense.

Section 4
Under the skin

IT'S ALL VERY WELL TO FALL in love with a kit car because of its shape alone. However, there are more important factors to be considered. A kit car that does everything you want it to might not be the car you imagined in your dreams. In this section, we'll initially take a look at the various different kinds of structures and bodies to be found in kit cars, considering their pros and cons.

These days, most production cars have something called a monocoque structure. This means simply that there is an overall bodyshell, usually made from sheet steel, which also serves as the car's structure. Bolt-on panels and wings contribute to the final shape and aerodynamics but the main shell is the strength of the car. The mainstream press often refers to a monocoque as a chassis but there are plenty of variations on this theme.

The monocoque concept isn't particularly new but it's a long

way from the old horse and cart-derived chassis. Yer average cart was made from wood, meaning that its structure was restricted to straight or curved beams, all jointed to each other and with the seating room attached to the top. The same principle was used for the early horseless carriages. Many 4x4 utility vehicles and trucks still boast a rudimentary ladder chassis – ie: a chassis resembling a horizontal ladder.

Somewhere along the line, things started to change, especially as sheet steel and related forming techniques became economically viable. Cars such as the VW Beetle and the Citroen 2CV used chassis with both sheet and tubular steel, combined to make a floorpan. They were strong but not particularly stiff. Therefore, a bodyshell, bolted onto the floorpan, had to add rigidity.

Modern cars seem to combine the floorpan and rigid shell into one unit which can be manufactured using the now commonplace sheet steel materials and complex forming techniques. Computer-aided design, together with a better understanding of stresses, combine to save raw material costs by getting these monocoque structures as thin and light as possible but still very stiff and strong – until the rust sets in.

That's why vehicles which are designed to last a good number of years without succumbing to rust problems, such as the Land Rover and most lorries, quite often have separate tubular steel chassis.

These chassis, usually rectangular hollow section steel, are thicker-walled and heavier than their monocoque counterparts. They take longer to

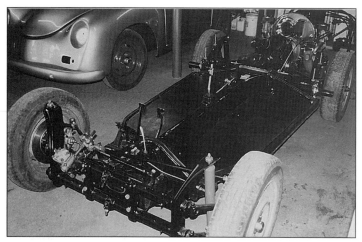

Not many kits retain that old kit car favourite, the VW Beetle floorpan, but with the simply removed bodywork, one can see the appeal of such an easy working platform.

Most chassis, and in particular spaceframes, gain their main strength from triangulation of relatively small chassis tubes. There's lots of bracing around the rear differential on this Dax chassis.

rust and can be readily repaired. The body, which doesn't contribute much to the vehicle's strength, is more or less a sacrificial component. One drawback is that monocoques tend to be stiffer and better suited to high-performance vehicles.

Somewhere in between the basic ladder chassis and the monocoque shell, there's a remarkable diversity of structures and many of them are to be found in kit cars and, indeed, classic cars of all kinds. Car and kit car designers, when unable to afford steel monocoque technology, have toyed with many different chassis designs.

What they discovered was that the basic twin-rail ladder chassis had to be made very big and heavy before it could be described as stiff. Chassis stiffness is desirable for most types of car because it enables the suspension and steering designer to rely on a stable platform for the suspensions at each corner of the car.

If the car flexes too much, then the positions of the suspension mounts will vary in relation to each other and the geometries will become inconsistent. This can easily lead to suspect or unpredictable handling and roadholding characteristics, more often felt as a springy or wallowy sensation when cornering.

That could be acceptable or beneficial for a long-distance, straight-line cruising vehicle, such as those big American cars, but terrible for a nimble roadster. British car enthusiasts are often connoisseurs of competent handling characteristics. Excess flexing can also lead to premature cracking and rusting.

Instead of making the ladder frame huge and bulky, with terrible weight penalties, designers found ways of strengthening the ladder with extra tubes inside, around and above it. Using a large x-shaped frame within or instead of the ladder frame made some improvements. This is known as a cruciform chassis. Other designers chose to reinforce the

Smaller kits such as this Caterham can reduce the size of chassis rails to a minimum yet still retain their stiffness. This in an ultra modern K-series powered car complete with catalytic converter.

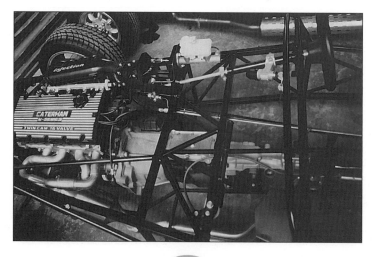

ladder by adding many more cross-bracing tubes and flat sections of sheet steel to form various box-section shapes.

In some instances, the twin-rail concept was dropped altogether in favour of a single central box-section known as a backbone. This backbone could be made from may small tubes arranged in a series of triangles a bit like the Eiffel Tower. It could also be made from sheet steel or a combination of sheet and tubular materials. Special subframes front and rear formed the suspension mounts, which were designed to feed their loads and stresses into the stiff backbone.

By far the most complex and sophisticated form of tubular chassis became known as the

spaceframe. This incorporates many triangulated lengths of steel tube welded together to create a stiff overall structure but without heavy materials. Careful consideration of the stresses applied to a car told the designers specifically where to put the tubes for the best effect.

Some incorporated a backbone section, others opted for a cage-like device called the perimeter spaceframe. Obviously, pure principles had to be compromised to allow room for such things as engines and occupants, so it would be more correct to say that such chassis are designed 'on spaceframe principles' rather than being true spaceframes.

A few were determined to go the whole way and create a monocoque. They couldn't use steel sheet as the equipment for shaping it properly is so expensive. They opted for fibreglass and the related composite materials. Colin Chapman was one of the pioneers of this technique with such cars as the original Lotus Elite. He also became a virtuoso of the steel spaceframe.

GRP monocoques are traditionally created by first making a hand-crafted, full-sized body shape from wood, filler and other odds and ends. It's called a buck. This is then smoothed and painted, covered with a releasing agent, gelcoat and GRP mat. When the GRP has

cured and is released from the original buck, usually in two halves, you're left with a mould. Cover the insides of the mould with releasing agent, gelcoat and GRP mat and you'll end up with a body shell the same shape as its buck. It's not quite as simple as that but that's the theory.

Various other moulded shapes will be required to add to the stiffness and functionality of the overall shell but it's a method that can produce a very stiff monocoque either with or without steel reinforcement. Longevity is assured as GRP doesn't rust but design or quality shortcomings can lead to cracking of the smooth outer gelcoat or even de-lamination in time. GRP isn't cheap compared to steel and can also burn very nicely unless treated with modern fire retardant resins.

As most kit car manufacturers have opted for their own types of steel chassis, the bodies are mostly not structural. They are often moulded GRP panels or complete GRP 'tubs', to be fixed to the body at key positions. Some manufacturers go for a combination of GRP mouldings, for the more complex curved shapes, and flat or formed aluminium panels, or even plywood, for the simpler shapes. Others use alloy or steel sheets in a structural capacity in the floor, bulkhead and tunnel areas.

In general terms, you'd choose a sophisticated backbone or spaceframe type chassis (with or without sheet reinforcement) for a red-blooded, sporting road burner. You might opt for a ladder or cruciform for a comfortable and unpretentious tourer or a big and tough ladder for a robust utility vehicle.

Chassis more complex than the basic ladder but not in the spaceframe league can create a good compromise between performance and a smooth touring feel but some of them are indeed capable of delivering excellent performance. Such kits as the JBA Falcon and Marlin Roadster spring to mind.

Choice of body takes a close second place to choice of chassis. Obviously, potential customers should insist on a test-drive to see if the overall body/chassis gives them sufficient legroom and headroom, as well as seat width. From the constructor's viewpoint, a body with more components will take longer to assemble than a single GRP tub but it probably won't be more difficult to get right.

Early impressions might lead you to believe that a single GRP tub is the only way to get a waterproof cockpit but this isn't necessarily the case. 'Flat-pack' bodies are much easier for one person to handle, trim and trial-fit. A tub can often require two or more people to lift it and it may have to be removed and replaced several times before fitting properly.

A lightweight body with interchangeable panels might be better for a competition-orientated car which may have to sustain damage regularly. A one-piece GRP body needs time-consuming repair after a bad crunch and it is

often quicker to replace the entire shell. A heavier and thicker body could be better for a touring car, helping to reduce road noise intrusion.

In favour of the one-piece or modular GRP tub is the fact that many manufacturers can offer these in gelcoat final colours. These are colours impregnated into the GRP resin, serving as a cheaper alternative to a professional paint job.

Most bodies which are offered as a selection of many different panels, especially those involving steel or alloy sheet, will need a paint job. If you're not game to try it yourself, it could well cost £1000 to get a professional to do it. We will consider the relative arguments for and against different body finishes in Chapters Six and Nine.

These facts may help you to get an overview if you're really not convinced about which kit car to choose. There are other equally important factors, though. In the next chapter, we'll take a look at costs and budgeting. You might want it but can you afford it? How can you choose the next-best thing? Hand in hand with the cost of the kit goes the cost of the donor vehicle and the mechanical components which you have to source for yourself. Some donors are more expensive than others. We'll take a look at the more popular examples in Chapter Three.

Top: GD 427 chassis uses backbone construction with a strong semi-monocoque body. Below: GRP laminating is an economical way of forming body shapes.

You can still get compound curves in alloy, though rarely, like this beautiful Teal Type 35 kit. Traditional alloy-rolling is a craftsman's art seen predominantly in the restoration business.

Chapter 2
BUDGETING

Section 1 : Between the lines
Section 2 : Hands on
Section 3 : Form filling
Section 4 : Tooling up
Section 5 : Grubby bits
Section 6 : Hidden costs

Section 1
Between the lines

OK, SO YOU'VE READ THE reviews in *Which Kit?* magazine, perhaps you've even got as far as visiting one or two shows and you're beginning to get some sort of idea as to which kit cars really take your fancy. *Which Kit?* will hopefully have given you some indication of cost but this can only be the roughest of estimations, usually based on what is going to be the cheapest route to completion. You may not want those bench seats and vinyl trim, you may end up with a tuned engine and you may find that before you even start the project you have to buy extra tools, paint the garage, put in some extra lighting etc.

But as your project grows from just a mere notion into something a little more tangible, the first green shoots of interest will usually manifest themselves

as a need to get brochures and other items of printed information. The conclusions that you draw from interpreting these brochures will usually tell you which kits you can and can't afford.

All too often, though, the manufacturers' brochures will only tell you a part of the story. The vast majority of amateur kit builders exceed the budgets which they had at first predicted on the strength of all this paperwork. There are a few knacks to interpreting such statistics and the key mistake is the presumption that certain items are included in a package even though they are not specifically listed.

Often we find that kit manufacturers will cut down the contents of their basic package to make it look cheaper than rival alternatives. Essential components, which you might presume are included, are not. Such things as windscreens, special exhaust systems, seats,

essential tailor-made mechanical parts, weather gear and conversions to donor parts often come as extras or options. Some might argue that this is done so that the buyer can more easily afford to get started and then pay the additional costs in stages.

In the first instance, you shouldn't make your judgement on the strength of the initial kit price alone. A kit that appears more expensive than your other choices may well work out the same at the end. If you are choosing between unrelated types of kit car, then it becomes

ever more important to look carefully at what you do and don't get in each case. On closer inspection, obviously, you might feel that the more expensive of your remaining choices looks, drives and generally feels better than the cheaper one!

We've taken information from a pair of (hypothetical) brochures to illustrate the point. First off, the listed contents of the basic kits and their prices. Next, the additional components to be purchased from the manufacturers to get both cars up to much the same level of

THE WHICH KIT? TIP
To double check that you've included everything in your kit car costings, dig out a back issue of *Which Kit?* which features the car and check over the pictures in the feature to see if there are any major components you've forgotten about (wheels and tyres, interior trim, bumpers and chromework, paint!)

At first glance you may think these two Cobra replicas would cost pretty much the same to build - you'd be very wrong! The Pilgrim Sumo (left) can be put on the road for as little as £7500 while a decent Dax Tojeiro will easily set you back £15,000.

completion. Last of all, the costs which the builder might reasonably incur to get each car up to a fully finished standard.

When interpreting price lists relating to kit cars or anything automotive, make sure you are aware of whether prices quoted include VAT or not. We've made sure that all the prices quoted on our example lists include VAT at 17.5%. Generally speaking, most kit car companies still seem to release prices that are plus VAT. You should also enquire of the manufacturers whether their prices are current and whether there is a price increase in the offing. There might also be special offers planned for future shows.

Ethical or not, the magic word CASH can work wonders sometimes. A popular story relates how one business quoted a very advantageous cash price to one of its

customers. They went a little wide-eyed when he mentioned that his job was with the Inland Revenue! Didn't make any difference to the customer though, we're all human.

Once you've sorted out the basic kit package you'll then be adding all manner of bits and bobs to the kit before you end up with a car you can drive. Very rarely will you find all the parts needed listed in a manufacturer's brochure pack. Obviously, some of the parts you will be getting from sources other than the kit manufacturer such as the donor car and perhaps aftermarket parts such as seats and instruments etc. Gathering all these components together and making an accurate costing is, as you can probably gather, an incredibly difficult, if not impossible, task.

Still, once you think you've made a decent stab at what the

car is going to cost you, then there are one or two other areas of the brochure you should check on. Another of the costs that might not be revealed properly is that of delivery. These are the initial delivery of the body and/or chassis and subsequent delivery costs relating to other mail order parts and other components that you might have to send to the manufacturer for modification.

The latter may not be so expensive, as you could travel to deliver and collect these parts. The kit itself might be cheaper to collect using a rented truck, the size of which can be specified by the manufacturer. If you are doing all of the running about, try to estimate total fuel costs for all the trips which might be necessary. There's also the question of insurance during transit. This must be clarified by

the manufacturer.

It certainly doesn't hurt to collect as many kit and components brochures as you can before you decide. They may cost you but subsequent savings due to wiser choices can save you a lot of heartache, if not money.

For instance, you should ensure that all the nuts, bolts and other fasteners you need are bought in stainless steel or other rust-resistant coatings if possible. (Be particularly aware that high-tensile bolts may not be rust-proof). Anything that can rust, will. It'll make the car look awful in a few days, even if it isn't used in the wet.

We will be mentioning other costs in subsequent sections, so don't go off half-cocked. Throughout your kit build, it's a danger to try and simply guess at the price of parts and services or to guess which of these you

The table below shows that kit A, a higher performance car with a paint finish, will probably be more expensive than kit B. The latter is more standard in specification. Having established this comparison, a test of the demo cars could well be the decider.

COMPARATIVE KIT PROJECT COSTS

ITEM	KIT A PRICE/SPEC	KIT B PRICE/SPEC	ITEM	KIT B PRICE/SPEC	KIT B PRICE/SPEC
Body/Chassis Kit	3000	3000	Rear Springs/ Shocks	In Kit	In Kit
Donor &			Rear Brakes	From Donor	From Donor
Reconditioning	500	500	Fasteners	20 (Most In Kit)	150
			Chassis Coating	In Kit	100
EXTRAS:			Brake & Fuel Pipes	In Kit	30
Windscreen &			Brake Flexi Hoses	In Kit	20
Frame	In Kit	250			
Exhaust System	250 (Tuned)	In Kit	**FINISHING COSTS:**		
Propshaft	In Kit	60	Final Body Colour	1000 (Paint)	100 (Gel Coat)
Wiring Loom	From Donor	100	Reproduction Parts	300	Not Applicable
Seats	50 (Mini)	200	Inner Wings	In Kit	50
Hood & Frame	200	250	Wheels & Tyres	275 (Capri)	400
Instruments &			Dashboard	60 (Walnut)	In Kit
Senders	250	From Donor	Full Engine Tune	100	
Switches	30	From Donor		100 (Twin Webers)	50 (Std. Carb.)
Fuel Tank	100	From Donor			
Lights	100	100	Comprehensive		
Rear Axle	From Donor	From Donor		400 (Fast Car)	250 (Ltd. Mileage)
Roll-Over Bar	In Kit	100			
Front Springs/					
Shocks	In Kit	200			
Front Brakes	From Donor	From Donor	**GRAND TOTAL:**	£6635.00	£5910.00

will need. If a manufacturer says that you have to use after-market wheels, for instance, check if they supply them and, if not, do they have to be made with a special offset? A wheel supplier will then tell you what the damage is in more specific terms.

Section 2
Hands on

CLOSER INSPECTION IS THE name of the game from now on. We're going to presume that you've narrowed down your choice to three or four kits. There's little point in offering you guidance as to what 'type' of kit car you ought to choose. That would take an entire book and most potential kit builders are fairly certain anyway. Now's the time to think about arranging a visit to the manufacturer's

premises to get a good look at its operation.

Although common sense can be the best overall guide to choosing between your remaining possibles, there are a few rules of thumb that are fairly unique to the kit building world. Most manufacturers in this trade are enthusiasts rather than entrepreneurs, finding job satisfaction more important than getting rich quick.

As a result of this, you won't find many showrooms with gleaming demonstrator fleets awaiting your pleasure. Many turn out a relatively small number of kits, relying on other work to bring in more business. Demo cars can often be daily transport for the boss or staff, although there are exceptions to this rule. Companies such as the mighty Westfield, Caterham and DJ Sportscars International all boast nice, large premises,

usually busy, with various staff members on hand to deal with your enquiries.

Looking at the other end of the scale, some companies may not have a demo car available at all. It may have just been sold or the company may rely on existing customers bringing their completed examples along. This is certainly far from ideal but neither should it necessarily be the end of your investigations. Inspecting a customer's car and chatting to him about the build can be of vital importance and we'll deal with joining the relevant kit car club later.

If you're trying to get an accurate comparison between a few companies, try to arrange visits in fairly quick succession, so that impressions stay fresh in your mind. It's best to go on weekdays as most visitors arrive on a Saturday and staff can be too busy to give much

time to each group - especially when it's a one or two person band. Always make sure that you have a confirmed appointment, especially if you're going a long way.

We would recommend that you start with a test drive. In most cases you'll be a passenger to start with, but most companies should let you drive the vehicle if they feel you are sufficiently serious about it all. However, it's surprisingly common for customers to damage or crash the really powerful cars, as they're just not used to real performance, so don't be surprised if you're not allowed to instantly pilot a 7.5-litre Cobra lookalike. It's not the same as your 16-valve Golf! Kit manufacturers have to be careful with their cars.

If you are permitted a test drive the first thing you must check is insurance. Either your

Always take the opportunity of sitting in the demo car even if you cannot drive it. Line of sight gauges are better but can easily become obscured (above). Offset gauges require more effort to read.

Above: Many smaller kits, such as the Caterham Seven, can be a tight fit. If there is no way of getting comfortable, look elsewhere. Below: Huge Beauford Tourer should be less of a problem.

insurance company must cover you or the kit manufacturer's trade policy must but, either way, accidents can happen and both you and the manufacturer need to be aware of who is liable. Do not assume that the kit car company's policy covers you to drive.

When you're out in the car you'll obviously be trying to find out whether it's a car that you can learn to like. After a lifetime of driving production cars, you might not fancy the firm ride and slingshot throttle response of a fast sportster. It always takes time to get to know a new and different car.

At this early stage, you might be more interested in seeing if there's sufficient legroom, headroom and seat width. Are the pedals too close together for your size of feet? Are the windscreen frame and sidescreens in your line of sight? Are the instruments obscured? Do the tyres foul the arches or chassis on full suspension bump, droop or

steering lock? Are the gear and handbrake levers in sensible positions for you? Is the soft-top a going concern? Do the windows wind up properly? Are there rattles, clunks and bangs from the suspension?

What you need to identify are any design faults, not those that can be put down to simple maintenance problems. Over-sensitive steering and hard suspension, for instance, are criticisms often levelled at some excellent sports kit cars by someone who's used to driving hatchbacks and other rather insulated vehicles.

A test drive can be a very good way to eliminate candidates on your list. No matter how good a company's service, price, quality and presentation, if you don't like the way the car

drives, and if you don't 'quite' fit in the driver's side, don't buy the kit. It'll be a disappointment in the end and you'll just sell it off.

If you can't get a test drive, still take the chance to go out as a passenger and do the best you can to feel the car's responses and to watch the driver's efforts. You'll still be able to pick out more obvious faults with the car from where you're sitting.

Make sure that you do get to sit in the driver's seat at some stage and take the time to look at the instruments and size-up the other controls. You'll at

least be able to tell if the cockpit is too small for you.

After experiencing the demo car, you should ask for a guided tour of the premises. Most kit car companies do all or some of their manufacturing in-house. This can include laminating GRP bodyshells and panels, storing, cutting and welding steel for chassis and special parts and often part-preparation of kit cars for customers who want some of the construction work done for them. Some companies, on the other hand, get everything made by external sub-contractors and simply ship out kits when all the necessary

Loads of spares mean less delay when you come to ordering parts. A company open day, such as this one at Quantum, is a great opportunity to see both the company and its customers.

Westfield's huge premises are the largest in the industry and clearly demonstrate the car's popularity and success. Below: GTM's showroom is small but tidy. Others may not even have such a thing.

components come in. Both have advantages and disadvantages.

A walk around the factory will give you an idea about how busy the company is and how much of their equipment is sophisticated or dilapidated. Tread carefully, though. It is generally correct to say that big, bustling factories produce popular and good quality kit cars (there have been exceptions). It would not be true to say that small, dusty nissen huts usually turn out rubbish.

Many kit car companies operate from small, quiet, untidy premises and many of them make excellent machines.

Some appear to be on the verge of extinction but have looked the same for decades! In essence, you can't really glean that much information from looking at a premises.

The fun starts when you manage to corner the boss or the sales-person and can grill them with a list of technical or financial questions you have prepared in advance, from looking at the brochures and, preferably, the build-up manual for your chosen model. After you've asked your own questions, try to get some more information about the demo car and the company itself...

Is the demo car representative of the kit specification you're thinking of building? If not, why not? Different engine, gearbox or other donor parts? Different wheels and tyres? Different body mouldings. Special custom-made parts such as exhaust, hood, springs and shocks, seats, trim, dash, instruments? Paint job or gel coat finish? How old is the vehicle and how well has it aged?

Do the answers lead you to believe that a car of this specification is going to cost a lot more than you'd bargained for? Do you need your car to have all this equipment anyway? What alternative components are there? It may turn out to be rather misleading as kit cars offer a

huge range of choice in their specification. Many dealers will offer to help you fit all manner of different engines if you can afford it.

Showroom vehicles are often dolled-up to prove just how far you can take things. Sometimes they're built down to a tight budget to show how little you need to spend. Don't presume that the basic kit listed in the brochure will leave you with a car like the company's demo model.

What about the company itself? What are the relevant facts here? How many cars have they sold? How many years have they been going? Have they designed their kits to comply with the relevant Construction and Use regulations? (You can do some simple checks for yourself using the statistics in Chapter 10 - take a tape measure). How long do they take to produce and deliver a kit? Do they have an up to date build manual? Do they offer quality guarantees?

Brochures (above) should be interpreted very carefully and costings and kit contents properly examined. Quality of these will vary enormously. Below: Build manuals are good for research.

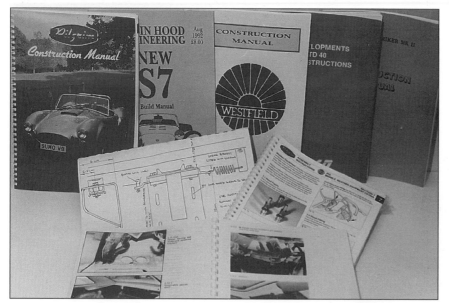

Information obtained from relevant owners clubs should be a vital part of your research. Below: A second hand purchase may eventually suit your needs and abilities better.

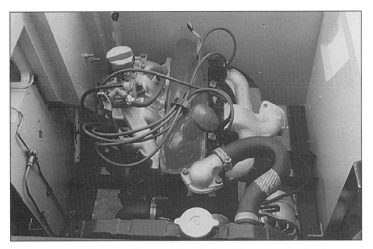

Ford's Kent X-flow is still a popular choice with many enthusiasts. Whilst some are used in standard form (above) many people take the opportunity to modify them to produce more power.

Insurance is best dealt with by the specialist kit car insurance companies. Shop around as prices can vary enormously. Classifieds can be a good source of donor vehicles.

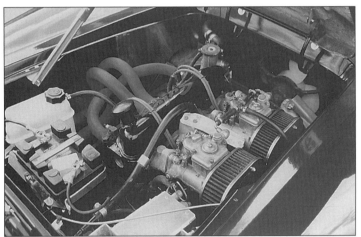

Will they refer you to an owners club or others who have completed their kits?

This last point is pretty major in many respects. If you take the trouble to note down some of the information given by the company's representatives on technical or other points, it's very interesting to put the same points to club members or owners of that kit on another occasion. If the word on the street is good, that's an excellent sign. Some manufacturers have their clubs to thank for many sales. A happy owners club means a good reputation for the business!

Go through these motions for all the kit car companies remaining on your list and you'll soon begin to get a clearer picture of the kind of thing you want - or indeed whether you're better off forgetting the whole

project. Decide now whether you're getting in way over your head.

Have you understood any of the technical terms used? Has your previous car maintenance experience not really been as deep as you'd like to think? Would it be better to get the company to do all the difficult jobs and pay extra to avoid the heartache? Would it be even better to buy a second-hand example and just maintain it rather than build it?

Section 3
Form filling

WHAT'S THE NEXT STAGE going to cost you? Well, you've already spent out on trips and quite a few brochures - and hopefully a few copies of *Which Kit?*! When you start to get really interested, there are

several more angles to the information-gathering game.

First off, you should, if you

haven't already, get copies of the manufacturers' build-up manuals relating specifically to the kits in question. Not to last year's model or 'the one without independent rear suspension.'

If the kit you're interested in is a relatively new addition to the range, then it is likely that

THE WHICH KIT? TIP
Don't be too concerned if you find it difficult to follow or understand some of the processes discussed in a build manual – it's often much clearer once you have the relevant components in front of you. However, photographs and diagrams are important, and if a manual is all text then it may be considerably more difficult to follow. Finally, skim through the manual to see whether it offers hints and tips on how to complete jobs. Merely describing what needs doing isn't always good enough

the manufacturer will not instantly have a build manual for that kit and you may have to wait. Kit car designers tend to have fertile imaginations and they're always improving

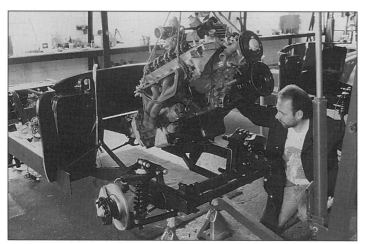

Having enough space to work on your kit is absolutely vital. If you are without a suitable garage, then you may well be better off to wait rather than try to build a kit outside.

Single garages are often very cramped. Make sure you've got at least half a meter on either side of the car. Jobs underneath the car need to be done with great care. Axle stands are a priority.

products where possible. If there's no manual on offer, it's all down to your initiative and contacts. Not the end of the world but you'll need very good support from the manufacturer and any other people who have already built an example of the kit in question.

In general, most build manuals cost below £20, with some manufacturers taking this off the kit price if you place an order with them. The extra details gleaned from the manuals will give you a better idea as to extra costs involved in the kit build and will help you to judge your ability to cope with the technicalities of the build.

There will inevitably be a further list of questions forming in your mind and these can be directed towards the manufacturer. You'll also need one or more workshop *(Haynes* type) manuals for the kit's donor vehicle(s).

It's an excellent idea to ask these questions while visiting the manufacturer or at one of the several kit car shows. *Which Kit?* usually lists the dates of such shows and it must be remembered that the manufacturers don't turn up at all of them. Sometimes they only send sales representatives to work the stand. Always, always verify this before going.

Once you've arrived, you'll also be able to cross-reference these questions and answers

with the owners clubs. They attend the shows faithfully and can be taken as the essential source of knowledge. Make sure you've got all the relevant

Donington (Derbyshire) in September. There are, however, plenty of others, some of them getting bigger each year.

You'd be well advised to join

only. Club membership fees are in the region of £5-£30 and well worth it for the information and organised meets that most offer. You might be referred to someone in your area who is building that particular kind of kit and who will let you come and have a look or even a drive. Extremely useful.

Other administrative costs to be incurred can also include insurance for the kit during the build-up. We checked (anonymously) with some of the various specialist kit car insurers as to their charges for insuring garaged kits. The results are included in the list at the end of the section.

While talking to these insurance brokers, you'd be well advised to get quotations for road use insurance. Bear in mind that limited mileage policies are available and that most kit cars can be built up using different engine capacities.

The younger driver (under 21 in particular) might be able to insure a kit fitted with a Ford Kent OHV 1100cc engine and then uprate it to a standard 1600cc or tuned Kent engine with very few fitting problems. We have found that insurance rates and options can vary widely for kit cars but the prices are by no means extreme compared with production cars.

There's even an option to insure comprehensively for

THE WHICH KIT? TIP
Don't automatically assume that the manufacturers you want to see will all be attending a show. More often than not, some will be present while others will not. Always get in touch with the show organisers to check that a specific manufacturer has booked stand space

questions firmly in mind before you go. Write down handy hints and contact addresses. Major shows of the year are Stafford in March, Scotland (Edinburgh) in April, Stoneleigh (Warwickshire) in May and

a club if you're serious about a certain kit because the better organisations will have printed newsletters or magazines listing useful build-up and maintenance tips. Back-issues might be available to members

Here's the Which Kit? *workshop, all ready to tackle our Caterham Classic. You can see we're spoiled for space, with acres of room and loads of storage space.*

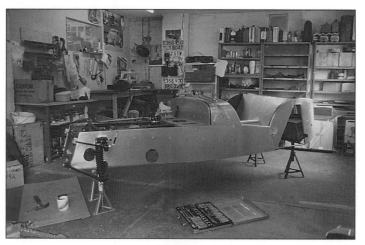

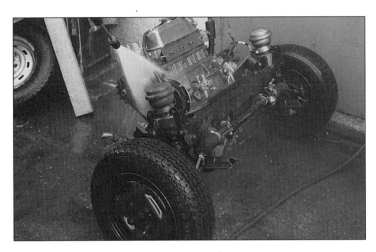

'parts only', leaving you to rebuild the car in case of accident. Make sure you'll have the time, energy and facilities should the necessity arise. It might turn out to be a false economy. High street insurance brokers who do not usually deal with kit cars can turn out to be particularly expensive compared with the specialists.

Other predictable paperwork-related costs will start to happen at the end of your kit build project. These are pretty much standard and are covered in more detail in Chapters 10 and 11. They are the costs of the MoT and vehicle registration. Single Vehicle Approval (SVA) is extremely immanent at the time this book was published and looks set to cost around £200, although your car will not then have to go through an MoT for a further three years (which can be offset against this increased initial cost).

Vehicle registration is currently included in the price of your first tax disc, again charged at the same rate as a production car (some three-wheelers may be an exception here).

You may drive the unregistered kit car to a pre-booked MoT or SVA test and drive it home if it passes. A registration inspector has to see the vehicle before registering it and can either call at your home or see the vehicle at the local Vehicle Registration Office's test centre - although you can't drive it there. More transportation costs may be incurred if the car fails its MoT or is inspected at the VRO's site.

Last of all, if you're really into the swing of things, you might put classified adverts in the local press or into the specialist magazines for a good condition donor vehicle, special donor

parts or an incomplete build project. The latter, you may have decided, could be a cheaper way of starting a project than buying everything new from the kit manufacturer. Beware of older models, as parts may no longer be available for these.

Section 4
Tooling up

EVEN IF YOU'RE NOT familiar with all the different kinds of garage equipment and DIY tools available to make certain tasks easier, there are many reference points when predicting costs. We will consider tools and other equipment in detail in the next chapter but for now we'll be taking more of an overview to show you how to structure your shopping list.

Most sensibly organised build-ups start long before the kit arrives at your workplace. Whatever route you take to get your donor vehicle components (see next section), it is advisable to undertake a certain amount of preparation work before they are all fitted to the kit's chassis, body or monocoque shell. Mechanical parts used second-hand must be all brought up to a good state of repair and should be made clean and tidy.

Some of the expense can wait until the kit progresses towards certain new stages. Some of it must be spent straight away. If you've purchased a complete donor vehicle which is running and road legal, it's an excellent idea to invest in a professional garage steam-clean of the engine and all of the running gear.

Above: Some jobs, such as welding and grinding, can be a serious fire hazard. You'll need a good size, non-water filled, fire extinguisher. Below: Logically stored tools will save hours of frustration.

Donor parts will often be covered in grim and a hired pressure washer is the ideal tool for cleaning them (above). You'll need to do a lot more than that to end up with something like this!

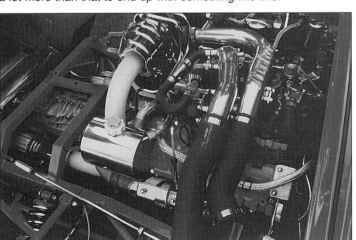

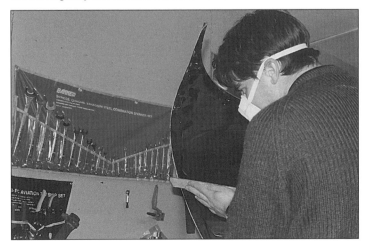

You might even hire a pressure-cleaning machine to do it yourself if you can't drive the vehicle to a garage. An adequate water pressure cleaner, while very expensive to buy, can usually be hired for around £20 per day plus the cost of chemical solvents needed. Don't underestimate the amount of grease and grime this will leave behind when you're done. It's a horrible job but well worth the effort.

After that, you'll need a basic set of tools to get the donor parts removed from the vehicle. Most kit manufacturers' build manuals will list the tools you need, including the more specialised stuff. The donor's *Haynes Workshop Manual,* which you should get, will also explain when any special tools are necessary. Don't forget to consult your local rental shop for prices of tool hire (especially for things like an engine hoist).

If you're starting from scratch, you could predict something like £100 for a good quality set of basic tools (see next chapter for more detailed lists). If you're considering an engine rebuild, then also consider getting a reconditioned engine instead. A full rebuild can cost you a lot more than a reconditioned unit or a guaranteed low mileage engine.

There's nothing to say that you have to find an old donor car and refurbish the bits. If finances allow it, why not go to one of several reconditioning companies?

If you have a normal bare garage with electricity, you don't necessarily have the room to build up a kit car. Most garages are single size and it's practically impossible to wield tools in the given space, let alone install a workbench and shelves. Many builders find that they need to move the car outside to work on it, especially when the bodywork is fitted. Do you have the external space? What about weather protection? Rolling chassis are much easier to cope with than bodywork in a small garage.

Setting-up expenses in these circumstances will include designing and making work surfaces that are collapsible, so you can get the kit back into the garage after work finishes for the day/night. High-level shelving can usually remain a permanent fixture and you need plenty of shelf space, as well as hooks and nails to hang things from the ceiling beams.

All this is basic DIY stuff and will cost you the price of a drill, tape-measure, spirit level, shelf brackets, Rawlplugs, screws, nails and wood or MDF for the worktops and supports. Much of what you use can be scrap materials saved from, for instance, a set of old melamine-covered kitchen units. £50-£70 should settle this early fitting-up. Less if you can borrow a drill and spirit level.

When you have your garage cleared of all the old, stored debris that seems to haunt garages, you can also take a long, hard look at the walls, ceiling and floor. The perfectionist might want to spend money on painting the walls and floor. This is a bit optional but you're going to be spending many hours here, so why not make it into a really tidy workplace?

White walls will also make the garage lighter and a painted floor will make it easier to find dropped nuts, tools etc.

It can also be a good idea to get an electrician to sort out a good spread of power points and a few well-spaced fluorescent tubes or tungsten bulbs/spotlights for the garage. It is essential to get a high-quality RCD contact breaker serving all of the garage power points - normal domestic fuses don't mean that you're safe from electrocution.

A few home comforts can make a lot of difference, especially when building a car over the winter months. A powerful heater is essential and you'll be glad to have some sections of old carpet to lie and kneel on when working low down. A water-container and an old electric kettle can save a lot of trips back to the house. Boot sales are an excellent place to find such things at minimal cost.

Some say that the best home comfort is a good set of locks. Make sure your garage has these as good tools are hot

Digging around old scrapyards may be your idea of fun, but it can also prove quite hazardous! Many modern breakers yards are actually well organised with components already stripped off the cars.

This Range Rover rolling chassis is destined to become a Dakar 4x4, but it's not a common donor, even if the 3.5-litre V8 engine is a popular choice with performance freaks.

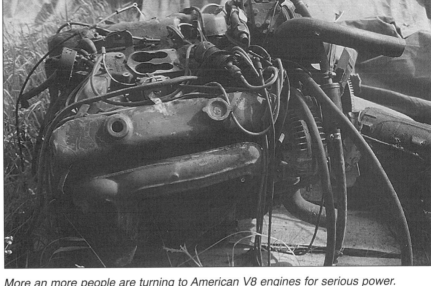

Above: The Ford Sierra, with its independent rear suspension, is an increasingly popular donor choice. Below: Jaguar XJ6 is a popular donor for high performance kits.

More an more people are turning to American V8 engines for serious power. Buying a cheap 'cut-out' (above) can be a good move but you can get caught out! Below: There are a large number of companies offering brand new American units these days.

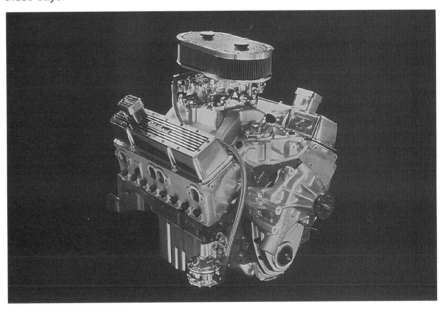

property. You can also get hold of some really good garage alarm systems these days that won't cost you the earth (certainly less than even a basic set of tools).

Tool racks can take the form of simple nails in the wall or elaborate wood creations. Make sure anything that's sharp is positioned safely. There should also be a proprietary first aid kit in an easily-reached position. A 10kg fire extinguisher suitable for electrical and fuel fires (not water or one of those tiny aerosol-sized hand-held jobs) is a must.

Other basics of garage preparation tend to be simple by-products of normal shopping trips and general domestic strife. These are detailed in the next chapter but in terms of accounting ahead, they aren't particularly important. Jam jars, margarine tubs etc.

If you're renting a garage, consider very carefully how long the build-up is going to take

you. If you can guarantee only one day per week working on the kit, it could easily take more than two years. Compare the price of a year's rental with the part-build costs quoted by the manufacturer.

It might be cheaper to receive the kit as a complete rolling chassis or to send it back for final body fitting, lessening the period of rental payment. What alternatives do you have if the garage owner wants you out and you're not ready? This can also be important for a garage borrowed from a friend or relative.

They can soon get tired if you overstay your welcome - especially when you start spraying and their beautiful state of the art stereo gets a mysterious dusting of yellow acid etch primer. In all

calculations of cost, remember to include potential disasters such as 'eviction' and quantify their potential effects in cash terms. You don't need many mishaps to start you off on the misery road - and the bank doesn't always listen sympathetically.

Section 5
Grubby bits

MORE COSTING RESEARCH can yield excellent returns when sizing up the bills you'll pay for donor parts. There is a wide selection of ways in which you

can buy donor parts and the best method depends on the kind of kit you're building.

Some kits require the majority of their donor parts from one single production car. Some need a small minority of bits from a second and/or third donor and some require a huge variation of parts from all over. Mid-engined cars tend to fall in the last category, they're usually the most expensive option.

Perhaps the easiest and most common example is that of the single donor kit. The majority of these still use Ford Cortina mechanicals from the Mk.3, 4 or 5 models. Ford

MATERIALS USED					
PART NUMBER	DESCRIPTION	QTY	RATE	£	p
	Pistons Set	4		243	53
	Balance Crank Ass.			99	37
	Bore + Hone Block + 04			50	00
	GASKET SET. Engine	1	S882036	82	52
	Oil filter	1		8	11
	Timing Belt	1		14	62

Performance tuning an engine can be an expensive exercise (above), but choosing the right engine in the first place may help matters. Below: Mildly tuned Lancia produces around 140bhp with over £1000 worth of goodies. Modern Vauxhall produces more as standard.

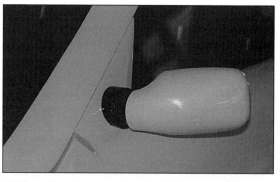

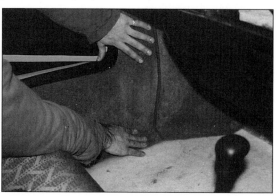

Odds and sods can soon add up. Colour coding this wing mirror is all extra expense. Below: Trim the car yourself or buy a pre-cut carpet set?

Sierra based cars are rapidly growing in popularity and, slightly strangely, Jaguar based cars are extremely popular (largely due to all the Cobra replica manufacturers). From here on your into other Fords, MGB, Citroen 2CV, Rover Metro, a host of other oddities and, let's not forget the oldest favourite of them all, the VW Beetle.

You have a lot more control over the project when you are looking for a complete donor vehicle. Watch out for manufacturer's estimates that you can buy one of those cars 'for under £50!' You might be able to but it'll cost you more at some stage. We would recommend that you look for a car that is road legal and running reliably - especially if you intend to use its engine and gearbox as well as the suspension components.

This is because you can more easily choose between available donors and you can get condition checks done on them by the AA or high street garages. Just putting it through an MoT test will give you some idea of the car's faults. Driving it around will help you to find others. It may mean paying £300-£500 for a Cortina but new and reconditioned parts aren't cheap. You could save a lot by choosing carefully in the first place.

Bear in mind that you should make it a matter of principle to renew or recondition the brake pads, shoes and hydraulics throughout, preferably the discs as well. The condition of these won't be of too much concern when choosing a donor. The wheels, tyres, exhaust, interior furnishings, lights and rust might also be irrelevant - maybe even the engine and the suspension bushes - but more faults mean lower price. Obviously, make it look like you want the car as daily transport.

The stakes are increased when you're after a Jaguar XJ6 or one of the newer models of donor vehicle. Properly maintained examples are rarely cheap. However, many don't get proper maintenance because of the prohibitive cost of parts and labour for these vehicles. Even if you get a reliable runner, you might still get a large bill for reconditioning.

Plainly, it might be better to presume that thorough reconditioning will have to be done, so buy a cheap wreck anyway. No point spending out on a beautiful and expensive Jaguar only to find that you still have to pay hundreds more in bushes, shims, discs, bearings and independent rear suspension (IRS) parts. *Which Kit?* magazine has details of specialist parts suppliers for Jaguar, along with many other makes.

Kit car manufacturers are often in touch with insurance companies and can get their hands on written-off examples of the newer types of donor car like the Sierra, Mk.3 Granada or Vauxhall Cavalier. Quite often, the mechanical parts are so new that you can get a good guarantee. It is better to get the whole vehicle delivered if you need the majority of its components.

You might be offered non-roadworthy and incomplete donor vehicles at knock-down prices. Worth considering if there's a good reconditioned engine/box to be had but be careful again. The complete donor will have a full set of washers, electrical components, bushes, cables, tubes, switches, instruments etc. which will cost you a lot more if you have to buy them separately. Worse still, you might assemble an important mechanical component that hasn't got a key tab washer, for instance. This could lead to a tragedy.

If you can't be bothered to do all the dismantling work on a complete donor vehicle; if you lack the space/tolerant neighbours/special tools/courage; if your kit car needs a selection of parts from more than one donor vehicle, you've still got a few options. They might be a bit more costly, though.

Option One is the local car breaking business. These days, there are many who offer an off-the-shelf service, so you don't

have to go around the water-logged scrapyards. They also have national database networks and can get the bits you need even if they haven't got it straight away.

When buying bits over the counter like this, be sure that you're given the bit you need and not the equivalent component from 'the old Mk.1' or worse. Make sure also that you get a receipt and the right to change it for a better component if it's unworkable. Things like differentials often have to be used before you know if they're any good. The onus is on the buyer to recognise exactly what is needed.

Option Two is to use one of the more service-orientated breakers advertising in the kit car magazines who will sell you a complete boxed set of reconditioned donor

components from one or more cars. This sounds like an excellent way of avoiding hassle, especially for hybrid kits using a variety of parts, but we have heard of instances where 'single' donor packages turn out to be a mixture of parts from slightly different models. The components may be freshly painted, but is that rust and grime underneath? Be ready to send things back.

The last big parts-buying pitfall refers to engines. If you're buying an engine separately or exchanging one with a reconditioning company, make sure that you know exactly what you're getting with the replacement engine. Specifications vary and you may well need to secure a whole host of ancillary parts elsewhere.

Cylinder heads, manifolds, alternators, water pumps,

starters, pulleys, belts, carburettors, mounts and brackets might all have to come from other sources. Check the warranty conditions carefully. Cheapest options can be false economies and we have heard of some dubious reconditioning companies.

Section 6
Hidden costs

YOUR FINAL SET OF COST predictions relates to the very broad areas of the construction jobs following the main mechanical tasks of completing the rolling chassis. They fall under the broad title of non-mechanical parts, services and tools. This is where the help of club members and others who have built up this kind of car before can be essential. You'll need an excellent imagination to

There's quite a large variation in the prices for insuring a kit while it's being built. Make sure you know exactly what sort of cover you are being offered and whether your garage's location is OK for the policy. You'll be keeping a lot of valuable bits in there.

INSURING A KIT DURING BUILD-UP

Quotes based on building a JBA Falcon with a total value of £6000.

INSURANCE COMPANY	ANNUAL POLICY PRICE STRUCTURE
Adrian Flux	£61.50 (£1/£100 + insurance tax)
Footman James	£36.90 (£6/£1000 + insurance tax)
Cheshunt Insurance	Unable to offer cover
Hill House Hammond	£65 (based on sliding scale)

Prices quoted were valid as of 07/1996

Cover includes fire, theft but check on accidental damage

Cover not possible if garage is not adjacent to home

Cover may not include theft of garage equipment and tools

You may not be able to cancel the policy if the project is finished early

Keep volatile fluids/materials out of the workshop

Keep a first aid kit in the workshop

Keep a fire extinguisher in the workshop (at least 3.5kg – not water)

guess at all the possible expenses here. Again, we'll look at specifics in later chapters.

Body fitting can also require a selection of adhesives, chassis tape, sealants, masking tape, face-masks, paints, sound-deadening materials, wood, aluminium sheet, fasteners of many kinds and a host of sanding and shaping bits to fit into a drill chuck. Your kit build manual should give you some idea of the kind of things you'll need. Many of them are readily found at motor factors or DIY shops.

You'll have to decide on the concessions you're going to make to quality and appearance beyond the call of duty. Perusing the cars on the club stands, you'll notice that many owners embellish their vehicles with extras like non-standard engine-bay cladding in alloy or stainless steel. People often know a source for such expensive things and can get them cheaply.

Once the body is fitted to the chassis, you could be looking at costs incurred by opting to do your own trimming and carpeting instead of buying the manufacturer's ready-cut trim and carpet kits. The kit car shows and mail order companies are an excellent source of material and specialist fasteners to be used for such jobs.

Hinges, mirrors, bonnet catches, bumpers, lights, instruments, switches, looms, soft-top weather gear and frames, wheels, tyres, exhausts, propshafts, seats, fuel tanks, filler caps, pipes and pumps, radiator grilles, electric fans, heaters, rubber hoses, panel edge trims, anti-chafing trims, fire extinguishers, security systems, stereos and paintwork. These are all additional costs and you can be well rewarded if you budget as high as possible for quality.

If the kit manufacturer does not supply specialist parts for the propshaft and exhaust, for instance, you could be into big expenditure to get them made for you. Electrical and paintwork jobs can also be expensive locally if the manufacturer can't suggest a good value alternative for you. Get quotes in advance to see just what your budget might have to be. Even at this stage of the cost estimating, you may have to change your choice of kit because you can't afford £1000 for the paintwork.

If you do have the time to frequent scrap yards, auto-jumbles and car boot sales, though, the time spent can yield excellent savings. We often hear of successful searchers who happen across an excellent set of lights, instruments, nuts 'n' bolts, rivets, tyres, wheels, seats or even a pile of stainless or alloy sheet. You can't include such windfalls in your budget but they do happen if you put the effort in.

We see it all too often but it's very common to see cars that have plenty spent on their mechanical build-up. Most kit builders prefer the rolling chassis stage of the build. Beautiful engines, suspension, oil coolers, remote filters, twin 40 Webers/Dell'Ortos, twin-cam conversions, blueprinting, rare live axle ratios, disc conversions etc. Then when they come to the jobs that make the car look good and go reliably, they run out of money. That's why some part-built kits for sale are excellent bargains.

It's heart-breaking to come to the 75% complete stage and realise that you'll have to compromise on the quality of the overall finish or interior (or indeed delay the build) for want of cash. Better to start off using a bog standard but functional mechanical stuff first. That can all be changed later. The car can be a going concern with good trim, carpet and paint the day it hits the road. That's why a lot of this preparation and research can really pay dividends in hard cash as well as in driving enjoyment.

Above: This Fisher Fury uses some original alloys which look great but can be bought for very little indeed. Below: If you budget carefully, you can avoid putting your kit in the Part Built Kits classifieds section.

Which Kit?'s editor, Ian Stent, bought this Transformer Stratos (lower left) as an incomplete project. Three years later, and with the help of Courtenay Garage's Bob Pilott, the car reached completion.

Chapter 3
SHOP FLOOR

Section 1
A good spot

YET ANOTHER KEY ASPECT of your forward planning relates to your proposed build premises. Where are you going to do all of that preparation and assembly work? We've heard about kits being built in all manner of places: the drive, the front garden, in a large garden shed etc. etc. What constitutes a suitable spot and what doesn't? Each option affects the overall cost of your project and the pleasure you derive from building a car.

Let's start with the essentials. The things that really are necessary for a smooth build-up. Your workplace must be weather-proof, even if you intend to build the car in one summer only. Wind and rain can ruin components as well as your resolve. You'll soon become disheartened if the simple act of working on the kit becomes a trial of your resilience.

Storage space is also important. If you receive the chassis first and the body later, when it's needed, you'll still need plenty of secure and dry shelving, boxes, racks or hooks where donor components can be kept. Some of the parts that arrive with the kit and during the early part of the build will be pretty expensive items that are attractive to thieves. Not least of these are your tools and power tools.

Heating, lighting and power can also be taken as near-essential. There are kit builders who have coped without these comforts but they're a rare and patient breed. Imagine drilling every hole by hand, using up torch batteries to illuminate the shadowed areas and freezing during the bitter winter.

Cordless tools have improved enormously in recent years, but they still don't have the umph of a mains powered equivalent and have a short-

lived charge. A row of car batteries can provide lighting but it's all pretty awkward and will slow you down no end. Heating's not so much of a problem because you can get such things as free-standing Calor Gas heaters. It's different if you can't get protection from the wind, though.

THE WHICH KIT? TIP
If you really cannot get hold of a decent garage at the moment, you would be much wiser to delay buying a kit car rather than struggling out in the open. After all, this is supposed to be fun, isn't it?

The average build-up will take somewhere between one and two years, so you should accept that there will be winter weather to cope with, along with short hours of daylight. This means that a covered area in the front or back garden certainly has its drawbacks

unless you really think that you can get the kit in and the finished car out by the time the weather turns nasty. Not to mention the difficulty in securing your possessions against theft and vandalism.

This all leads us to say that the minimum acceptable build premises is the standard domestic garage attached to a house. If such a garage is too small to allow you to walk and work around the kit, then it must be accompanied by a drive or car port into which the chassis can protrude to leave some work room inside the garage. Again, there will be weather

En-bloc garages are far from ideal. They usually do not have any power and are very prone to vandalism and theft. Storage is also very limited and location is away from your house.

You must at least have room for a workbench at one end. Some limited storage can be had underneath it. Make sure you carefully label boxes for later identification of their contents.

problems if that area is not covered.

A surprising proportion of kit builders find that they have friends or relatives who are in a position to give them the use of a garage or workshop building that fits the bill nicely. It's worth travelling a reasonable distance to work on the kit if the alternative at home is too inflexible for a smooth operation. You just have to make sure that possible time scales are agreed with the lender of the garage and arrangements are made vis a vis electric bills etc.

If you do borrow a garage or even rent one, be sure that the owner knows that kit building will be taking place and this involves use of volatile fluids (petrol, solvents etc.), it creates noise and floors can and do get contaminated with oil and grease. Work surfaces will also get splatterings of oil, grease, GRP dust, paint, thinners, steel swarf and other nasties. Not everyone will be aware of what car building involves.

You can always say, in your favour, that you will improve the premises before you start the build and leave it in better condition than when you found it. The next section will be

THE WHICH KIT? TIP
Where bodywork is liable to get damaged during the build, you can tape sheets of bubble-wrap over panels to permanently protect them. Equally important might be to stick thick foam to the garage walls to protect the door edges when they open

detailing such improvements and they could bring a reluctant owner round to your way of thinking.

How much room is enough room in a single garage? Your chosen kit build manufacturer should be able to give you the dimensions of the kit as a rolling chassis and with the body fitted. If the size of the garage leaves only room to walk around the kit, you know

that you'll need a covered work area outside the garage to leave you room for a work bench inside. You'll get cold in winter and during evening sessions and the garage really only serves as storage for the kit.

The ideal minimum single garage leaves you at least two feet either side of the kit and room at the end for a permanent workbench running the width of the garage. You'll be able to work on the car with the garage doors shut and won't continually be tripping over and scratching the gel or paint when the body is fitted. There will be mains electricity, good locks, a

We're going to bang on about this, but it's vital you keep the workplace clean on a daily basis. You'll also need a major spring clean at various times throughout the project.

Above: Only the very lucky few will have a workshop like this one. More often it's a case of rolling the car out of a single garage to get more room.

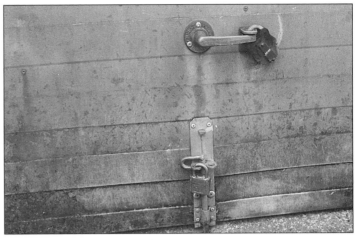

Above: Many power tools that you use can be potentially lethal, especially with a lead in this position. Below: Buy a decent circuit breaker and then make sure you use it!

Above: Your garage will house lot of expensive machinery. Some decent locks are a basic requirement. An alarm may be worth considering. Below: Painting walls will lighten a dark garage.

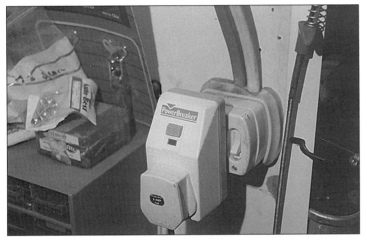

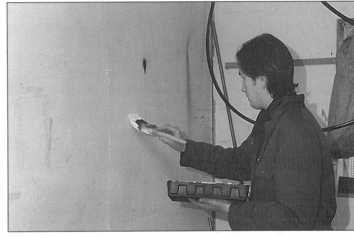

leak-free roof and places to put shelves for storage. Lots of items can be suspended from roof beams and supports.

Where bodywork is liable to get damaged during the build, you can tape sheets of bubble-wrap over panels to permanently protect them. Equally important might be to stick thick foam to the garage walls to protect the door edges when they open.

Needless to say, the best work premises come in the form of a double garage, an unused farm building, a generous corner of an industrial unit or, better still, a purpose-made wood or wood/brick building on your own land which might masquerade as a larger than normal garden shed. In the last instance, beware of planning regulations and access to the road when the kit is complete! Don't paint yourself into a corner...

Take no chances when deciding on a place to start building. For most of the build-up, your kit will not be street legal and moving it, and all of the bits and pieces that go with it, is a difficult job as well as confusing. When all your little tubs, boxes, shelves and tins have got mixed together, who knows where that packet of M6 x 25 cap screws went?

Section 2
Garage into workshop

SOMEHOW, THE GARAGE usually gets ignored and remains well down the list of jobs for the house-maintainer. When there's the prospect of a kit build in the offing, though, attitudes change. It's no longer on the remote edges of your awareness and your property. It's about to become the centre

of all activity. Girlfriends and wives beware. That garage, in its capacity as build centre, and maybe even refuge, is about to be smothered with affection and attention.

This is the first real nitty-gritty hands-on work for the aspiring kit builder. The following section lists a (sometimes rather idealistic) set of jobs that can be undertaken to make the garage into an effective workshop for the car builder. Your budget may require you to choose between them and to restrict yourself to certain priorities rather than do the whole lot. This is down to your own judgement.

Whatever garage you've managed to get your hands on should first be ruthlessly cleaned out. If you're to be serious about kit building, then this space should be out of bounds for normal garage

activities for the foreseeable future.

Toys, bicycles, lawn mowers, boats, drum kits, barbecues, garden furniture and garden tools should go. It might mean a second or new garden shed, a good loft re-think, a car boot sale or a visit to a charity shop but it has to be done very well.

A beautifully built kit car doesn't necessarily indicate that the builder's workplace was militarily tidy. You can be pretty sure that a badly built kit car, on the other hand, was done in less than clinical conditions. There are exceptions but this is a pretty firm rule of thumb.

Once the place is EMPTY, it needs a thorough spring clean. It is essential to get eye protection and a nose/mouth mask with replaceable filters for this job. Get a broom and sweep the ceiling (yes, ceiling), walls and floor. Remove the

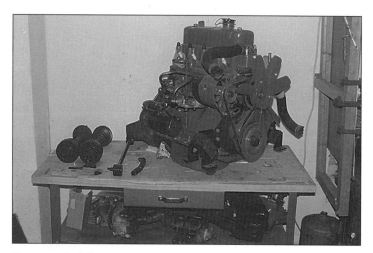

If you are building a workbench, make sure it can withstand some large weights. It may also be a good idea to cover the top with a temporary surface which can be thrown away.

When you are painting donor parts, it's a great idea to hang them up using coat-hanger wire. It means you can paint the whole part and not just one side.

worst of the dust with a brush and then vacuum everywhere if possible. If you think the ceiling might be asbestos, stop work and immediately get help from an expert (the council can help or try *Yellow Pages* under Asbestos Removal to find out if it's a harmful type).

If there is any evidence of roof leaks or other water

garage. Some around the car at waist height and some for the workbench at head height.

They must be out of the way of possible splashes, spillages and damage from heavy tools such as jacks and axle stands used low down. A good spread of power points means that you'll be less likely to be trailing extension leads all over the floor.

The power circuit should have a high quality RCD circuit breaker at its source to prevent electrocution. Normal household fuses aren't enough to guarantee safety and, for the sake of £80, a good RCD creates great peace of mind. A cheap RCD can be too sensitive and might need constant re-setting.

Before you start filling the garage with equipment, there are still several possible improvements. Make sure that all the doors lock securely. If you're building a valuable kit, you might want to put in a burglar alarm as well. Those tinny up and over type doors are usually very easy to break into and a few bolts and padlocks will at least delay the burglar a bit longer. Don't forget

those natty movement detectors which turn on an exterior light - a good deterrent in many places.

Painting and decorating next. Concrete floors often produce an endless supply of dust and soak up oil and other liquids for an awful visual effect. Nasty if it's not your garage. Once the floor is clean, dry and dust-free as possible, use some proprietary concrete stabilising paint. This can be applied with old rollers or large brushes. Ventilate the place well while doing it or you might get a touch high.

The same stuff can be used on the walls to make sure that dust production will be kept to a minimum. This is very important if you're to be doing engine dismantling or bodyshell painting. Perfectionists will then cover the floor in a proper concrete floor paint of the lightest possible colour. Two or three coats of white, for instance, will help to spread the available light in the garage and will make it much easier to find dropped components, nuts, bolts, washers, rivets, tools etc.

Light-coloured wall paint will also help to make the best of the lighting and the general effect is to make the workshop a brighter and cheerier place to be in. You can use an exterior grade masonry paint for the walls (and/or ceiling) as this is more robust and sometimes

THE WHICH KIT? TIP

If you are not prepared to spend time and money making sure your garage is fully sorted prior to the kit arriving, are you really ready to take on a kit build up at all? Do the whole job properly and the chances are you'll end up with a car to be proud of

intrusion such as rising damp etc., get it sorted out now. The effect of damp air can be terrible. Symptoms include mildew on trim and carpet, rust on anything that hasn't been painted properly, damage to power tools and even a health hazard. The workplace must be made dry before the next step. Ventilation, especially with a powered fan, is a big bonus.

A qualified electrician should be called in to check out your garage's electricity supply. While the expert is there, you should get some installation work done so that there is a selection of power points in the

Even when you have the car up on axle stands, the chances are you'll be spending a lot of your time on your knees. Some old carpet tiles are a good protection.

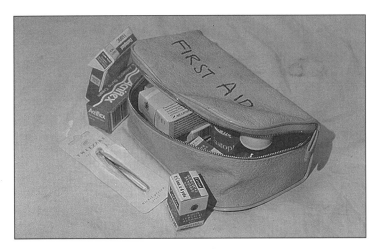

involving engine and brake parts that have to stay totally spotless.

Wall shelves can be made entirely from new or scrap wood or you can get the cheaper and less 'stylish' steel angle

If you're lucky enough to have beams or RSJs running across the ceiling, they should be extensively used for hanging components from. Beware the strength of older or narrower wood beams. You will need

cheaper than interior emulsion. Remember that there's always the option of re-painting in more subdued colours when you've finished.

By now you will know if there's room in the garage for the kit and your necessary storage space and worktops. If there is, then mark out the dimensions of the kit on the floor and design your shelves, racks and tables around the car for best access and least awkwardness. You must have space to lie down, walk around and stand up without continually smashing your head on something. Watch out for eye-level corners and sharp edges of shelves and racks.

A work surface can take the form of a heavy wood or steel-topped table that can be moved around or mounted to a framework permanently set

against one wall. An ideal worktop would go across one end of the garage, perhaps with a lifting section if there is a back door. It must be sufficiently strong to support a proper vice and heavy suspension items such as a live axle. You might even need to put the engine or gearbox up there so make sure of it at this stage and not when it's too late!

It's a good idea to give the main work top an interchangeable surface of thin ply, board or plastic. If you spill something like oil, battery acid, brake fluid or paint onto this surface, or drill into it once too often, it can be replaced quickly and cheaply. The main table surface gets protected and you've got the option of a totally clean new work top when you start on jobs

brackets to support the loads. A tool hanging panel, probably positioned by the worktop, can be made from a plywood sheet mounted to a timber frame. You can then use nails or screw-in hooks in the plywood to support all manner of tools.

(bent coathanger wire) hooks for hanging up painted parts to dry. Ceiling mounted hooks and 'cradles' are also good for storing longer items such as exhausts, rolls of carpet and trim and even complete GRP bodies if there's the headroom.

Shelving can make life much easier in the garage and can be obtained very easily. You may even be able to get some second-hand from office clear-outs.

Above: At best you will cut yourself and get splinters. At worst...it doesn't bear thinking about. A basic first aid kit is essential. Below: Barrier cream really protects your hands.

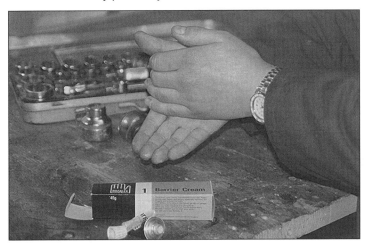

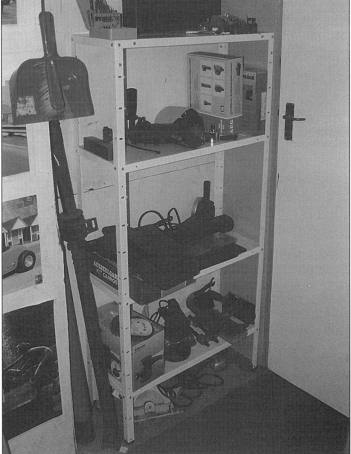

If you're lucky at a car boot sale or a liquidation sale, you might get a complete set of Lin Bin-type plastic storage bins and the relevant wall-racking to support them. This kind of thing is the Rolls Royce of storage stuff as the containers can be lifted away from the racking for perusal, they're strong and take up very little space. There's all manner of special plastic storage boxes for smaller nuts, bolts and other fasteners that you'll be amassing during the build-up.

If your work place is too small to keep the kit fully inside while working on it, you'll have to be careful to design the surfaces and other features so that the kit can be easily pushed back inside for storage at the end of the day's work. You might opt for a demountable table that bolts together by hand using large coach bolts and butterfly (wing) nuts. Make sure that all the mounts are strong enough for the loads to be exerted on the table.

You might finish off the garage 'furniture' with a stool and some carpet, carpet tiles, old duvets or sleeping bags on which to kneel and lie for the more awkward jobs. It's nice to work on a car lifted to chest level but that is a luxury reserved for the garages with such lifting equipment. We

When the going gets really mucky, some impermeable gloves are a real boon. These are the disposable type doctors use and can be bought in large boxes. Use once and throw away.

have to crawl around at axle-stand height and make do, unfortunately.

Section 3
Safe haven

SAFETY CONCERNS SHOULD be examined next, before you get the chance to really damage yourself for life. It doesn't cost much to get your workplace up to a high level of safety as most measures involve common sense and preventative equipment rather than subsequent expensive cures.

In the first instance, you should have a full domestic first aid kit at an accessible place in the garage. These are available

from good chemists etc. You should add to this extra materials or chemicals to deal specifically with workshop situations.

These include dust/swarf/GRP in eyes (Optrex and the like); bandages and wadding for deeper cuts that you might get from a Stanley knife or power tools such as a jigsaw; water for instant relief of a burn; sterile pins/needles to remove splinters; liquid antiseptic and disinfectant and a good-sized tub of mechanic's barrier cream to apply to hands or any skin which might come in contact with grease, oil, engine grime, paint etc.

Prevention is definitely better than cure, though, so there's a list of stuff you'll need for

protection. Most of these things are readily available from good DIY shops, motor factors and industrial suppliers.

First off is a good pair of safety goggles. Look for a ventilated pair with an elasticated headband. They are less likely to mist up and usually offer protection from sides, top and bottom as well as front. These should fit without interfering with a face mask that snugly covers both nose and mouth and uses throw-away filters. Remember to buy some spare filters straight away. Don't forget a pair of ear defenders. Power tools working on steel, alloy or wood can create a huge noise.

Other items of protective 'clothing' might include a selection of impermeable gloves such as rubber gardening or dishwashing gloves. The tighter-fitting variety can be worn when doing more intricate work. In the *Which Kit?* workshop we use the tight fitting gloves that you see doctors using. You can buy them in large boxes of 100 for not very much money at all and they really save your hands when you're painting donor parts etc. Barrier cream helps but we've found it wears off quite quickly. You don't want prolonged or regular skin exposure to old oil, grime and other kinds of fuel and solvent. You can soon get used to gloves.

Sparks from either a welder or grinder will fly out in all directions and can smoulder for ages. You simply must use appropriate eye protection at all times.

With many potential fire hazards in the garage, not least of which is the car's fuel system, having a decent sized, non-water filled fire extinguisher is a must.

Above: All of the above are hazardous to your health. Below: Never rely on a jack, always use axle stands.

Above: You'll need all manner of tools during the project, but most are typical DIY stuff. Those that are not can always be hired. Below: This good quality ratchet was bought separately to the sockets.

A good boiler suit helps a lot, especially the kind with lots of accessible pockets and an integral hood. Some of the kit car shows have stalls selling nearly new overall for under a fiver, which seems excellent value. Working under a messy donor vehicle can soon have your ears full of gravel and worse. A long scarf helps to stop it all going down your shirt but keep the scarf well tucked away when close to any machinery or power tools. A tight fitting hat will also keep most of the grim out of your hair.

Good boots with steel toe caps and thick soles will serve the joint purposes of stopping your toes from getting crushed and insulating your feet better from the cold of the floor. Cold feet can often, in many senses, be the end of many a day's kit building.

You will be working with such things as white spirit and paraffin to degrease and clean up many of the donor parts and other things that might need painting. You might also have paint thinners such as cellulose. These should certainly not be stored in the workplace but kept outside any building. A lockable cabinet at one well-chosen extremity of the garden should considerably reduce the hazard of explosive fumes and flammable liquids. Remember that paint must be protected from frost.

When you are using these volatile liquids in the work place, make sure you are aware that the vapour from them is more dangerous than most of the liquids themselves. The vapours, in sufficient concentration, can explode. Solvents can also mingle with your body fat having been inhaled - the brain can be affected in this way.

Provide adequate ventilation. One aperture, with or without a fan, is pretty useless if there's not another opening to allow a through-flow of air. Beware heaters which use flames and certainly don't ignite one soon after using solvents as there could have been a vapour build-up. Power tools and switches can also create sparks.

If a fire starts, one of the quickest measures you can take is to cover it with an easily accessible fire blanket. These are usually sold in tubes or in wallets for wall-mounting. A good (10kg/15kg minimum) fire extinguisher can save the day. Small aerosol types won't. Make sure you tell the supplier that the extinguisher must be suitable for fuel, electrical and GRP fires. Avoid pressurised water type extinguishers at all costs.

If you're going to be doing welding, make sure you have the requisite dark goggles, gauntlets and heavy 'spark-proof' hat and overalls. Welding with gas or electricity obviously increases the fire risk. Keep an eye on inflammable liquids and materials like the floor

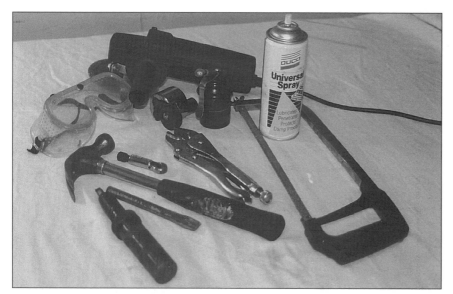

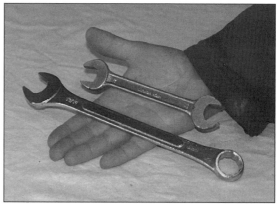

Above: Open/ring spanners are preferable to just open-ended ones. Quality can vary enormously. Below: A selection of pliers is handy.

Above: The heavy brigade! When things get tough you can always resort to violence. Hammer, chisel, mole grips and grinder are typical tools of the trade. Below: A decent set of screw drivers is a worthwhile purchase.

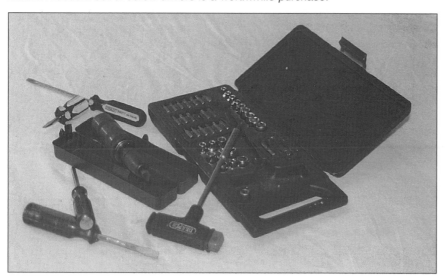

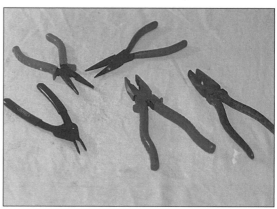

coverings mentioned earlier and make sure they're out of harm's reach. A weld (or grinding) spark will happily travel the whole length of your garage and more.

Section 4
Capital equipment

NOW'S THE TIME TO START stocking up the work place with your own selection of tools. As an example, we will assume that, like most kit builders, you will be getting at least one complete donor vehicle to dismantle or some heavy donor parts supplied by a vehicle breaker. Obviously, the kit builder who spends out on

buying pre-cleaned and refurbished donor parts, or even new components, will save on tools, materials and time spent in the garage.

Having equipped your garage with electricity, heat, security and safety needs, there's a relatively simple list of tools that you'll need for dismantling the donor vehicle. Many of the tools are common to most donor vehicles, although there are also special tools listed for many. The *Haynes Workshop Manual* is good at explaining how to avoid buying or renting some of these special tools, so make sure you get one even if you already have the official workshop manual for the donor.

A trolley jack and four axle

stands in good condition are prime requisites. Don't be tempted to use the simple mechanical jacks that are supplied in vehicle tool kits and don't use a bottle jack. They are OK for changing a wheel but are too unstable for lifting more than one corner of a vehicle. Never get under a car unless it is properly supported by wheel ramps and/or axle stands.

Absolutely avoid supporting a vehicle with any kind of brick or wooden blocks. These can crumble or split without warning. When you are working under a vehicle, it is also a good idea to slide old wheels underneath (stacked in pairs) as a secondary fail-safe in case the vehicle shifts off its supports. Extra axle stands of a smaller size can also come in handy if you're removing the engine, gearbox or live axle from

underneath. You don't want any of these falling onto your head as you take out the last mounting bolts!

You should, by now, have established whether the parts you are working with need metric or AF spanners. Often you'll need both types. Don't be tempted to buy the cheaply-priced 3/8" or 1/4" drive socket sets even though they are often sold with a huge selection of peripherals. The drive size relates to the dimensions of the square peg of the ratchet handle which slots into the sockets. 1/2" drive is the best all-round size and you pay more for these initially. They're cheaper in the long run.

A good socket set will include a ratchet and direct drive handle, a long and a short extension bar, a universal joint, hexagon-shaped socket heads (as opposed to the more common double-hexagon sockets), one or more common spark plug sockets and socket sizes from 10mm to 21mm and

3/8" to 15/16" AF. A smaller size socket set can be handy for minor nuts and bolts below these sizes and you may still have to buy separate larger sockets in some instances.

Along with the socket set, you'll need the equivalent sizes of AF and/or metric ring/open spanners. Most good sets of ring/open spanners will come in a kind of tool roll with sizes at least equivalent to those in the main socket set.

Tool kits owned by professional mechanics often have special 'stubby' ratchet handles for the socket set, about fist-sized for limited access applications. They also have short and long, cranked and curved ring/open spanners for odd situations. These, by and large, can be considered as luxuries, but they certainly have their uses.

When dismantling donor parts, it is immensely helpful to have exactly the correct size of spanner and socket for the job. A nut or bolt with a rounded-off hexagon is not the end of the world but it does create a lot of difficulty and can be expensive to rectify. Don't try to get away with that old set of Whitworth spanners your great-grandfather left behind.

A complete set of cross-head and slot screwdrivers is a boon. Using the wrong size of screwdriver can be as damaging as using the wrong spanner. Opt for a set with a square or hexagonal shaft so that you can turn them with a spanner or a mole grip if necessary. Some makes of screwdriver are designed so that the metal shaft extends through the handle to a metal surface at the top of the handle. These are much more resilient to hammer blows if the necessity arises.

Bear in mind that there are plenty of kinds of cross-head screws. Phillips, Pozidriv etc. are different shapes and the cross-head screwdrivers you get may be a compromise design. You might still need to buy odd cross-head screwdrivers to suit certain bolts.

A set of metric and/or AF Allen keys is handy as some cars are equipped with hexagon socket cap screws and you may well be using such fasteners later in the build anyway. There's an increasing variation in the types of socket cap screw, so be prepared to buy special keys if necessary.

What happens when things don't go your way as you dismantle the old donor parts?

THE WHICH KIT? TIP

Buying a really good quality socket set can sometimes be a case of taking out a second mortgage! They ain't cheap. Whilst they are unquestionably a good life-long investment, a slightly more affordable route might be to buy a really good ratchet and buy cheaper sockets separately. It's invariably the ratchet that breaks on a cheap set

---

Spring compressors can be obtained quite cheaply but must be used with extreme care. Never compress a spring with anything other than a dedicated spring compressor. It will end in disaster.

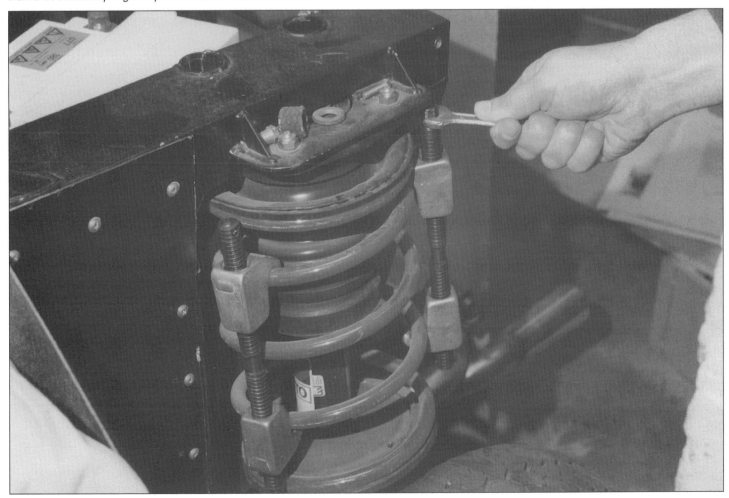

If you have taken the trouble to steam clean the donor and coat all relevant fasteners in a releasing oil before starting, your job will be much easier. However, it doesn't always work smoothly and some fasteners and components won't be budged with mere patience and regular tools.

It's pretty certain that you'll need 'less precise' back-up tools to shift stubborn or damaged fasteners. Adjustable open-ended spanners are available in a number of sizes. The better ones will have less play in the jaws and will therefore be less likely to round off hex heads.

A good set of mole-grip pliers helps as an extra pair of hands if you're tackling a bolt with an inaccessible nut. Clamp the moles onto the inaccessible end to secure it while turning the bolt etc. A good quality mole

wrench won't pinch your hand when squeezed shut and will be easy to release from its locked position.

Engineer's pliers and side cutters are essential and generally the bigger the better. Insulated handles are better and the more expensive types will have harder cutting edges and more precise gripping jaws. Under the 'pliers' subheading come such things as needle-nosed pliers and external or internal circlip pliers. Some jobs will be impossible without them.

A wire brush has a hundred uses for dismantling and cleaning parts. If you're removing a bolt which has a lot of visible thread, the dirt on that thread can clog the nut and make removal difficult and slow. Brushing around the thread with the wire brush cleans the muck off and speeds up the job. A large selection of drill-mounted

wire brushes is always useful.

When push comes to shove, such tools as universal nut splitters and ball-joint splitters are essential. When a nut becomes impossibly rounded, you can simply break it off by using the nut splitter. This is like a garrote. A collar sits around the nut and a small blade is tightened into the side of the nut using a spanner.

The ball-joint splitter is not a destructive tool but simply helps to concentrate the effort needed to separate conical ball-joints from a tapered interference fit in a suspension upright or other suspension arm. These joints are usually very stiff and you're stuck without a special splitter.

A hammer is often useful and you should have two types at least. The first is a normal steel-headed ball-pein hammer and the second is a copper and hide-faced mallet. Heavy steel

hammers can cause cracks, especially in castings, that might not be visible and will later lead to failure of that component. The hide/copper mallet offers a damped impact less likely to cause damage. A succession of light taps is preferable to a few heavy blows.

Among the other dismantling tools that can come in handy are the junior and full-sized hacksaws with replacement blades, a 'tommy' or extension bar that will fit over the handle of your socket spanner to give a better mechanical advantage, and a decent set of levers (such as car tyre levers) for budging jammed components. Try not to use a nice set of screwdrivers as levers!

Even if you've got decent garage lighting, a mobile light with a generous length of flex is helpful for illuminating underneath a car. Make sure

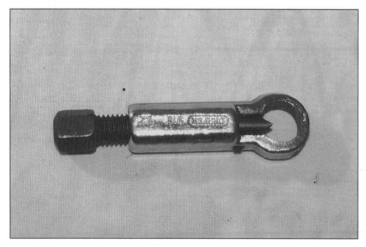

Above: If, during donor refurbishment, you need to use a nut splitter, buy a good quality one. Below: Alternatively, buy refurbished donor parts from someone like Kit-Fit.

Above: Engine block supported by its bell-housing mounts on a special stand. Vital for any rebuild. Below: Use a vacuum cleaner to remove brake dust. Never blow.

you get spare bulbs and a holder which properly protects the bulb and allows you to clip it to handy positions out of harm's way.

The materials you might need include a selection of (old or knackered) paint brushes, degreasing fluids or white spirit, aerosol and liquid releasing oils such as WD40 or Plus Gas, plenty of rag (old cotton bed sheets and towels are excellent), masking tape and a marker pen for labelling – especially in the case of wiring looms and electrical components and their contacts.

Sealable plastic bags which you can label are essential, as is a host of jam jars and other containers for storing the parts you have dismantled in good order. No matter how good your memory, you'll soon forget which bits go where if you don't write it all down clearly. It might be an idea to buy an exercise book and describe or sketch assemblies that you have to dismantle. These provisions will take a lot of the pressure and guesswork out of subsequent reassembly.

When working on old donor components, make sure you start off by coating your clean hands in a good barrier cream. Make sure it gets under your nails and a good way up your wrists. An alternative is to wear impermeable gloves. Old engine oil and grime are particularly harmful in regular doses. Clean your hands using a proprietary mechanic's hand cleanser such as Tufanega and make sure you get the residues out from under your nails so that you avoid prolonged exposure. Any skin irritations should be referred to your doctor.

If you are dismantling a donor vehicle with suspension coil springs, don't underestimate the force that these springs exert even when the vehicle is suspended off the ground. Don't dismantle double wishbones, rear axle assemblies or McPherson struts without first compressing the springs with a set of proper spring compressors. Makeshift attempts using rope tourniquets, levers, G-clamps, cramps and bits of hooked wire will probably end in disaster.

A suspension spring which suddenly sets itself free can hit you or others with a force of hundreds of pounds, easily stoving in your skull, snapping your neck (or worse)! With universal or specific spring compressors, such springs are closed up to allow dismantling of the suspension and then are slowly released until free of compression force.

Some engine and gearbox units are removed by lowering to the ground on a suspension subframe, some are removed from the bonnet aperture. Study your *Haynes Workshop Manual* carefully to see if you can get them out underneath as you're removing the suspension. Whether you're lifting up the engine and 'box or lifting the car body out of the way, get proper lifting equipment.

When working around a car you often find you need lots of different tools. Having some sort of tray or stand can be useful to keep everything together and avoid those times when you spend ages looking for something you only just put down!

A block and tackle can be very purposeful but not if they're suspended from a weak wood or metal roof beam (weak doesn't necessarily mean small here). Best bet for most is to rent a hydraulic car engine hoist locally, along with chains or straps for heavy-duty lifting. It's rarely worth buying one of these as the decent-sized types you can rent are usually very expensive. The cheaper types aren't always up to the job.

If you are going to be doing a large amount of engine work, though, it is worth buying a proprietary engine stand. These resemble a stubby metal windmill on wheels and allow you to bolt the engine to a support using the holes for the bell-housing mounts. Adjustable arms allow for different hole patterns and the engine may be rotated on its mount for access to all areas. Much better than crawling around on the floor or perching it precariously on a gritty work top.

Bear in mind a few safety tips. The underside of a car which is covered with road grime will also be contaminated with the asbestos dust from the brakes and the clutch. Concentrations of asbestos dust are to found on the wheels and within the brake drums and the bell-housing. Use your face mask when dealing with these parts. Don't blow dust off them - get a garage vacuum cleaner for all workshop dust.

Hazards also come from fuel in the tank, carburettor and fuel lines and from battery acid in and around the battery. Dispose of all these fuel reservoirs quickly, storing them, if necessary, outside for the ventilation. Remember that it's the vapour which can be explosive and a stray spark from an electric grinder will be enough to ignite it. Old or new engine oil is not particularly volatile but does burn. Recycle the old and store the new safely. Regular brake fluid often strips paint nicely.

Traces of acid from around the battery will eat through clothes and materials over a period of weeks or days. Dispose of old car batteries at the relevant council recycling facilities. Connected batteries can cause electrical fires if the wiring loom is short-circuited during dismantling. Make sure a reusable battery is topped up, charged and stored away in a dry, ventilated area. Most batteries produce explosive hydrogen gas, especially when being charged.

Section 5
Services

OK, SO YOU WANT PRISTINE results but you either can't or don't want to get really stuck into the dirty bits. Fair enough - this is supposed to be fun, so

Above: It's extremely unlikely that you'll have your own engine hoist, but they can be hired very cheaply from your local hire centre. Below: Be extremely careful when dealing with fuel tanks. Vapour is very flammable.

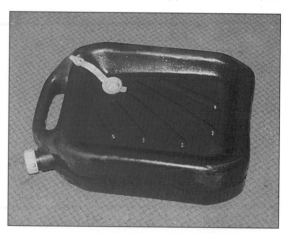

Above: Special oil draining container is a neat idea. Below: Cover battery terminals with tape to avoid accidental shorting-out.

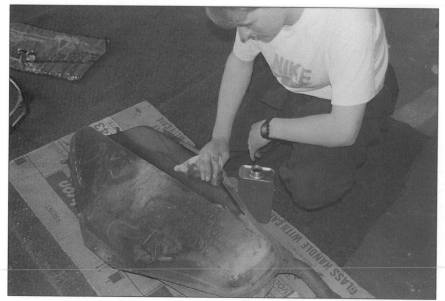

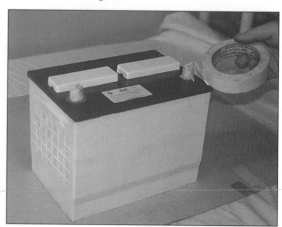

If you don't want to get involved with all the grubby bits, there are several ways of avoiding this part of the build. One is to buy everything from someone like Kit-Fit.

Above: Alternatively, you can buy a kit where everything is ready to fit, as with Which Kit?'s Caterham Classic. Below: A company like CRA Engineering will even build your car for you.

if you don't fancy doing a particular job, get someone else to do it! Some kit builders prefer the finishing and trimming jobs, some prefer the mechanical side, some prefer to drive the car and leave the build and upkeep to someone else.

At this early stage of the project, when the kit builder is amassing the donor parts needed for the kit, there are still lots of options for those who can afford them. In the first instance, the supplier of the kit may well offer a complete rolling chassis preparation service with reconditioned or new parts. Assembly might be done by the kit manufacturer or by a recommended sub-contractor.

It's a neat way to sidestep all the time and effort of cleaning, reconditioning and fitting donor parts. There's also the added advantage of getting all the bits from one source. If anything goes wrong, you know where to point the finger.

You might choose to take a middle ground. The engine and gearbox can be sent away as exchange units or for specific re-working at a local engineering company. That would leave you to take on the suspension components and other more minor jobs.

As we have mentioned, several vehicle dismantlers

advertise 'boxed sets' of donor components in the kit car press. They can also supply you specific items on request. Make sure you know whether the price includes VAT, reconditioning, painting, delivery, warranty and whether the items are supplied as exchange or outright purchases.

All those hours of hard graft can be avoided if you can afford professional steam-cleaning, shot-blasting and powder coating. There are many methods of cleaning car components using shot, sand, grit and other abrasives under pressure. Carburettors and other engine parts with hidden oilways and apertures can be cleaned with special ultra-sonic equipment or acid baths.

Powder and/or epoxy coatings are sprayed and oven-baked and are usually far more resilient than painted finishes. Such services can be found in *Yellow Pages* or via a club or the kit manufacturer. If you're building a car for ultimate longevity or concours presentation, they're seriously worth consideration. Prices vary widely, so shop around.

Make the acquaintance of your local tool hire person and find out just what kinds of automotive tools are available. If your donor engine requires special equipment for correct

dismantling, reassembly or tuning and adjustment, it's possible that the hire shop can get them. You probably won't be the first person to have enquired after such tools, especially if it's a popular engine or suspension system. Your local garages might also offer expensive specialist tools for hire.

Items such as torque wrenches, spring pre-load gauges, run-out gauges, hub pullers, slide-hammers, vernier gauges, clutch aligners, void bush removers/installers, compression testers, basic electrical diagnostic equipment, air compressors, spring compressors, power tools, transformers and even generators can be rented if the retail price is too high.

Your technical manual should tell you which components are simply too

much for the amateur car builder to attempt at home. Differentials, steering racks, exhaust gas analysis, electronic ignition or fuel injection repairs, crack testing, steering and suspension geometry measurements, alternator/dynamo repairs, block and head skimming, hydrolastic suspension pressurising, instrument calibration etc. are best left to the experts with their expensive equipment.

This chapter should have given you a good idea of the equipment you do or do not need in order to set up your build premises properly for the start of your project. We will be dealing with extra tools, equipment, techniques and sub-contract services in subsequent chapters, so don't presume that you've already got everything that you need!

Chapter 4
DONORS

Section 1
The choice

ONE OF THE MOST COMMON letters we get here at the *Which Kit?* office relates to choosing a suitable donor car for your project. Almost without question, each week will see a number of people writing in asking if there is a kit to suit this or that (donor) car. All carefully maintained by the family and used as the trusty daily workhorse for the last 15 years, the old Volvo estate, Toyota Celica, Triumph Acclaim, BMW 3-Series has finally failed its MoT on grounds of terminal body rot. Engine and running gear have many excellent years of use ahead of them, we are told, so what kit can they build out of their old family friend? The answer, more often than not, is not a lot.

Think about this for a minute, you are in the process of committing yourself to several thousand pounds' worth of investment, hundreds of hours of work and yet you are willing to limit your choice of project to perhaps just one kit because it happens to use the engine and suspension from your MoT failed Nissan which is worth no more than £150 at best! You're quite right – it makes no sense at all. Get your £150 quid and buy the donor car that suits the kit you might actually like to drive.

Kit car manufacturers will have thought long and hard about the donor car they base their kit on and the chances are they'll have chosen a base car which was produced in huge volume, is easy to find, cheap to purchase, offers the use of as many components as possible and will be around for many years to come. Hardly surprising, then, that the most popular donor car for many years has been the trusty old Ford Cortina. It's now being caught up and overtaken by another Ford model, the Sierra, but there are also several other donor cars being used, from seemingly exotic models such as the Jaguar XJ6 to rather more basic runabouts such as the old Citroen 2CV.

Because the average kit builder isn't going to invest much less than £5000 or £6000 in the project, it has to be well researched. The prospective buyer must check that the donor refurbishment and the relevant kit components are within the right price bracket and that the level of skill needed to work with each is realistically available.

Armed with your £5000, therefore, you know that you will not be able to satisfactorily complete a Jaguar-based Cobra replica - even if the neighbour has an excellent XJ6 going for a couple of hundred quid. However, if the family living opposite is trying to get rid of a Marina or a Cortina at the right price, then you could be into several good kits with a head-start.

It doesn't take much common sense to realise the kind of features that will send your budget skywards. Many different types of body/chassis kits have a similar price tag. Something expensive that needs Cortina suspension, and the donor engine as well, may cost less than a cheaper kit which requires a Rover V8, independent rear suspension, wide wheels and a tailor-made radiator etc.

Your level of ability is another important factor even if your budget is pretty robust to start with. We would certainly recommend that first-time kit builders cut their teeth on something easy to handle. Undoubtedly, there are those who can jump into the V12 deep end and come out smelling of roses. However, the majority will reek of something rather less appealing.

There's a large section of the kit car market supplying kits which are cleverly designed to

The old faithful Ford Cortina still rates as one of the most prolific kit car donors still in use. They are gradually becoming a little more difficult to find.

The Jaguar XJ6 is a surprisingly popular donor choice. You'll usually find them underneath high performance kits such as the Cobra replicas.

The Ford Sierra is becoming an increasingly popular donor and it seems likely that it will take over from the Cortina fairly shortly as the donor car everyone uses.

The VW Beetle's removable body made it the ideal donor car of the 'seventies but only a handful of kits still use it - usually for early Porsche replicas such as the 356 and Spyder.

use assortments of suitable donor parts, as well as parts specially made by the manufacturer for that kit. Most of the mid-engined kits fall into this category, as well as some popular sports models and real performance machines.

Deciding whether or not you have got 'what it takes' isn't just a question of being able to interpret a donor's *Haynes Workshop Manual* and the kit's build manual. It also requires some hands-on experience to see whether you can relate the

you service a basic engine such as a Ford Kent or Leyland B-Series? How does a clutch work? Where is the water pump? Should an earth wire be large or small? What is crankshaft end-float and what does DOHC stand for? Stumped? You will be!

No matter how many hours you spend gazing at brochures, manuals and asking kit manufacturers for their opinions, you could be on the brink of an expensive mistake. Perhaps it might be a good idea to buy a popular donor vehicle such as a Cortina, running and fully MOT-tested? You could get the *Haynes Workshop Manual* and practice all kinds of maintenance, service and major

repair jobs on it just to see if you can do it. Obviously, welding sills won't be one of the key tests here.

If you're really serious about your intention to build a kit car, this experiment will be relatively cheap. If you end up bodging most of the jobs, even with good advice and technical reference books available, then you lose the few hundred quid you spent and perhaps get some money back on spares value. It will have saved you thousands wasted on a failed kit. Let's face it, some just do not have the manual aptitude.

If you achieve a good level of success with the potential donor (there are bound to be some mistakes) then you might want to use it as the basis for a first project or you might sell it on in good nick for a fair price before going a different route.

The beginner or the builder with a limited budget should never be seduced into going for a really fringe kit just because the body shape looks superb, the price is cheap or the staff are really nice. When you're on a tight budget, that's just the time to stick with the established names where decent support and a well proven product should go most of the way to ensuring you don't end up putting an advert in *Which Kit?*'s Part Built Projects section of the Classifieds.

Once you have decided on a

THE WHICH KIT? TIP
When you come to strip out your donor, be utterly comprehensive and remove every last grommet and seal, you never quite know when it will be just the thing you are looking for at a later stage during the build

Usually, it is the car enthusiast's past experience at maintaining or rebuilding production cars which will help to sway the vote one way or the other. If you've owned and maintained Escorts and Cortinas, then you're bound to feel more confident with them. Some are happier with the Leyland group products and will stick with Mini, Marina, Triumph, MGB etc.

If you've got plenty of experience with many different types of car, then you might well feel confident enough to tackle a hybrid kit or any other offering. The real problem comes when you have the enthusiasm but not the real experience. You might turn out to be an automotive genius or you might swoon at the first real problem.

theory to the practice.

Can you understand how to trace and rectify a knocking noise from the rear end? Can

The Beetle based Nova was one of the first bulk selling kit cars. Many people fell for the exotic lines but early cars were difficult to build and Beetle underpinning was disappointing.

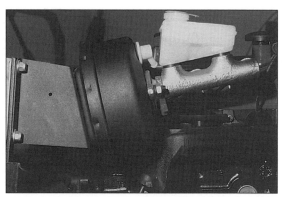

Even the best donor car will require a degree of refurbishment. Vital brake components such as the calipers, servo and master cylinder will need careful checking. If in doubt - replace it.

Above: Remove absolutely everything from your donor car - you never know when something may be useful. Below: Ford Pinto (1600 and 2000cc) is most common Cortina installation.

kit and its donor vehicle(s), there's the hunt to buy and strip the donor so that the parts you want can be repaired, cleaned and painted in preparation for the rolling chassis assembly.

Let's take the example of the Cortina at first. We'll also look at Jaguar, Sierra and Mk.2 Escort hunting in later sections and throw in some advice about other cars and engines that might be of interest.

Section 2
Cortina

WHEN A KIT IS DESCRIBED as Cortina based, it usually indicates that the base vehicle can be the Mk.3, 4 or 5 Cortina.

The kit will probably accommodate most or all of the engines fitted to those models by Ford. (To our knowledge, there are no kits built from Mk.1 or 2 Cortinas). There might also be an extra set of engines to choose from and you might also need more minor donor parts from other vehicles.

Ford's Mk.3 Cortina was introduced in 1970 with estate, four-door and two-door saloon models. Engines were primarily 1300cc and 1600cc pushrod Kent OHV 4-cylinders and Pinto 1600cc and 2000cc SOHC 4-cylinders. From September 1973, all 1600cc models used the Pinto OHC unit. Manual and automatic gearboxes were used.

The Mk.3 disappeared in 1976 to be replaced by the Mks. 4 and then 5, which used much the same mechanical components with revised body shapes. There were detail variations in the mechanical parts used and a manufacturer might specifically advise you to be on the lookout for a Mk.4 or 5.

The largest engines to be fitted to standard Cortinas in the UK were the German Cologne pushrod 2.3-litre V6s, offering better torque and refinement than the 2-litre Pinto but creating a weight and economy penalty. The Cortina was killed off in the early eighties to be replaced by the Sierra range which appeared in 1982.

In most cases, you'll do yourself a favour by ignoring the older Mk.3s and looking for a good Mk.4 or 5. The latter is still commonplace on the road

and you'll pay higher prices for them as many will be 'going concerns' for some years yet. The rust blight was a little less rampant on later models.

Very few Cortinas have been professionally maintained to a high standard and the newer models, with fewer miles, are less likely to have been compromised by the not-so-good or not-so-rich amateur mechanic.

We would always advise you to buy a model which is running and can be test driven with the engine at full running temperature. It's the best way to tell if there's something disastrously wrong with the engine, gearbox or axle.

Presume that you will have to refurbish the brakes, suspension and steering components as a matter of course. It won't matter too much, therefore, if they are trashed.

If you're looking for a bargain running Cortina with all suspension and brake parts still

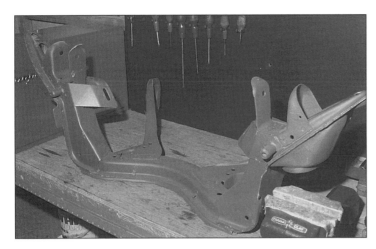

in good condition for instant re-use, then you should consider whether you have saved enough money for a decent build-up yet. Chances are, you will be very lucky to find an example in tip top condition for reasonable money. Economising on reconditioning can be very hazardous.

John Froggatt of Kit-Fit, the trade's leading supplier of reconditioned donor parts for Ford based kit cars, says that there are several key points to look out for in any Cortina you might consider buying. You might add these tips to your own specialist car buying repertoire.

First off, the Cortina front crossmember is quite often damaged. There's a write-off factor of around 40% relating to second-hand crossmembers, mainly due to a combination of kerb impact damage, rust and

extreme wear from neglected and non-existent bushed joints. Look very carefully as the crossmember is usually filthy.

Check the points where the front tie rods mount to the front of the subframe. The large rubber bushes wear out and crumble away, the tie rod thread gets worn and it can slot the crossmember holes.

A knock-on result might be excess wear in the lower wishbone (or track control arm) bushes. Has the lower wishbone split anywhere? Look carefully and clear off grit with a wire brush if necessary.

At the back end, check for oil leaks at the front and rear of the differential. The back plate can become porous and may need replacement. Oil leaking around the differential nose/flange will probably mean a new seal at least. Oil seeping onto the brake shoe backing

plates might also mean a specialist reconditioning job.

A whirring, grinding or vibration from the rear might mean an differential replacement. OK if you've budgeted for it. Clunks and bangs can be propshaft bearings and suspension bushes, all of which should be replaced anyway.

1600 Cortinas will usually have a Salisbury Type A rear axle with a 3.89:1 differential ratio. The *Haynes Workshop Manuals* will describe how the axles differ visually. The 2-litre models usually have Type B axles with 3.44:1 or 3.7:1 differential ratios. Make sure the kit manufacturer recommends a specific ratio best suited to your choice of engine, gearbox, wheels and tyres.

When checking the OHC Pinto engines, make sure you

do it with the engine starting from cold. Keep an eye on the oil pressure light before you turn the engine over. The oil pressure light should go out after the engine has turned over for only a couple of seconds, even if it hasn't fired yet.

If the warning light stays on until the engine catches or the revs are increased, it can mean that the crankshaft and related main or big-end bearings will need reconditioning. Oil leaks from the head, sump or other seals and gaskets are cheap to fix and the jobs are relatively easy.

When the engine fires up, immediately take it up to pretty high revs and turn the ignition off. Switch the ignition back on again just as the engine stops turning, so that it doesn't catch and start again.

If it's cold, the oil pressure light should stay off for three or

Front subframes are very prone to rust and damage. Check thoroughly. Below: Front tie rods can also be damaged at the subframe mounting points.

Above: The rear diff backing plate may well be leaking and can become porous. Below: Perhaps one of the Pinto's most renowned weaknesses is a worn camshaft due to poor lubrication.

four seconds. If the crank's knackered, it will already be on or will come on after only one or two seconds. If the engine is hot, this should still take two or three seconds to be comfortable. If the oil level is below the dipstick, the engine has probably been well abused in its recent life.

Start and rev the engine again. A tapping, clicking or loud rattling from the top of the engine will usually indicate a worn-out camshaft, not just valve rockers out of adjustment. Neglected or infrequently used Pintos can suffer from very poor camshaft lubrication and the cam must subsequently be replaced. Even properly rebuilt Pintos can retain a slight cam tapping.

A rough compression test can be done by seeing how long the engine runs on after the ignition has been turned off. If the engine takes two or three seconds to come to a halt, then compression probably isn't good and a rebore and pistons are on the cards, possibly a cylinder head refurbishment as well. An engine which stops very sharply from hot or cold, and possibly with a brief shudder, could well have a good compression.

Vulcan Engineering, the Ford tuning specialists of Hanwell, West London, tells us that kit builders should stay clear of the 1600cc Pinto OHC engine fitted

Above: Original mounting points for an engine and gearbox will often be removed and new ones supplied in the kit. This original Cortina gearbox crossmember is unlikely to remain.

to Cortinas, Sierras and Capris etc. They are inferior to the 2-litre variant in many respects and the only benefit is the possibility of cheaper insurance. Even that might be offset by the extra reconditioning bills!

The company confirms that camshaft failure is pretty commonplace for the Pintos and that you should do your best to get the donor which has a twin-choke downdraught carburettor rather than the single-choke Motorcraft downdraught.

If you are looking for the rare 2300cc V6, we would advise you to watch out for bad oil pressure and blown cylinder heads caused by possible overheating. Most owners say that this is an excellent, free-revving and low-maintenance

engine but it will obviously be more complex than the Pinto, much heavier and nearly completely untunable to boot. Sounds much better but exhausts are more involved. Less engine bay room because of V format.

If you have access to slightly more specialised equipment, check compression of each cylinder and look for a difference of no more than 15% between the lowest and highest. You might be able to get an oil pressure gauge and sender which can be used to replace an electric warning light sender. Some OHC Capris have these as standard. Test oil pressure with engine hot.

Particularly good news for Pinto engine users is that there

is a simple conversion to a five-speed gearbox if you're fed up with the Cortina's four-speed restriction. A fifth gear is particularly useful if you have a lightweight kit with wheel/tyre diameter restrictions (under-gearing from a four-speed box on a light vehicle might be offset by an increase in wheel diameter specified by the manufacturer).

1600 and 2-litre Sierras were often fitted with an optional five-speed gearbox. These boxes were common to both models, although there were various four-speed options as well. JBA Engineering of Standish, Wigan, makers of very popular Cortina and Sierra-based kits, tell us that fitment of the five-speed gearbox from these Sierras is a pretty straightforward swap-across.

Keep your Pinto's flywheel, friction plate, clutch cover, release bearing, actuating lever, bellhousing and starter motor and bolt on the Sierra box. The first-motion shaft is the correct length. The Sierra gear lever will appear 5/8" further back and the propshaft may well need shortening by the same amount. You will probably need chassis alterations to accommodate the new gearbox crossmember and its revised position.

The sliding splined propshaft forward section will slide into the tail end of the Sierra box if your

You'll often find different carburettors fitted to an earlier or later version of the same car. Standard twin choke (below) is the best Cortina carb. Auto choke can be changed to manual.

Few Cortinas ever had a five-speed gearbox. Using the Sierra 'box is quite straightforward and retains the Cortina's original bell-housing. It's a popular conversion.

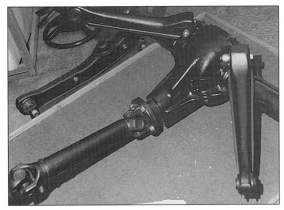

Above: Propshafts will often have to be shortened. Several companies can do this for you. Below: Thorough reconditioning is only route to reliability.

Above: This is the standard Sierra front disc, upright and caliper assembly. Drums are the standard rear fitment although 4x4s and other performance Fords offer rear discs. A worthwhile option when using high performance engines.

prop donor was a 2-litre Cortina. If you are using a 1600 Cortina donor, then you will have to get a new prop with a 2-litre or Sierra splined forward section. The relevant 1600 or 2-litre Cortina clutch assembly can be retained or you can opt for the equivalent 1600 or 2-litre Sierra assembly.

Terry Nightingale of Terry Nightingale Autocraft, Saffron Walden, Essex, tells us to use the common five-speed boxes from the 1600 and 2-litre Pintos. Watch out for the (rare and highly saleable) MT75 performance box fitted to Cosworths as there can be extra expense incurred in fitting these. You can tell they're special as they have an integrally cast bellhousing.

Watch out also if using the five-speed box from the Cologne V6-equipped XR4i and Capri 2.8 models. These have a longer first motion shaft protruding from the gearbox and you need to compensate for this with a special spacer between the bellhousing and the block.

This will set the gearbox even further back.

When dismantling Cortina suspensions, expect some very recalcitrant components which will do everything in their power to block your gentle efforts. We have mentioned the subframe failure rate above. You're immediately at an advantage if your kit doesn't need the Cortina subframe.

Small M6 bolts retaining the lower mounts of the front hydraulic shock absorbers are often jammed tight into the lower wishbone. If they shear off, then you've got trouble getting the holes drilled and re-worked.

Kit-Fit recommends that you use caution if applying heat to help free components. Suspension parts involve a fair amount of rubber and, unless tidied before dismantling work, a

fair amount of oily grim will also have collected around them. Using a standard gas blow torch can set the whole lot alight.

A tighter flame from a welding torch or similar is safer but you might just have to settle for soaking the whole lot in releasing fluid and hoping for the best later on.

Much the same story goes for the lower rear shock absorber mounting bolts. These can also be extremely difficult to remove and flame is equally likely to set the whole lot off. Top quality spanners with single-hex heads, releasing fluid, a wire brush and patience

could reward you. If not, there are sources such as Kit-Fit who will supply dismantled and reconditioned parts to order.

Section 3
Sierra

EVEN IF THE SIERRA GOT A proper slagging for its road manners, it is a quantum leap ahead as far as engineering sophistication is concerned. The Cortina might be easy to service, cheap and blessed with excellent parts availability but it's an engineering nightmare of the most cynical order.

Comprehensive reconditioning can be very satisfying. This refurbished Jaguar rear suspension looks terrific after many hours of work.

More and more modern kits do not use the donor's front subframe and mount suspension directly onto the new chassis. Below: Complete Sierra rear suspension set-up including De-Dion tube.

These engineering shortcomings are responsible for many of the major and minor faults to be found in the suspension, engine, road manners, gearboxes and bodyshells - not just the age, neglect and high mileage of many remaining examples.

Ford's Sierra, which arrived in 1982, covered a lot of new ground and was a real trend-setter in its day, especially with its apparently aerodynamic bodywork. The models with which kit builders will be mainly concerned will be the 1.6 and 2-litre Pinto-powered versions, the 2.3-litre V6 Cologne-powered version and the 1.8-litre CVH SOHC-powered version. (Some donors will be fuel-injected models).

These are all rear-drive cars with front-mounted in-line engines and a selection of manual four and five-speed gearboxes or automatic boxes. You will have seen the other XR4i, XR4x4, RS500 Cosworth and Sapphire Cosworth versions and most of these will have various different mechanical parts possibly not suited to the kit destined for a standard Sierra donor.

Estate versions also feature slight detail changes in the rear suspension system and there have been several design changes over the years. Be careful to know exactly which models/years the kit manufacturer specifies when you're out bargain hunting

because there's a good chance you'll be buying a crash-damaged vehicle to take advantage of the low price. If it's the wrong sort, you might have a problem moving it on.

Up until recently, crash-damaged Sierras were generally the only ones which fell into the

predominance of the Pinto engines is also a big plus point for keen car maintainers.

You have to be extra vigilant when looking at crashed cars for sale. Roll-over damage promises better suspension condition that side or end-on impacts. It might be better to see if the kit manufacturer can offer you checked and warrantied donor parts approved for resale by insurance company car breakers. Some of these have

correct donor vehicle price bracket but second-hand prices have tumbled in recent years to the point where decent running examples can often be found for under a grand. They are easy to maintain in most cases and the

crack-testing facilities to be extra-sure.

Common casualties in Sierras are the fragile front subframe and, subsequently, the steering rack. These can both be damaged if the former is caught on a curb stone or other obstruction. Kit-Fit tell us that the front lower track control arms and bushes are regularly replaced for safety's sake.

The company also says that the rear end is generally in good condition, with little trouble coming from the differentials, half-shafts or propshaft. The 1600, 1800, 2-litre and 2.3-litre models are all fitted with unequal length 'double-tripod'-jointed half-shafts.

No-maintenance tripod joints allow the bearings at the differential ends to slide and compensate for suspension travel by altering the half-shaft acting length. The half-shafts themselves are different lengths so that the differential flange can be positioned in the centre of the car, giving the propshaft a pretty straight run to the gearbox.

Different types of half-shaft attachment are used for the XR4i and other performance Sierras and for the Mk.3 Granada range. These are called Lowbro joints and feature cap screw fittings at the differential ends, rather than just a sliding spline fixing.

Depending upon the make and model of kit, the manufacturer might instruct you to ignore the rear DeDion tube, the front McPherson struts, the subframes, coil springs, rear shock absorbers or the rear trailing arms.

You might have to secure the wiring loom, complete dashboard with switches and instruments, front seats, uprights and hubs, rear lights etc. Such factors will affect your donor-buying assessments. Never use the seatbelt components from a crashed car.

Increasingly, kit car manufacturers are appreciative of the high engineering standards reached by the Sierra's designers. Having based models on Cortina machanicals in the past, many have found that the Sierra comes out way ahead.

The 1800 CVH installation, while rating high on reliability and practically as easy to maintain as the Pintos, is a boring and gutless unit with not much tuning potential. It's better than the 1600 Pinto, has far less scope than the 2-litre Pinto, is lower than both and has less character than the 2.3 V6.

Don't choose a fuel-injected Sierra engine if you are not confident enough to rework the complex engine wiring loom to the requisite shape and manage all of the dedicated sensors and senders which are involved. Remember that not all Sierras have five-speed manual boxes and that a four-speed or automatic box might be wholly inappropriate for your kit car.

The fact that so many new kit cars are based around the Sierra is hardly a surprise. With independent rear suspension as standard, endless tuning potential thanks to performance models such as the Cosworth and typical Ford affordability in terms of parts supply, the Sierra is allowing kit car designers the chance to develop new kits which have greater ride refinement; modern facilities such as central locking and electric windows and all at budget prices. No two ways about it, the Sierra will remain the staple diet of the kit car industry for many years to come.

Section 4
Jaguar

OF ALL THE MANY manufacturers who make

This awesome Jaguar V12 looks amazing in a Dax Tojeiro Cobra replica but the engine is frighteningly expensive to work on and a nightmare in plumbing! American V8s offer more affordable power and are easier to deal with.

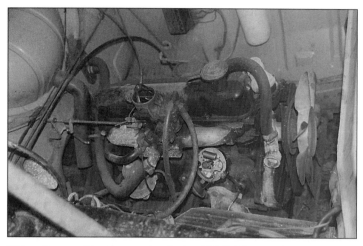

This rather sad looking engine is the OHV X-flow engine fitted to most old Escorts. Be very wary of using an engine in this condition and expect a complete rebuild.

The result of some serious graft on an old 1600cc X-flow can be amazing. This terrific looking unit fitted to a Tiger Super Six produces 135bhp of flat out exhilaration.

Jaguar based kit cars, most say that their customers will simply buy a donor, strip it and unquestioningly recondition and modify all the required parts. Some customers don't even buy the donor but just order reconditioned parts from the manufacturer. Strange behaviour? Extravagance or caution?

It seems obvious that kit builders looking for Jaguar based kits are in the higher budget bracket. It is possible to buy, strip, clean, check and reassemble Jaguar parts at home, especially as the high street cost of reconditioning is prohibitive. You don't get into such a project without knowing the potential costs.

However, kit car companies making kits for the Jaguar base can often offer very competitive prices on reconditioned parts, exchange or outright. Much better than Original Equipment or high street prices. It's often difficult to refuse the offer.

Most kit cars which use Jaguar/Daimler parts, as we have mentioned, will need the suspension and axle components from the post-1974 S3 saloons with straight six twin-cam or V12 engines. The entire XJS range is also suitable for most Jaguar based kits.

A good proportion of kits will need shortened rear half shafts and 'wishbones' and that job has to be done by the kit

manufacturer's recommended specialist - not just any welding shop. The Jaguar front and rear suspension subframes are usually not required for the kit build.

In most cases, the heavy and very expensive engines and gearboxes will not be appropriate for the kit in question as there will either be insufficient room or the builder will find it more economical to sort out a British or American V8. Very few builders are lucky enough to find, afford and commission the legendary V12 but the costs and complexity are phenomenal.

It's quite common for kit builders to treasure the Jaguar separate gauges, main instruments and switches from

This is the spring hanger on a Escort rear suspension set-up. These donors use leaf rear springs but often it's only the axle that is used with a new location.

the dashboard. The steering column, column stalks, related wiring, pedal box, fuel pumps, propshaft, rare manual gearboxes, brake components and other selected trim items can also come in handy.

A kit car such as the Aristocat, from Autotune, will benefit from most of the donor parts, including engine and box, so you'll have to be more choosy when looking for the donor. Try to get a good, running example. Autotune's Anthony Taylor will give you excellent advice relating to the Aristocat donor search.

Most Jaguar specialists, such as Classic Spares in Hertfordshire, find that they very rarely break a Jaguar and find terminal damage to the drive or

suspension components. They're over-engineered and immensely strong because the Jaguar is a very heavy and powerful car. Most un-crashed donors will supply parts suitable for standard reconditioning, no matter how rusty the body looks.

At the front end, you'll usually find that the front upper and lower balljoints will need to be replaced and that the wishbone metalastic bushes will also have to go. Special tools and or sub-contract 'pressing' services might be needed to fit the new bushes or remove the old ones. Steering racks from the Jaguars are hardly ever used by kit manufacturers.

Jaguar's independent rear suspension system really can defeat the less-than-confident amateur. You'll often need a good three-claw puller to dismantle the hub assemblies and there are also various shims to be dealt with.

Oil seals, felt washers, universal joints and bushes of different kinds can be worn out and the amount of time taken up by the repairs explains why kit builders tend to sub this work out to the trade rather than take it on at home.

If you're lucky, you'll need to recondition only a few parts and will save money. If you're unlucky, it'll cost you more to do all the work yourself. You may even increase the cost by damaging something expensive or you might compromise safety by overlooking a difficult and essential job.

There is a selection of differential ratios available to Jaguar based kit builders and the most common of these is probably the 3.3:1. You can also find the 3.54:1, 2.88:1 and there's even meant to be a very rare 4.55:1 from some export 2.8-litre models. Find out if you're better off looking for a specific ratio in the first place.

Although the Jaguar might seem like an extravagant choice of donor, there is much to recommend it. The earlier bodies rust away like crazy, creating a good supply of MoT failures, and the independent rear suspension is sophisticated, strong and offers optional diff. ratios and Powr-Lok limited slip capabilities.

Jaguar's front suspension is the timeless and super-smooth double wishbone system which can be adapted to give excellent anti-dive geometry while retaining road feel and steering

sensitivity. Suspension units are coil-over shocks all round, making it easier for kit manufacturers to alter rates with new parts without changing geometries detrimentally.

Because the width of the Jaguar is usually wider than the kits which use its components, kit manufacturers redesign the steering geometry (with varying rates of success) to use a narrower steering rack. As we have mentioned, the rear suspension arms and half-shafts (which themselves act as top arms) often have to be carefully shortened to give a suitable vehicle track.

Some have criticised this shortening process as expensive, structurally fallible and liable to cause more exaggerated camber changes from full bump to full droop. We

have heard of only one or two cases of re-welded Jaguar rear suspensions breaking and these might even be put down to excessive horsepower or unlucky and sudden grip at the rear wheels causing too much stress for any rear assembly to handle.

In an effort to save money and time for the kit builder, some manufacturers have redesigned their kits to accept the full-width Jaguar front and rear axles. It might alter the look of the kit, especially if that kit is meant to be a lookalike Cobra or other classic car, but it really does simplify matters.

All in all, the Jaguar stuff

remains popular for those looking to use high-power engines. The closest available alternatives, Ford's current IRS Granada and Cosworth Sierra, only offer indifferent front suspension and relatively limited horsepower handling capability.

Section 5
Ford Escort Mk.2

MANY KIT CARS USED TO BE described as Escort Mk.1 or 2 based. These days, sadly, the Mk.1 Escorts are usually so old and knackered that it's difficult to see the point of using one as

This is the front suspension of the Escort, as fitted to a Rickman Ranger. The upper mounting bracket has been incorporated into the chassis.

Above: Here you can see how the leaf spring is attached to the live axle along with its rubber bump stop. Below: Reconditioned front subframe. Front mounts are for steering rack. Check carefully for rust and damage.

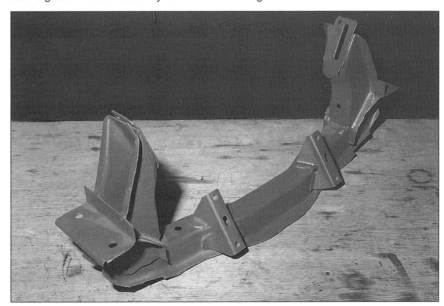

your main donor.

Needless to say, there will still be some well-maintained models out there with good running gear and engines but there are front suspension differences that make the Mk.2 a better bet. More reconditioning parts are available for Mk.2 running gear.

Don't turn your nose up at the offer of a good engine, gearbox or rear axle from a Mk.1, even if you do intend to go ahead and get a Mk.2 donor anyway. There are some handy axle ratios available from Sport or GT Mk.1 models.

Although it has declined as a main donor for kits, the rear drive Escort is still very sought after as an engine donor. The predominant engine fitments were the Ford Kent X-flow pushrod OHV units in 1100cc, 1300cc and 1600cc formats, the latter being a very popular unit to this day, especially in GT format. The rare RS2000 Mk.2 was fitted with the 2-litre Pinto and the Mexico 1600 is also a valuable find.

Automatic or four-speed manual gearboxes were all a bit of a let-down but we can get around that. Ford's Kent engines, which were also present in the Capri and Cortina ranges, are fabulously easy to work on for the aspiring amateur and the 1600 and 1300 variants have been graced by the availability of a huge selection of affordable performance parts and modification services.

The 1100 doesn't really rate in anyone's book but as all the engines have basically the same fitting requirements, we think that an 1100 unit could be a good insurance-saver for a young driver who could then upgrade to the beefier 1600. The 1100 is also very common and good examples can still be found.

They are all lighter than the lumbering great Pinto OHC units and share the all-iron construction for heads and blocks. This makes it easier to clean off gasket surfaces without scoring them. It also makes for more robust spark plug threads and less likelihood of head-warping after overheating episodes. Alloy heads, as fitted to the CVH units, are light but much more fragile when old.

Vulcan Engineering says that the archaic basic engine design usually leaves a large piston-to-bore clearance which can lead to excessive blow-by gases entering the crankcase. Pintos are better in this respect. A compression test showing around 130 PSI per cylinder will probably mean a rebore.

Watch out for a flywheel ring gear damaged by the inertia starter. Fitting a new ring gear can be a tricky job and many will send it away to get it done. Because the line stopped so long ago, it's likely that most of the engines will need some kind of reconditioning.

You would probably spend up to £500 on a comprehensive standard rebuild if you did the splitting and reassembly yourself. This is one of the

Compared to the Pinto (left), CVH units are expensive to tune and even then cannot match it for power output. Pinto may be a little tall for some kits.

American V8s, such as this Ford 302ci example are increasingly easy to get hold of and offer relatively cheap performance. However, this exhaust system will be anything but cheap. Looks fantastic in this GT40 replica.

easiest engines to work on.

If you want more horsepower, having reconditioned your engine, the best initial move is to use the Escort GT twin-choke downdraught carburettor and relevant inlet and exhaust manifolds. Two side-draught Weber or Dell'Orto twin-chokes on a special manifold can work wonders when properly tuned and a flowed head makes a big improvement.

When you come to the realm of camshaft uprating, things can start to get pretty involved if the job is to be done properly and prices will also start to creep up. There's only so much that the standard engine will take, so you will have to end up reinforcing certain areas if you increase the horsepower by much.

If you're happy with the standard 4-speed gearbox, fine. However, Terry Nightingale

Autocraft (TNA) will tell you how to fit the beefier four-speed boxes from the Pinto engined Fords. The company also explained to us how to fit the Sierra's five-speed gearbox (not MT75 box).

TNA can supply a kit of parts which includes a special heavy-duty 7.5" friction plate, standard 1600 Kent clutch cover, standard Sierra release bearing and a 2-litre Cortina bellhousing and actuating lever. This uses the standard 1600 Escort's inertia starter. Consult the company about specifications and the possibility of part-kits for the conversion.

Rear drive Escorts are equipped with coil spring/McPherson strut front suspension on a steel subframe which also supports the engine. Mk.2 models feature a lower track control arm located by inboard rubber bushes,

outboard balljoints and a rubber-bushed anti-roll bar. The upright (or stub axle assembly) is integral with the McPherson strut tube and front brakes are solid discs.

Rear suspension features a selection of live axle types (and differential ratios) located primarily by two longitudinal single or multi-leaf cart springs. Rear shock absorbers are telescopic and rear brakes are drums.

The kit manufacturer should specify exactly which type to look out for and whether it has a servo or non-servo braking system, the correct differential ratio (most common are 4.125:1 and 3.89:1) and the correct springs at the rear.

There are variations in the types of propshaft fitted but the Mk.2s generally have two-piece units, with a central support bearing. A multitude of detail

variations can be found in the electrical equipment, loom specifications, engine compression ratios etc.

The most prized find is a good or reconditionable 1600 engine with the legendary 711M identification number on the block casting. These blocks are said to be the toughest of the lot and more capable of withstanding extra bhp.

If your kit requires Escort rear leaf springs, we would recommend that you use only the estate or van single leaf types, preferably a new pair instead of worn out 'flat' ones. Saloon single and multi-leaf springs are notoriously soft, even when new. This was fine for the unpretentious standard Escorts but usually isn't so good for a more robust or sporting kit car.

Mk.2 McPherson struts are OK most of the time but a

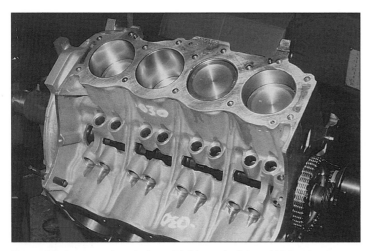

Rover V8 is a popular choice with kit car builders. Whilst the bores are usually OK, timing chains are prone to wear. Major rebuilds on the Rover can be expensive.

All reconditioned engines from Roverpart are run-up on the test bed prior to being sent out to customers. Back street bodgers unlikely to do the same and may well prove a false economy.

collection of moisture-retaining grime in the lower coil-spring retaining cups may cause these to rust through. Other rust victims are the drum brake backing plates at either end of the live axle and the front suspension subframe.

Kit Fit reports that the fallible brake back plates and the shields for the front discs are no longer available new. Nor are the rubber bump-stops. The front subframes can look really sound when still covered in grime but when they come back from the cleaning sub-contractor, loads of rust holes can suddenly be revealed. Rust can also cause subframes to become rather thin.

Rear axles and differentials are usually not too bad but listen for grinding noises and watch out for oil leaks at the outer ends of the axle tubes and at the differential flange.

There seems to be no shortage of second hand, pattern or reconditioned parts for the Mk.2 Escorts but firms will increasingly demand exchange components, especially engines and axles, as the new supplies dry up. New 1600 engines seem to have been all bought by the likes of Caterham.

You might find yourself crawling around scrap yards to get the bits you need and Ford

dealers will probably stare blankly when you ask for a special part. If you have real trouble, try other kit manufacturers who use the Kent series engines, they might be a lot more familiar with the bits you need - and they might own the last stocks anyway.

When the last of the rear drive Escorts clanks its way into a scrap yard, it will be a sad day for motoring history. It won't be long before kit car enthusiasts will be mourning the passing of a car that lit the flame in so many of us and was so tolerant of our early attempts at home maintenance. It was a much better design than the Cortina and no-one will miss the upstart front drive Escorts when they leave us!

This Rover V8 has a special inlet manifold for twin-SU carbs which helps to lower them under the bonnet of an MGB. May well be a suitable conversion for many kits, too.

Section 6
New kids on the block

THIS SECTION DOESN'T AIM to outline every donor car currently used by kit car manufacturers but it's interesting to see that new kit cars are increasingly being based on really quite modern donor components. Modern kits such as GTM's K3 and Midas' Coupe have stringently adhered to the single donor policy and have made outstandingly comprehensive use of their Rover Metro donor car. Typical of many modern kit car manufacturers, the GTM/Midas kit packages include every last bit and bob not to be found on the donor

car so, once you've bought the kit and sourced a donor there should be no more mucking around collecting extra bits. To make life even easier, several kit car companies can put you onto to a recommended supplier of ready stripped donor packages.

The Alfa Romeo 33 range is another modern donor that has found its way into the kit car market via Minari Engineering's pretty Road Sport. Once again, as much as possible is gleaned from the single source and Minari is more than happy to supply everything else you need in a single package.

The later Granadas have found their way into various kit cars, and in none more comprehensively than the amazing Royale Sabre. This classic tourer bristles with modern features such as central locking, electric windows, 2.9-litre injection engine and ABS brakes! All thanks to its modern underpinnings.

As we try to look towards the future it seems increasingly likely that modern front-wheel-drive cars will become the donors of tomorrow. And with the handling limitations of the FWD configuration we are already seeing companies moving the engine and front suspension to a mid-engined configuration in order to

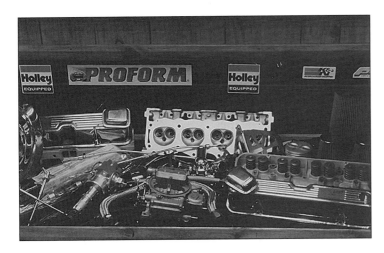

achieve higher levels of handling and individuality.

Section 7
Engines aside

MORE AND MORE manufacturers and builders are looking to alternative engines from those supplied by the main donor and we'll look at one or two of those here. Over the years, there have been a vast array of Fords fitted with the 1300, 1400 and 1600cc CVH engines, first seen with the front-drive Mk.3 Escorts and Fiestas. Inevitably, the kit car trade has made use of this source of engines, even though they would normally be pretty useless because of their front-drive gearboxes.

Only the special Sierra 1800cc CVH variant had a rear drive box as standard. (We mustn't forget that the excellent Quantum monocoque kit uses the CVH front drive units complete). Terry Nightingale Autocraft to the rescue yet again...

This company will sell you either a Ford kit with a heavy 'cruising' flywheel or its own full or part kit to fit the Sierra five-speed gearbox to the CVH block. You'll be accumulating a CVH clutch cover, special friction plate, special release bearing, a Sierra bellhousing and a Cortina starter with an adaptor enabling it to fit the Sierra bellhousing. Problem solved.

CVH stands for Compound Valve Hemispherical head. These single overhead cam (alloy head) units were introduced as replacements for the Kent series OHV engines and have been a pretty big disappointment in general. Even with a neat appearance, easily maintained belt-driven OHC and multiple valves, they sound like a typical economy Japanese unit and have very little character. Just what the fleet buyer ordered.

The top-of-the-range XR2, XR3, XR3i and RS1600i are a bit more interesting than the boring 1300s and 1400s. Their main virtue is low maintenance, plentiful supply and some after-market tuning capability, predominantly for the 1600cc versions. (Avoid any complex EFi versions with flywheel-operated, distributor-less ignition systems).

Think carefully if you have a choice of different engines for your kit and performance is your goal. Vulcan tells us that the CVH really doesn't return very good value for money as it is inherently not a particularly powerful engine.

You might get 125bhp from a 1600 CVH motor with twin Webers and the whole tuning kit and caboodle fitted. A 2-litre Pinto with 'merely' a single twin-choke carburettor, after-market cam and special head can put out 135bhp and cost less!

If you're after a V8 for a muscle car, you'll hear plenty of reasons why you should go for the American models (usually 350ci Chevy or 302ci Ford). Big bhp, some have more compact V angles, relatively cheap, loads of torque, very reliable, possible 20mpg, manual boxes available but still fun with auto and loads more new and second-hand bits being shipped in from the 'States every day.

However, there are reasons why the Rover V8 comes out tops for many kit builders in the UK. The biggest reason is that it is phenomenally light, being an all-alloy engine with alloy

Above: Front drive Mini engine is being used less and less but can still be found in a number of kits. Below: 1700cc Marina Ital engine is a popular choice for the Marlin Roadster.

Above: With the Rover V8 being such a popular unit, there's no shortage of performance parts. Below: Ford Granada 2.9-litre V6 is another multi-cylinder option - seen here in a Pilgrim Sumo.

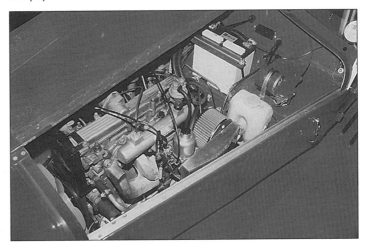

heads. Chris Crane of Roverpart International Ltd., Horsford, Norwich, estimates something like 110kgs without gearbox and manifolds. This is lighter than Ford's Pinto fours and bodes well for good power-to-weight ratio.

Some lighter kits capable of accommodating a V8 engine would simply sag under the weight of an American cast iron unit. Chris, in fact, wonders why people go for the big bhp US motors when they carry a self-defeating weight penalty. However, he does deal in Rover V8s and kit builders do have their reasons!

According to Mr. Crane, the typical second hand Rover V8 unit will be, or will once have been, fitted into a Rover SD1 saloon car. It will probably have an automatic gearbox, twin SU carburettors and it will probably still be running. You might find earlier V8s in earlier Rovers but stick with the SD1 unit if you can. The Rover V8 engine is still produced for the Range Rover and for TVR but you're unlikely to find one of these cheap.

A very small percentage of Rover V8 engines are unserviceable. The main cause is frost damage due to insufficient anti-freeze. Cracks between the core plugs each side of the block toll the bell for the Rover. Ex-Range Rover

Ford Cosworth Turbo is remarkably affordable if you are after some really serious performance. Installation can sometimes be a little complex, especially where space is limited.

engines, always heavily burdened, can suffer from the odd connecting rod through the crank case and this also means bye-bye in most cases.

It seems as if most newcomers to the Rover V8 are somewhat seduced by its torque and power when they first test-drive the engine donor. Even if it's down to 120bhp from a standard rating of about 160, it can still impress many of us.

Be cynical, though, and drive a hard bargain. There will usually be something that needs servicing or maintaining on the engine you're looking at. Most of them are high-mileage motors - 'genuine' low-mileage examples are like rocking horse shoes.

Typical age and neglect-related shortcomings include worn or non-existent cam lobes (these engines are single camshaft, pushrod OHV units), worn out main and/or big-end bearings (causing a loss of oil pressure), loose timing chain and possibly oil leaks partially caused by inherently high crankcase pressure (a blocked breather flame trap or carbon-clogged carburettor bases).

These are the main recurring faults but there may well be other minor or major setbacks. Valve, valve guide and/or valve seat wear, worn rockers and/or rocker shafts etc. Bores are said to be a low-problem area and although there are eight cylinders, it isn't meant to be a difficult engine

to service if you can follow a *Haynes Workshop Manual.*

The more impecunious kit builder might 'get away' with a strip down, thorough clean and degrease, new camshaft and followers, reground crankshaft, new bottom end bearings, new main bearing cap bolts and refaced valve seats.

Chris warns that reused main bearing cap bolts have a tendency to break when the engine first gets hot, or a short while after the rebuild. This causes severe internal damage leading to a written-off engine or a big bill.

The oil pump, once cleaned out, will not self-prime unless it is packed with Vaseline when you put the engine back together. Roverpart can supply a handy tool for priming the oil pump without having to dismantle the engine. The problem doesn't occur when the oil is drained for an oil change.

Those imported American parts are originally destined for American cars fitted with the Buick alloy V8 from which the Rover 3.5 was developed. The engines share many standard and tuning parts but the American stuff is cheaper by far.

If you really want to take advantage of that power to weight ratio and aren't happy with endless bottom-end torque

300bhp John Eales prepared Rover V8 makes this Westfield one of the fastest cars in the world - period. Cost of carburettors alone is enough to give you heart failure.

Vauxhall Astra/Cavalier twin-cam is an increasingly popular power unit and offers cheap performance in largely standard format. Turbo version is a rarity but superb if you can find one.

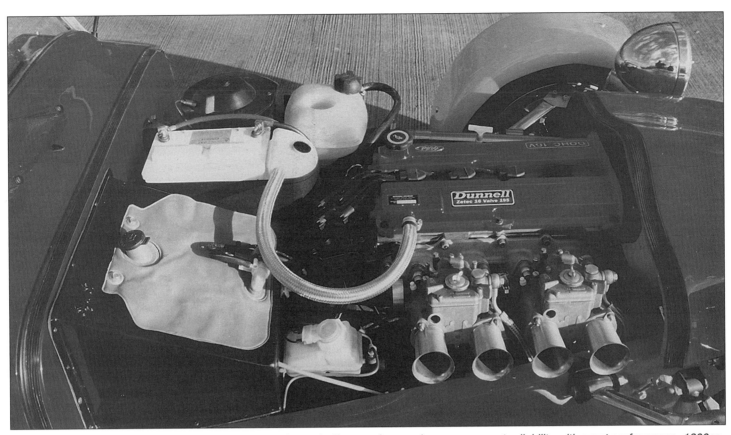

Modern Ford Zetec engine is proving extremely popular and offers modern engine management reliability with great performance. 1800cc more affordable than 2-litre version but still plenty powerful enough. Twin-carb conversion usually necessary.

and 160-odd bhp, you can get a whole multitude of performance bits that you can fit yourself with specialist advice over the phone from folk such as Chris Crane.

If you don't want to do any of the preparation work and can afford a professional job, Roverpart can organise a pick-up and delivery service as well. If you need to buy an engine, Rover specialists will usually have a stock of second-hand units to work on but as the supply inevitably dries up, you'll probably be under pressure to find an exchange unit.

More serious after-market tuning is abundantly available for the Rover V8 from all kinds of sources, JE Motors, Real Steel etc. Rumour has it (could this be from Rover V8 specialists?) that a bored out 3.9-litre Rover V8 tuned for something like 220bhp and 270lb/ft torque can still return 35mpg when you take it easy! When you consider the weight advantage of kit cars over the Rover's donors, this seems to be a more reasonable theory.

What can you do if you don't want an automatic gearbox? Apparently, there are several sources for the five-speed manual gearbox which is compatible with the SD1 V8. Try the five-speed TR7s, the FX4 London Taxi, the five-speed Sherpa van and any of the five-speed Rover SD1s, including the straight-six models. There were also some four-speed manual six-cylinder SD1s.

Trouble is, you'll definitely need the bellhousing and the flywheel from the V8 manual SD1 in order to fit any of these manual gearboxes. They aren't too common and high demand means a high price, even for second hand stuff of possibly dubious integrity. It's better to get to get a complete manual V8 SD1 donor so that you can be sure of all the peripheral parts for the job.

Don't forget that the Rover V8 is also a good prospect for the mid-engined super-kits and it is often grafted onto a Renault 25 or 30 transaxle or a special racing transaxle for this

purpose. When pricing up mid-engined fitments, make sure you know about the cost of a special exhaust, proper cooling equipment, transaxle, clutch assembly and gear linkages etc. There's a large quantity of special equipment needed.

What are the disadvantages of the Rover V8? Well, once you've established that you can afford a 'worst case' reconditioning scenario, there's very little to be said against the alloy V8. Problems occur when kit builders and manufacturers try to shoehorn the Rover into an engine bay that just isn't wide enough.

It is a wide 90-degree V, which reduces the overall engine height immensely compared to some of the American 60-degree stuff. However, if the engine bay is too narrow or otherwise restrictive, you may well find yourself with a 'conflict of space' situation.

That means that the steering column or the brake master cylinder touches the exhaust

manifold, the carburettors want to protrude through the bonnet, the engine/water pump pulleys want to pierce the radiator, the oil filter must be replaced with a remote kit etc. etc.

Don't think that you're sunk if you're not using Ford or Rover engines. Go to the kit car show club stands or some of the races in the 750MC's two kit car series and check out the hardware in the limited and unlimited classes. It'll open your eyes wide.

Many kits which are designed for a four-cylinder, front-mounted, in-line, rear-drive power train can be equipped with various donor engines of that configuration. Ask the manufacturer for advice when deciding what you want to fit. Chances are that the fitment might be possible, even if it costs you more for a special set of engine mounts and you can't use the off-the-shelf wiring loom.

Rear drive Fiat Mirafiori twin-cams, complete with a suitable gearbox from the donor, are excellent engines and pretty

Fiat twin-cam has become increasingly popular for small sevenesque kits. The addition of some twin-carbs and a performance exhaust making for very respectable performance. Engines usually come with a 5-speed gearbox as standard.

powerful in standard form. We once had a meagre 1600cc version fitted to a Sylva Striker and a set of 40 DCOE Webers really made it fly. Sounded superb and was totally reliable, if a little thirsty.

Both the Leyland A and B series engines from the Marinas are fitted with rear drive gearboxes and are easy for the amateur mechanic to dismantle and maintain at home. The A-series units can be particularly highly tuned thanks to all the interest from the Mini fraternity.

Leyland's rear-drive 1700cc O-series SOHC four fitted to later Marinas and the larger Itals (as well as the Sherpa vans) is a simple-to-maintain and very reliable unit. It is not a favourite of engine tuners, meaning that major parts usually have to come from the super-expensive Unipart outlets.

Think of other rear-drive production cars and you could have found an interesting donor for the engine and gearbox. The large Volvos are rear-drive and feature engines up to V6 (Renault unit with a rear-drive gearbox).

The Granadas can yield the Pinto or the Cologne 2.3, 2.8 and 2.9 V6s. These are cast iron, extremely heavy and offer little performance advantage. The older Essex V6 from 3-litre Capris is even heavier but has a better reputation at tuning houses.

Older Toyota Celicas and modern Supras provide interesting rear-drive twin-cam engines, with the six-cylinder, 3-litre Supra and the 2-litre Celica units providing excellent performance. Watch out for the expense of Japanese or other imported spares.

On the subject of big-budget twin-cam engines for rear-drive, you can consult your kit's manufacturer if you want to use such power units instead of a V8. You can get a 2-litre Cosworth Sierra unit fitted with twin-choke carburettors instead of the turbo and injection if you want a simpler life.

Vauxhall's 2-litre Astra GTE twin-cam can also come carburettor or injection-equipped with a rear-drive gearbox. It has been used to devastating effect by Caterham in the HPC and JPE models. The conversion is ferociously expensive, though. So are various Cosworth BDA, Lotus TC and other variants which you can still get hold of from time to time.

Kits using the VW Beetle transaxle or other production or special transaxles can be treated to a whole host of engine fitments. Alfa's excellent flat-four produces superb performance in 1500 and 1700cc formats, especially the later 16-valve 1700 from the 33 range. Even the Beetle engine can be sensibly tuned and balanced for a respectable output. Air-cooling limits reliable states of tune but the price is right.

There's the Ford range again, adapted for rear or mid-engined use. The Lancia twin-cams with their own front drive gearboxes are popular mid-mounted fitments, as are American V8s and some Japanese engines, including the Honda V6.

One of the most convenient choices for a fast, mid-engined kit is the complete Renault V6 (25 or 30 models more common) and its dedicated transaxle. Parts are expensive from Renault or from after-market tuning houses but you save the price of a transaxle conversion kit and special clutch assembly.

The alloy construction of the engine and the gearbox creates a lightweight ensemble and it's also a good space-saver as it's only three cylinders 'long' each side. Much good use of these engines, usually in 2.7-litre format, has been made on track and road.

The list goes on and on. Some manufacturers are more willing than others to consider special engine fitments, so be very careful if you decide to end up going your own way. If the manufacturer, who knows the chassis and suspension better than you, expresses doubts about using such a powerful engine, you'd better take note.

Chapter 5
RUNNING GEAR

Section 1
Framework

AT THE END OF A successful and tidy clean-up programme, you should end up with a garage or workshop relieved of the ravages of donor equipment refurbishment. The parts themselves will have been neatly finished, hung, shelved, boxed, folded, laid out, leaned up and generally stored away. Once-dirty floors and work surfaces will have been swept, vacuumed and de-greased. Tools will have been replaced. We may bash on about keeping everything clean and tidy, but it really is important.

Unless you're going to be working with a kit that requires extensive GRP-related jobs and unless you'll be doing your own spray-painting in that garage, you've completed the messiest bits of the kit build already.

As this end to donor parts refurbishment comes into view, you may well have taken the opportunity to finally order your chosen kit, so that the whole kit, or the first part of it, would be ready as and when your workshop was cleared for action again.

Now starts the intricate bit. You must make sure that the high standards of care lavished upon the donor parts, reinforced by early stores of enthusiasm, are maintained for the rest of the build-up – even if the enthusiasm pales now and then.

If you've ordered a kit with a separate steel chassis, the latter could arrive in various guises. The most basic are the ladder and cruciform frames. They are also the simplest to handle and work on. Next, in order of complexity, are the simple perimeter frame, the backbone and the spaceframe.

Some chassis embody certain aspects of different types. You can get a perimeter frame or spaceframe with a structural backbone section, for instance. Any or all of these steel chassis types might come with (or might need the addition of) specially designed steel and/or alloy sheet as reinforcement.

There might be a floorpan type chassis to replace the original and rotting equivalents from such traditional donors as the Citroen 2CV/Dyane range or the VW Beetle. Similarly, there might be a semi-monocoque arrangement in sheet steel (or maybe even alloy) wherein folded and welded sheets of steel have been used to form the structure, which could well be lighter than the straightforward ERW (Electrical Resistance Welded) tubes used to make the majority of tubular chassis.

Other kinds of chassis sometimes used in kit car manufacture are the GRP/composite monocoque and the donor car chassis. Relatively few kit cars are still designed as rebodying concepts for existing donor chassis made by production car companies but there are a few (the American Pontiac Fiero being particularly responsive to this treatment). On the other end of the scale, the high-tech science of designing and manufacturing light and strong all-GRP monocoques (structural shells) is getting more and more important for the kit car trade.

We will be considering GRP monocoques later in this chapter. Initially, we'll be dealing with steel chassis and how to set up your workshop to cope with them properly. It's not just a case of 'get the chassis in the garage and bolt the bits on.' If you intend your kit car to be presentable and rust-free in the long-run, then there are plenty of ways in which a little extra time, effort and money spent will soon be justified – especially if you have to sell the car.

If your budget can run to it, and if you can't afford the time to prepare a steel or steel/alloy chassis, then you should make

This Mig welded chassis is being assembled on a chassis jig to ensure uniformity of production. It's a traditional ladderframe design which requires larger section tubing to give it strength.

These are Westfield chassis awaiting powder coating. Their spaceframe construction means lighter and smaller tubing can be used to gain excellent torsional rigidity and strength.

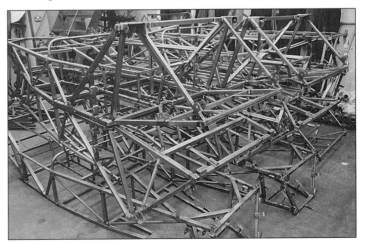

sure that the manufacturer delivers the chassis with a proper 'powder' or epoxy coating. There are several equivalents to this but in essence it's a process whereby the chassis (or other component) is firstly de-greased and thoroughly cleaned off.

finish. Other techniques might involve heating up the chassis and then bombarding it with powder-form plastics which melt to a smooth finish on impact with the chassis.

The third professional rust-preventative treatment offered by some manufacturers is

THE WHICH KIT? TIP

If you can stretch to it, we'd recommend getting your chassis powder or epoxy coated. Some people will swear by other means of chassis protection but we've always found powder and epoxy coating to be long lasting and chip resistant. It also looks much neater than hand painting or galvanising

When properly dried off and dust-free, the chassis might then be painted with epoxy spray paints and oven-baked to assure the durability of the

galvanising. This isn't such a favourite with all manufacturers because the process can, through the use of hot dips, warp thinner steel tubes and

sheet. It must also be assured that the each tube has an opening or vent to avoid explosion during the dip treatment. Therefore, the more robust or larger tubes lend themselves to this process.

If you can't run to the above, then try to get your chassis delivered with at least a brush-painted coating – especially if it is to be stored for any length of time before you get to work on it. Usual coatings are red oxide primer, other metal primers, black exterior gloss paint and even the very dubious quality 'hammer finish' paints that seem to be so popular. Avoid ever using the latter on steel chassis if you can, they often seem to become brittle and chip off easily in time.

If you must receive the chassis with absolutely no coating of any kind, then it should be painted with

something immediately as steel will rust very quickly, even if stored out of the rain and wind. Once the rust has a firm hold, then your job becomes a lot harder to remove all traces of it prior to finishing the chassis. Chemical rust 'converters' that we have tried seem to have a very low success rate, so physical removal of rust is a complete necessity in the end.

Section 2
A good coat

SO WHAT'S THE BEST WAY to set up a steel chassis in the workshop? The majority will probably opt for a set of four axle stands with the extendable centre sections set for maximum height. With a couple of helpers, it is usually possible to lift and manoeuvre the average kit car steel chassis. The

If you're preparing the chassis yourself then you'll be using harmful chemicals and dust. Always wear a good quality nose and mouth mask as well as some eye protection.

Top: Galvanising is another alternative to powder coating. Below: Having cleaned off the worst with a rotary sanding disc (below left) more careful preparation is done with abrasive paper.

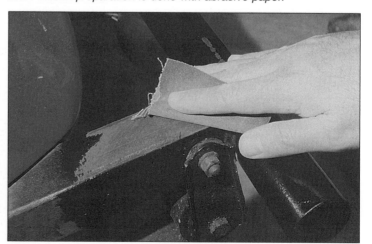

manufacturer should be able to give you precise details of how many persons are needed to safely move the chassis.

Axle stands are an acceptable way of supporting the chassis, especially in the early stages of assembly work when heavy suspension items must be bolted to it, usually from underneath. However, it can also be advantageous to get the chassis up higher, during the cleaning and painting processes for instance.

This is where trestles come in handy. Not the precarious and lightweight fold-away trestles you might use to support the tables at a wedding reception. We're talking about solidly made timber A-frames with heavy cross-bracing. They're easily made in the garage and the materials (timber, glue, screws) won't cost you anywhere near as much as a set of axle stands. They will allow you to support the chassis three or four feet from the floor and you can work on it standing up rather than crawling around on the concrete.

Let's take the typical scenario to be a steel chassis supplied without coating and with some rust already setting in after storage. Once the structure has been supported on its trestles, stands or otherwise, the prime job is to clean it down to shiny, bare metal surfaces and then paint it with the best combination of long-lived rust-proofing materials that you can readily get your hands on.

The same might go for the more perfectionist builder who wants to make sure that everything ends up in top condition. Not being satisfied with a painted finish done by the dealer, the builder might want to take off the old paint and start again from scratch.

The best weapon for all of these jobs is a drill-mounted wire brush. These wire brushes come in a selection of shapes and sizes and you can just about guarantee that you'll find a shape to reach into all the angles of the chassis. You might already have discovered their usefulness in cleaning off the donor parts. If you're re-using wire brushes from the earlier operation, make sure you de-grease them by immersion in white spirit. Let them dry off naturally before re-use.

Obviously, this kind of tool must be used in conjunction with the usual safety equipment. A nose/mouth mask with filter, a pair of protective goggles and gloves. You might also prefer ear defenders if you're using any power tools for prolonged periods.

Some simple scheduling can be of use here. It is preferable to apply your first coat of paint in the same day as you expose the bare metal of the chassis. (A hot, dry summer day being better than a damp winter one). If it takes a whole day to wire-brush the chassis, and you won't get another day's work in for a week or a month, then clean and paint half the chassis that day and do the other half at the next opportunity.

Above: Corners and seams can be prepared with a drill mounted wire brush. Below: Degrease the exposed area with white spirit before painting immediately afterwards.

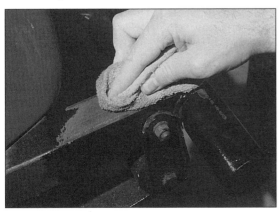

Above: Using a proper metal primer is extremely important. Below: Apply the primer in several thin coats rather than one thick one for the best results.

Take the chance to smooth off any sharp edges and corners on the chassis while you're at it. This can be done with a hand file, sanding block, drill-mounted sanding disc or similar tools. Unless the build manual specifies otherwise, these sharp edges and corners are usually undesirable as they are dangerous and can also act as stress-raisers in some circumstances, possibly giving rise to a stress crack. Paint will also rub or flake away from sharp edges in no time letting the rust start up again.

With the chassis sitting on its trestles or stands, only prepare the surfaces which can be easily reached with the chassis that particular way up. No point struggling to finish surfaces which will be revealed when the chassis is turned over on its supports.

You will find it relatively easy to get down to a shiny metal surface on the main chassis tubes. It will be more difficult to clear away the hidden corners and angles. Do persevere here though. Rust will often start in inaccessible parts of the chassis which have not been properly treated. Imagine where water and perpetually damp road grime will collect in normal road conditions. These are the places which have to be properly treated beforehand as you might not be able to reach them when the car is completed.

When cleaning a steel chassis, you may notice that some or all of the steel has what appears to be a thin and sometimes flaky metal skin around it. In some places this thin layer will come away easily and in others it seems to be more stubborn. It's called mill scale and is a residue left on steel tubes during the manufacturing process.

Try your best to get rid of the mill scale as it may flake away later, leaving part of the chassis exposed. In various places around a chassis, there will also be small metal globules attached, usually near the welds. This is splatter from the welding process and can usually be removed with a scraper such as a wide cold chisel. Again, removal will help the longevity of the paint surface in some cases.

When the chassis, or an appropriate part of the chassis, has been cleaned off, make sure that it has also been de-greased. Wipe it over with clean rag soaked in white spirit or similar. Don't use the heavier petroleum based solvents like paraffin, kerosene or diesel as they leave some oily deposits behind, rendering the chassis unpaintable. They're OK for degreasing engine and mechanical parts that you don't want to paint.

Choice of paint for steel chassis varies widely. Our pet hates, as we have mentioned, include rust converting fluids and hammer finish paints. They just don't seem to work in the long or even medium run. If your chassis is all steel, it's a

Above: Two coats of exterior grade gloss paint should be sufficient. Using two different colours will help you cover the chassis evenly. Below: When you start panelling the chassis use a sealant between chassis and panel.

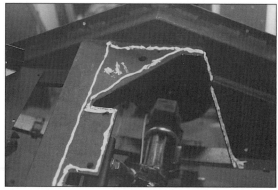

Above: Sealant will not only stop any ingress of water but also reduce squeaks etc. Below: Careful preparation prior to painting a chassis will pay dividends.

One way of avoiding any chassis preparation is to buy a kit with a fibreglass monocoque. This GTM Rossa K3 has no metal at all in its main structure. It also comes in a gelcoat colour and does not require painting.

good idea to start with a primer for exterior steel surfaces. Be aware that there are primers specifically for aluminium alloy as well. Such paints are usually available at local DIY outlets. Observe the thinning instructions for brush or spray application - spraying can make a visual difference but isn't really needed here.

You might opt for more than one coat of primer just to be sure. It usually follows that two or several coats of any properly thinned paint work better than one thick coat. Avoid depositing paint into threaded chassis holes or captive nuts etc. Tape them over, push grease into them or plug them somehow. A paint-filled thread, especially a female thread with one closed end, can slow things down a lot and might require the use of a tap and die set to get right.

Two or more coats of simple

exterior grade gloss paint seem to be an excellent way of giving the chassis a good long-lived covering. It stays pretty flexible, it's cheap and easily obtained in lots of colours. If you're taking

THE WHICH KIT? TIP
To help keep paint and grime out of threaded chassis holes, use an old bolt (perhaps from the donor) and screw it in finger tight to ensure the thread remains clean

the wise precaution of applying more than one coat, buy two slightly different colours. Try painting black onto black – it becomes very difficult to see where you have and haven't painted.

Final weather-proofing can come in the form of thick, black bitumen or bitumastic paint often sold as car underseal. It's

not particularly pretty but it's effective after a couple of generous coats, especially in the areas which won't be seen too often. There are higher-tech underseals used by modern car

manufacturers which appear to be relatively thin and translucent fluids. Not impressively thick like the black stuff.

These newer generation underseals, usually available from main dealers and good motor factors, are easily applied on top of your gloss paint and have the cunning knack of closing up scratches in the

surface of the underseal caused by stone impacts etc.

To further the cause of rust-proofing, some kit builders will also treat the inside surfaces of chassis tubes with injected Waxoyl, which can be purchased in a complete kit for home application. Be careful here as many chassis tubes have closed and sealed ends which will need drilling for Waxoyl application. Be aware that a hole drilled in a seemingly innocent location could eventually lead to a failure of a chassis tube or weld. Check the best 'safe' areas to drill with the manufacturer of the kit.

If you are ordering a chassis which comes with aluminium or steel panels, or even other body panels finally fitted by the manufacturer, you should make sure that the chassis has been properly coated before those panels are affixed. In many

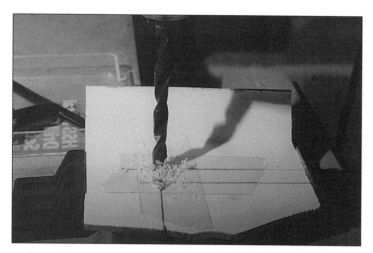

Above: There's a knack to drilling through fibreglass. Always drill from the gelcoat side and never use a brand new drill bit as this can snag in the gel and cause cracks and chips to occur.

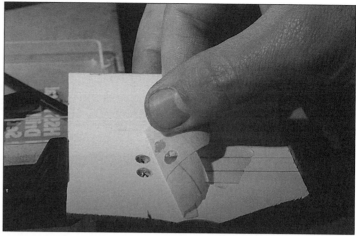

Above: Masking tape helps stop the drill from slipping as well as helping to avoid chips. You can also draw on it more easily with a pencil to mark the exact drill point.

cases, such panels are alloy and are attached with pop rivets and more technique than you might know. To get them all off again for a paint job would be a major task in many circumstances.

Alloy panels are best cleaned and then keyed with fine wet and dry abrasive paper before degreasing and initial painting with something called acid etch primer. Follow instructions carefully and use impermeable gloves, face mask with a good filter and generally avoid inhaling the vapour or getting the stuff on your skin. It isn't particularly friendly.

Etch primers use an acidic action to key themselves chemically into the surface of the clean alloy. They therefore become a very durable base for subsequent coats of paint. Again, your local DIY shop or an automotive paint specialist can supply you with undercoat for the alloy panels treated with the etch primer and then an exterior grade gloss paint will do nicely.

Don't let anyone tell you that alloy is rust-free. Most of the sheet alloy you will be supplied for car building purposes will certainly crumble away if not properly protected. If you are attaching any alloy panels to steel chassis, it's a good idea to use paints, other coatings done by the manufacturers, mastic etc. between the mating faces of the steel and alloy.

In some cases, it might be possible to use a thin chassis tape or other layer of unperishable insulating material between the surfaces. This will help to stop or slow down electrolytic corrosion which can occur when a tiny electrical current is passed between the two metals.

It is inevitable that the chassis will get scratched during the construction of the kit but it is essential that it gets its main rust-proofing done correctly and right from the start. Touching up the scratched areas is no great hardship. Although the bodyshell and interior will be the most often looked at parts of the kit, there's little more disturbing to the eye of the car enthusiast than a rusting structure. It's

The chances are you will still be left with unsightly fibreglass slivers on the underside of the panel. It's best to remove these with a foam sanding block (opposite page top left).

very difficult to put right after the rest of the car has been finished.

Section 3
Skin deep

SOME KITS WHICH USE A complete GRP bodyshell as the main structure of the vehicle will not obviously need protection from the ravages of the weather. Or do they? Look a bit more closely and you may well find that the mechanical parts used include front and/or rear suspension subframes from a donor. These are usually fabricated in pressed and spot-welded steel shapes.

Subframes are designed to carry a complex suspension set-

up (and even an engine) on a frame that is itself easy to remove from and attach to a car. If your subframe(s) are in good condition, it's an excellent idea to give them the same anti-rust treatments that you would give to a steel chassis.

Some GRP monocoque shells use steel components to help spread the load at a point of high stress concentration. Seatbelt mounts, suspension fixings, hinges, engine mounts, steering column mounts. Often, these steel plates or members will be laminated into the GRP and will therefore be mostly insulated from corrosive water, salt and air. If they're not, then make sure that they get the treatment.

What about the GRP bodyshell itself? For non-monocoque GRP shells, we shall be discussing techniques in Chapter Six. However, some of the hints and tips we will cover here will also apply to any GRP structures.

You might suspect that a GRP shell really isn't as indestructible as some of its reputation suggests. Although it doesn't suffer from anything like rust, it can still be adversely affected by the elements and is simply not as robust as steel or alloy bodywork because of its brittleness and inability to tolerate localised stresses. Gelcoat colours are also unpredictably liable to fade or

change colour due to the effects of UV light.

Most GRP shells are hand-laminated using a selection of body moulds. Usually, one surface of the resultant moulding will be smooth and gelcoated, the other will be relatively rough, showing the chopped strand mat or the woven rovings used. In some cases, the coremat reinforcement material is also evident.

Having dealt with any metal chassis components, there is still a small list of ways in which you can make your GRP shell more weatherproof. You might be able to see, in areas of visible GRP mat, that some strands protrude loosely or rigidly from the main mouldings. Beware of these and wear gloves and a breathing filter. GRP, especially when cut or drilled, creates a fine dust of

needles which is harmful to both skin and lungs.

These residual fibres, along with the untreated edges of GRP can actually absorb water through a kind of capillary action. If the water then freezes, damage to the moulding can result. That's why it is worthwhile painting the underside of the GRP shell to seal up most of the possible areas of water ingress.

Having sanded away the rougher edges and spikes of mat, painting the underside of the bodyshell is not a high-tech pursuit. You need to end up with a durable waterproof finish in the right places. Exterior grade undercoat and gloss should be OK although some makes might be specifically unsuitable for plastic surfaces. Normal black underseal is also useful. Check on the can and then on a small piece of scrap GRP.

Painting GRP also has the knock-on effect of preventing obvious light transparency through wings, bonnet and boot panels. Be careful not to apply this paint in areas which are close to the exhaust and engine. If there is a chance that a GRP surface will get hot due to radiated or convected heat from engine or exhaust, take steps to ensure that the affected area is covered with fireproof material supplied by the various mail order specialists advertising in the kit car press. See Chapter Six for more details on this.

Stone chips and subsequent 'star crazing' is another common fault with GRP. If the bodyshell has no protective inner wheel arches, a stone picked up by the wheel can hit the underside of a moulding and cause the smooth top gelcoat to erupt into an unsightly crack like a tiny

window shattering. This star craze is time-consuming to repair, especially if the gelcoat colour must be matched, and it gives away the vehicle's GRP construction.

Painting won't protect the GRP from such impacts so you might be well advised to protect the underside of the affected panels by sticking on a shock-absorbing section of light foam. This foam must be waterproof, preferable fire-proof and not obtrusively thick. About 3/8" - 1/2" thick should be enough if the foam is relatively firm and springy. You might even want to paint over it to hide its presence.

A GRP monocoque shell is also a good prospect for trestle support. If you must use axle stands, make sure they are supporting strong areas of the GRP and don't rest under a section that might be too thin

During the process of a typical build you will be doing a lot of drilling for rivets etc. A decent drill sharpener is money well spent. Below: Typical selection of useful drill mounted tools.

Below: Just because GRP doesn't rust, don't think it cannot get damaged. Flying stones hitting the underside of a wheelarch will cause cracks on the top surface. Rubber matting may stop this.

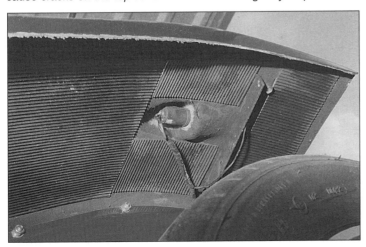

and weak. Alternatively, place wooden planks across the car from one axle stand to the other to help spread the load.

When preparing to work on the monocoque shell, it is a good idea to equip yourself with masking tape, a few good, soft pencils, a drill-sharpening machine which will offer the facility to sharpen your drills at different angles to suit plastic cutting, a vacuum cleaner, a hand drill, a countersink bit and the usual safety equipment.

If you must use a power drill, make sure it has adjustable (not just two-speed) settings so that it can be used slowly and very cautiously at the start of the drilling. If you have to drill through the gelcoat surface, drill from the gel side and tape the area with masking tape beforehand. This will help stop the drill bit from slipping and also help with gelcoat from chipping. Better results can sometimes be had by carefully drilling out the hole with successively larger drills until the right size is obtained

Sharp drills prepared with the wrong angle at the tip will be more likely to chip and shatter the gelcoat. Very blunt drills might require excess pressure to cut through, thus cracking the gel around the hole.

Make sure that you then countersink the gel side of the hole, especially if you are to use

Load spreading washers in the foreground will be a vital purchase. Buying in zinc coated or, preferably, stainless steel will be the key to maintaining your car's rust free status.

self-tapping screw through the GRP. Although we would always recommend avoiding self-tappers into GRP, there are some instances in which a bolt cannot be used. Always use load-spreading washers when screwing or bolting through GRP as pinpoint stresses are very likely to cause cracking. The washers should be as wide as reasonably possible.

Hole-cutting saws can be used for the larger apertures but large-sized drills can make a hash of the GRP, especially if they catch in the hole and then cut sideways. If possible, use a pencil and compass to mark out the larger holes and drill repeatedly through the circumference with a small drill.

You will then be able to cut out the 'disc' with a fine keyhole saw, small round file or scrolling jigsaw. The final edge can be tidied up with a flap-wheel sander or files and sandpaper.

Caution when cutting is the name of the game with GRP. Measure and re-measure. It's possible to repair extensively abused GRP but it is time-

consuming if you're after a good visual result. Much easier to take off too little and cut again than to take off too much and have to rebuild it.

Always wear the gloves and face mask and make a point of vacuuming the car, worktops and garage regularly and often when cutting or smoothing GRP. The dust can be very fine and light, settling everywhere. Certainly not ideal when you want to undertake subsequent mechanical jobs involving bearings and engine/gearbox internals.

Do not leave GRP shells under plastic sheets or tarpaulins when they are in direct sunlight. This can cause rapid deterioration of the gelcoat colour. High temperatures accentuated by a plastic sheet can also cause a moulding to settle and warp.

THE WHICH KIT? TIP
When protecting GRP panels against accidental damage, cover them with large sheets of bubble-wrap packing material and hold in place by taping onto the underside of the panel rather than the smooth gelcoat side

When a shell or panel is stored away, ensure that it is properly supported at all of its extremities, protected from accidental scratching (tape an

Escort axle with original mounting brackets ground off and a Fisher Fury 5-link rear location system welded on. This gives a much more precise location to the axle.

This is an independent rear suspension set-up for a Dax 40. It's fully adjustable and will need careful and expert adjustment for perfect on-the-road results. Comes complete with anti-roll bar.

Above: Reconditioned Marina axle shows new U-clamps, bump stop and aluminium block to lower the ride height on a Marlin Roadster. Below: Various hydraulic dampers for the Cortina.

Many kits you'll come across use aftermarket coil-over dampers such as this Spax unit. Springs are adjustable to alter ride height while damper can also be adjusted for firmness/softness.

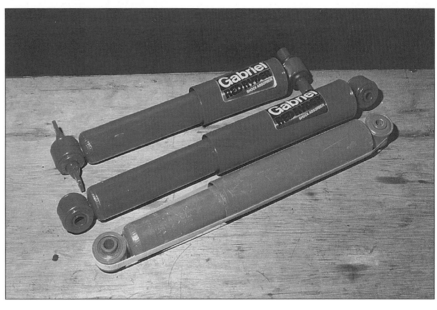

old blanket or sheet to it) and preferably in the shade. They can be stored out in the open but not with a close covering - watch out for the ice damage which might be done to an unpainted shell.

Section 4
At the back

AT THE FINISH OF YET another stage, you'll now have a chassis or monocoque shell supported relatively high on trestles or stands and sporting a lovely weather resistant coating where necessary. In most cases, this marks the stage at which things have to be bolted on to the structure. This is where you reach for the supply of ready cleaned and reconditioned donor parts you prepared before the kit arrived. You did, didn't you?

Now's the time that the manufacturer's build manual starts to come in handy and the *Haynes Workshop Manual* tends to slip more into the background. You'll need to know the order in which things are attached. You'll need to know when to tighten which bolts and to what torque. It's very important to know the order in which things are bolted together.

Which special components are needed from the manufacturer? Which new components are needed from sources other than the donor? What special fasteners have to be brought in as extras? You'll thank yourself for reading the manual in advance and preparing all the stuff in the garage. If you haven't taken the opportunity to prepare, then you will end up doing a lot of running around purchasing, ordering and waiting for stuff while the build stagnates.

Those of you who have chosen to take on a mid-engined kit might be starting to get a little uneasy at this stage. Your mate's live-axled Westfield or Pilgrim Sumo doesn't look anywhere near as complex as yours. Look at those various radius rods and wishbones. U/Js, bearings, hub carriers, half-shafts, discs, calipers, Watts linkages, A-frames, Panhard rods, coil-overs etc. etc. How complex can a rear end be? We'll get on to that later.

To start with, we'll look at the basic standard or modified rear live axle fitment. Live axle usually means a straight beam axle which contains a (near-) central differential, half-shafts within tubes, bearings and brake components. It is an unsprung mass, ie: it is separated from the car's body/chassis by the suspension.

The functions of the live axle include distribution of torque to the rear wheels, maintenance of zero castor, camber and toe-in angles at the rear wheels and, through good location, a firm platform for the absorption of torque action and reaction from the differential and brakes under acceleration and deceleration. It also serves as the lower

Above: Here's a standard Cortina rear axle with its four locating arms (three visible). Spring sits on the lower arm on each side (arrowed). Below: This modified Cortina axle shows a 5-link set-up with coil-over. Great improvement.

Here's an unusual rear suspension set-up. Sierra based IRS using fabricated lower wishbone and hub carrier with new coil-over.

mounting point(s) for the rear springs and hydraulic shock absorbers.

Some live axles are fitted with leaf (or cart) springs. These are single or multiple strips of spring steel, varying in width and/or length, and can be described as semi-elliptical. They usually curve downwards from their extremities towards the ground in the normal rest position.

Some kits still use such leaf-sprung live axles from donor cars such as the Escort Mk.2, Marina/Ital and MGB. These are probably the simplest transplants onto the kit chassis. It's usually a question of lowering the chassis to a reasonable working height and

then putting each leaf spring into position.

The live axle can then be carefully lifted into position on top of the leaf springs and bolted into place with the requisite U-clamps. Your refurbishing schedule should have left you with a separate axle, leaf springs, shock absorbers, new U-clamps, the donor's high-tensile suspension bolts (if in good condition) or new replacements.

When the leaf springs are held in place, their mounting bolts should be pushed home, with the self-locking nuts attached but not tightened until the car is resting on the ground under its full weight. Tighten the bolts prematurely and the

flexible bushes in each end of the springs will be badly twisted as the car settles down. This will lead to premature failure of the bushes, which aren't cheap. They're also difficult to fit.

Yet another way of suspending the back of a car from a live axle is via coil springs and suspension arms. The ubiquitous Cortinas Mk.3, 4 and 5 have this system. Instead of the axle's location being provided by the springs, as in a leaf spring system, separate pivoted arms are bolted between the axle and the body/chassis to restrict the axle's movement predictably.

In the case of the Cortina, there are four of these arms, two shorter arms reaching diagonally back from the body to the top of the differential housing (semi-trailing) and two longer arms reaching directly back from the body to the lower

outer ends of the live axle (trailing arms).

The Cortina's hydraulic shock absorbers are attached to the axle via special brackets and the coil springs actually extend between the trailing arms and the body. Neither the springs nor the shocks offer any axle location. This is done (albeit rather clumsily in the case of the Cortina) by the four locating arms - each of which is equipped with large and compliant bushes.

The kit manufacturer may choose to emulate the standard Cortina axle mounting set-up by putting the chassis mounts for the locating arms in the same relative positions as those of the Cortina. Some manufacturers, not happy with the Cortina geometry (or unable to fit the standard arms in the given space) use their own trailing or semi-trailing arms, springs and shock absorbers.

The Cortina based Rush, from DJ Sportscars, is an example of a kit that requires modification to the Cortina rear suspension. Throw out the old suspension arms, springs and shock absorbers, get new multi-purpose brackets welded to the axle casing and attach the live axle with DJ's own system of four trailing arms, Panhard rod and special coil-over springs and dampers.

Unlike leaf springs, coil springs have to be artificially compressed in order to get them into position prior to pushing home the rear suspension mounting bolts. This calls for special spring compressors. The kit manufacturer will tell you the best type to use for your front or rear suspension. They're usually a pair of external compressors or a single internal compressor.

The external compressors usually look like a couple of long hex bolts. Onto each of these bolts have been screwed two nuts which take the form of stubby hooks instead of hexagons. One of the hooks

has a reverse thread. When you turn the hex head of the long bolt, the hooked nuts will either converge or diverge. All you do is position the hooks on the coils of a spring, one compressor each side of the spring, and compress the spring by tightening the bolt.

Not as simple as all that, though, as you have to be careful where on the spring to position the hooks. Once you've compressed and removed an old spring, for instance, you might find that it has not fully extended even when the hooked nuts are as far apart as they can go. You've effectively run out of thread on the bolts.

The only realistic answer is to put the springs back into their original locations, release the tensioners and re-tension the springs with the hooks starting off closer together and

equidistant from the centre of the bolt.

Bear in mind that a compressed coil spring is a very dangerous item. Just because it appears to be near the full

alone wreck a good set of compressors.

Some spring compressors are internal, working through the centre of the spring, so you need only one per spring. For

THE WHICH KIT? TIP
Don't get confused when people talk about shock absorbers and dampers. They're actually the same thing even though calling a damper a shock absorber is technically incorrect. In fact, it's the spring that deals with shock forces while the damper unit does exactly as its name suggests - controls the spring from simply bouncing up and down out of control

extent of its uncompressed length, it doesn't mean it's safe to simply keep on unwinding the spring compressors and let one hook come off the threaded bolt. Forces like this can kill, let

the front springs of the Cortina, this is by far the best type as access to the outside of the springs can be hampered by the suspension components.

Increasingly popular with kit

Above: This Jaguar differential, with its in-board brake discs, is used in many Cobra replicas. Below: These specially fabricated tubes are used in the Caterham DeDion rear suspension set-up.

A mid-engined kit, such as the Tornado TS40, will be more complicated to sort than a simple front engined project such as this Eagle RV.

manufacturers is the independent rear suspension (or IRS). It is a concept adopted by production car manufacturers to remove the unsprung weight of a live axle and to refine rear suspension feel.

The Sierra, Granada and Jaguar/Daimler are the most common rear-drive IRS systems used by the kit car trade. (Jaguar's S3 version most commonly used by the Cobra replicators is an exception to the rule as its half-shafts also double as locating arms for the uprights).

Essentially, you will find that the differential is in its own cast housing. This has been specifically designed to bolt into the car's structure and those mounting points have been reproduced in certain kit car chassis so that the differential unit can be swapped across easily.

Extending out from the differential you will have a half-shaft each side. These may not be the same length, so make sure you know which goes where. At either end of each half shaft there will be a universal joint. The outer half of each outer U/J will be attached to a spinning, bearing-mounted hub, to which the wheels are attached. The hubs and their bearings are supported in cast or fabricated hub carriers or rear suspension uprights.

The job of the suspension components in an IRS system is to locate these hub carriers in relation to the chassis and to each other. To this end, the hub carriers will be designed with plenty of lugs and apertures to accept the wide variety of locating arms available.

Caterham's 'DeDion'

specification cars have a tube which holds the uprights in the same relative positions. This acts a lot like a well-located live axle but without the unsprung weight.

In the case of a mid-engined kit car, of which there are many, you can get a system similar to that of the front-engined, rear-drive IRS of the Sierra/Granada. The big difference is that instead of a solid-mounted differential, there's a unitary gearbox or transaxle with integral differential. The half-shafts will originate from this, usually to a recognisable outboard system of hubs, bearings, carriers and suspension arms or wishbones.

Kit builders might want to study such assemblies in advance and talk to others who have dealt with them. It is known that the Jaguar system can, in some cases, be

particularly difficult to work with, requiring the use of special tools which the amateur builder might not be able to access or afford. The Ford equivalents are easier for the home builder to tackle with few or no special tools required.

There is a small but increasing number of front-wheel-drive kits on the market. They use various different types of rear suspension system. Some might opt for a dead or beam axle with a Panhard rod; the Fiesta type, for instance. Others might use the Mini subframe and rubber doughnut suspension. There's the 2CV and Renault 5 system broadly involving trailing arms which act on transverse torsion bar springs.

Because there is no drive to the rear suspension systems of front-drive cars, the components tend to be lighter and much

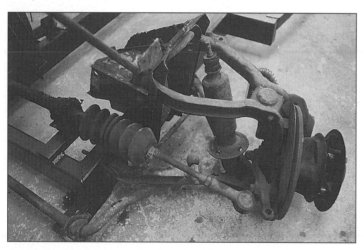

Above: Various donors offer their own front wishbones such as this rather tired looking Triumph set-up. Below: Note how the design varies from the heavy Cortina wishbone arrangement.

Top: In some cases the manufacturer may mix donor suspension parts with specially fabricated components. Alternatively, it may be case of starting from scratch to get a better result (below).

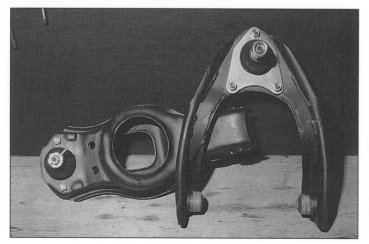

more easily mastered than their rear-drive counterparts. Caution must still be exercised when working with the springs or unitary coil-over shock absorbers.

Section 5
Up front

ALTHOUGH THERE ARE many variations on the theme, a build will usually continue with the addition of the front suspension and other related parts. Luckily for everyone, there's a wide variety of different front suspensions used by kit manufacturers. The Cortina based system must currently rank as the most widely used, followed by Jaguar, Sierra, Escort Mk.2 and Triumph Herald/Vitesse based assemblies.

The simplest way of transferring a donor car suspension to your kit car chassis or monocoque is by taking a whole subframe, with

everything on it, and bolting it to the kit. This is possible with the Cortina and Escort subframes, not to mention the Mini equivalent.

Whereas the Mk.2 Escort front suspension uses full-length McPherson struts and therefore cannot be fully contained within a subframe, the Cortina uses a more compact double wishbone-type suspension and can. The lower arm of the Cortina front suspension does not actually take the form of a classic wishbone but is a pressed and fabricated steel track control arm.

You will notice that the Cortina's lower arm is fairly beefy as it carries the lower mounts for the front coil springs and the telescopic dampers. The Escort has a forged equivalent which

looks much more compact and does less work - the spring seats and hydraulic shocks being incorporated in the McPherson struts themselves and not acting on the lower suspension arms.

If you're using a complete Cortina subframe, you'll find that it can probably be affixed to the kit's chassis with just four large nuts and bolts. Whereas quite a few kits use the Cortina subframe in full or part, many will (sensibly) opt for different (re-rated) springs and/or dampers as it is unlikely that their kit will weigh as much as the donor Cortina.

Such kits as the Rickman Ranger and White Rose Husky will use the whole Escort front subframe but the chassis are designed to provide top mounts for the McPherson struts which extend up to about the same height as the top of the engine or higher.

Even if the subframe mounting holes themselves vary in position, only due to Ford manufacturing tolerances or even accident damage, the top mounting hole spacings for the Escort struts can vary and the manufacturers will specify what action is needed to check for the right hole pattern.

Basic uprating of brake components may be possible by using parts from different models (Ford Sierra to Cosworth). Going to dedicated aftermarket suppliers can be very expensive, as well as unnecessary.

Above: The most commonly used front upright is the Cortina item and there is little variation from model to model. However, other parts such as these clutch actuating arms (below) will vary. Be careful.

Don't be confused if the kit instructions refer to new engine mounts or to the removal of the engine mounts on the donor subframe. Many standard production car subframes are designed to support the engine as well as the front suspension. Kits using these subframes often have a revised engine position, usually for better weight distribution or ground clearance, so the part of the subframe used for mounting the engine is no longer needed.

Some of the more perceptive manufacturers and kit designers will have noted that a Cortina subframe with standard wishbones will adopt a different suspension geometry at rest if the spring lengths are altered or the spring rates reduced. The worst examples of this will display quite extreme negative camber at the front wheels ie: the front wheels will lean inboard at the top. It's as if the car was heavily laden at the front and looks pretty weird.

Once the manufacturer has redesigned the front suspension geometry to cope with shorter and/or softer springs, without a drastic negative camber, it will become apparent that the fixed position wishbone mounts of the Cortina subframe are no longer relevant. In fact, the whole subframe might as well go in favour of a special pick-up points designed into the chassis or monocoque. The standard wishbones can be retained or replaced by new items.

Take a look at Pilgrim's advances in altering the standard Cortina front suspension. The Mk.5 Bulldog has been the company's best handling car yet. Others have gone so far away from the Cortina standard assembly that only a few of the original components remain...

This takes us into the field of double wishbone front suspension. When a manufacturer wants a sporty road-going kit which is subject to space or height restrictions under the bonnet (or boot), then double wishbones are usually the answer. If the designer of such a suspension knows the ins and outs, then the requirement to stay with one donor for front suspension parts goes out the window.

Some manufacturers might be able to stick with the uprights, brakes, steering rack and track rods/ends from one donor, others might mix 'n' match to suit the new suspension geometry, vehicle width, performance, price etc. There is a surprising degree of standardisation by the production car manufacturers, even between marques, and new transferable parts are being discovered each day.

If you're building a high performance vehicle, for instance, the manufacturer should be able to tell you whether you can uprate donor components safely using off-the-shelf parts from that donor's manufacturer.

Examples include the wide variety of differential ratios

Always renew essential suspension, braking and steering parts such as these tie rod ends (above) and ball joints (below). Much easier to do the job now and avoid potential accidents later.

This weird looking upright is a modified Escort front strut which has been converted into a stub axle for use in a Sylva Striker. Works very well.

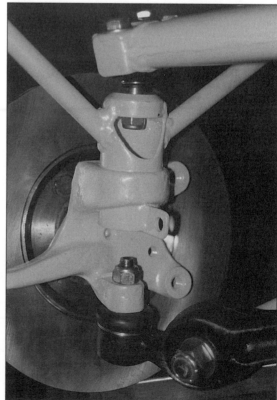

Above: This may be one way of lifting an engine into place, but it isn't one we'd recommend! Below: Hiring an engine hoist is not expensive and makes life considerably easier and safer.

Going mid-engined will often introduce new expense. Above: Cosworth turbo engine fitted to a Porsche transaxle. Below: Ford Pinto onto a Renault 'box for the same reason. Neither cheap.

available from Mk.2 Escort donors. Some have larger rear drum brakes. An estate donor might offer you a bigger servo for the brakes, stiffer springs, heavy duty shock absorbers etc.

DJ Sportscars, among others, can modify a Cortina upright (primarily for its Rush kit) to accept the standard calipers but with better discs. You'll need to use a selection of off-the-shelf wheel bearing components specified by DJ. A simple and cheap tuning modification. Chapter 12 deals with other tuning techniques which might be applicable to your kit car.

NB: An upright is generally taken to be the front stub axle assembly in most rear-drive cars like the Cortina but it can also describe the hub carrier (the part to which the outboard ends of the suspension arms are attached) in front-drive and IRS systems.

In some cases, there is no handy donor upright to fulfil the task in hand. The manufacturers of higher budget kits might be able to afford to get the right part manufactured for them at great cost. Others can improvise. One or two manufacturers have hit on the idea of converting the lower part of the Escort Mk.1/2 McPherson strut into a conventional-looking upright.

Originally, the Escort front stub axles are inseparable from the strut tubes. Answer? Cut the bottom of the strut tube and design a new top ball-joint mount which can be welded or bolted to the remaining part of the strut tube left with the stub axle assembly, which already has a tapered hole for a lower ball-joint.

As most front double wishbone systems use production car ball-joints at their outboard ends, this has been a

very acceptable modification when carefully designed. The Sylva Striker has been an excellent example of this.

When assembling new front suspensions with double wishbones, be very sure to follow the manufacturer's recommendations as to how to tell the difference between each wishbone and how, therefore, to mount them in the correct positions. Most wishbones will have metalastic inboard mounts and, like rear suspensions, the mounting bolts relevant to these bushes must not be tightened until the vehicle is standing unsupported under its usual load.

A loosening and re-tightening exercise is recommended when the springs have bedded down a little after a hundred miles or so. This is not necessary for ball-joints, which swivel without tensioning a bush or spring, and

can therefore be finally tightened before the vehicle is resting on its own wheels and suspension.

An increasing number of kit cars is being sold with adjustable front and/or rear suspensions. Traditionally, the kit builder would merely have to guesstimate the front toe-in until the vehicle could be taken to a specialist for final setting. Now builders are facing adjustable castor, camber, toe-in, ride height (usually including spring rates) and damping.

If you're not sure what to do with all this adjustment capacity, make sure the manufacturer of the kit tells you how it is meant to be set up and who has the equipment to do it properly. There are camber measurement gauges for home use at affordable prices but measurement of castor and toe-in can be a bit trickier.

Before you fit your donor's engine and 'box, take the opportunity to check the condition of the clutch. It'll be much easier to change now than when everything is in the car.

Also take the opportunity to check the ring gear and flywheel for any wear or damage. There's nothing worse than coming to drive your kit for the first time and getting nowhere!

Bad errors in setting up can cause dangerous handling faults and it isn't just a question of measuring how many 'visible threads' there on each opposite of the suspension wishbone or ball-joint extension. Some higher-tech tyre-fitting services or main dealers can measure all appropriate geometry angles for you and even alter them to suit your manufacturer's recommendations. Don't trust your own 'instincts' in adjusting these components.

Other problems can be caused when you re-use old ball-joints and wheel bearings to save a few bob. A collapsed wheel bearing can cost you a replacement stub axle. A broken ball-joint can let a wheel half fall off. Not something we'd recommend!

The position of the steering rack in relation to the front uprights is also a primary factor in determining a vehicle's road manners. The rack is attached to the steering arm of the upright via track rods and track rod ends. The latter effectively make the rack adjustable for length and are used to adjust wheel toe-in or toe-out (front-drive cars often have front wheel toe-out).

As each of the uprights moves up and down in the prescribed arc of travel, the track rod must follow that arc. If the arcs of movement followed by the track rods do

not coincide with those of the uprights (or more specifically of the steering arm ends) then the toe-in/out will alter as either of the front wheels approaches full bump or droop.

The net effect is called bump steer. A vehicle might be OK in a dead straight line on a smooth surface but a change in vehicle attitude (sideways roll or front to rear pitch) might create an unwanted and uncontrolled steering effect at the front.

This bump steer can be cured but the process can be complex. You might have simply omitted spacers that were meant to raise or reduce the height of the steering rack. Design faults with the kit might have meant that the steering arms or the track rods used are

the wrong lengths.

The rack itself might be the wrong length or it might be too far forward or back to create coincidental arcs of travel at the steering arm. Consider the kit manufacturer's demo car carefully before choosing. You don't want to end up trying to rectify this kind of problem.

Section 6
Engines and 'boxes

A STEEL CHASSIS KIT WILL now have started to look like a large go-kart without wheels. To sceptical onlookers, you haven't really progressed much and it's still a long way from being a finished car. We know different, though, don't we?

You may well find that your engine's standard oil sump may be too low to the ground when fitted in your kit. Shallow sumps are offered by a number of people and are a very wise investment!

For the mechanically minded, who might previously have spent a lifetime fixing and replacing the filthy and unattractive suspension components of the family hatchback, a gleaming tubular chassis equipped with new and/or reconditioned and painted suspension parts will look a treat. No asbestos dust, oil, grime, tarmac, earth, grass, manure and selected shreds of wild or domestic mammals to mess things up – yet.

If you're building a monocoque, then it will hardly have changed visually. You might now notice a set of stub axles within the wheel arches. Beware if your car is still on trestles. Try to lift the previously lightweight structure from its perch and you may find that you are no longer able to. Call in muscular helpers or risk doing your back!

Now's the time to think about fitting the really heavy stuff; engines and 'boxes etc. A live axle or complete subframe may have been the heaviest thing you've dealt with up to now. You'll soon realise that even the smallest engines are actually quite heavy.

It's more likely that you'll be working with the more traditional four-cylinder engines that have cast iron blocks and cast iron heads. Some of them will boast alloy heads but the Rover V8, Renault/Volvo V6 and Jaguar

V12 seem to be the only all-alloy engines regularly found in kit cars.

By far the most popular kit car engine is the in-line four-cylinder Ford Pinto OHC. This is available in 1600 or 2000cc versions, manual or automatic 'boxes, and originates from the Ford Capri, Granada, Cortina, Sierra and 2000cc Mk.2 RS Escorts. The Pintos are absent from Mk.1 Escorts and front-drive Fords.

They are closely followed in the popularity stakes by the in-line four-cylinder Ford Kent X-flow OHV motors found primarily in the Mk.1 and Mk.2 Escorts in 1100, 1300 and 1600cc variations. Also commonplace are the Rover V8s, in all their different guises, the American small, medium and big block V8s from Ford

and General Motors, the European Ford Cologne V6 2.3, 2.8 and 2.9-litre units and various twin-cam fours from Fiat, Lancia, Alfa, Toyota and even Ford/Cosworth.

Don't forget other British offerings, though. Many manufacturers offering kits for four-cylinder in-line engines with rear-drive gearboxes will give the customer a fairly wide choice of available engines from cars old or new. Westfield Sports Cars has conversions to put the Ford CVH SOHC engines from front-drive cars onto rear-drive gearboxes. There's the 1800 CVH already fitted with a rear-drive 'box on the Sierra 1.8.

Leyland has manufactured the A-series engine (commonly up to 1275cc) for both front and rear-drive applications and the

B-series motors are a popular rear-drive choice (from Marina, MGB). The 1800cc B-series was replaced by the reliable and easily maintained O-series 1700cc SOHC engine found in Marinas, Itals and even Sherpa vans.

For the manufacturer producing a front-drive or mid-engined kit, there is a good deal of choice. Various front-drive engines/gearboxes are relatively easily converted to mid-engined, rear-drive applications. The Mini, Metro and the Lancia Beta/HPE twin-cam are good examples of this.

Other manufacturers have chosen to take front-mounted engines and use them for mid-engined purposes with a special gearbox and conversion – instead of opting for the mega-buck Hewland or ZF racing 'boxes. The gearbox/transaxles from the Renault 20, 25 and 30

are used with conversions to operate with the Rover V8, assorted American V8s, various Ford fours and you can even use them with the original Renault V6 engines. Don't forget the Beetle transaxle for smaller capacity engines.

When it comes to fitting the engine and gearbox, (two more items that you'll undoubtedly have ready and waiting amongst the reconditioned, cleaned and painted parts prepared before your kit arrived) there are elements of both caution and hit 'n' miss to be considered.

In the case of most kits it is probable that the engine will rest on two mounts and that there will also be at least one gearbox mount or cross-member for extra support. In some cases the engine mounts, usually pressed or welded steel brackets, which bolt to the side

Top: This is Caterham's own specially designed dry sump arrangement with unique bellhousing. Below: Not an engine you'll find very often at the breakers. Right: Various Ford engines looking for a home.

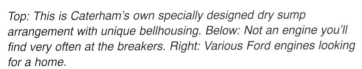

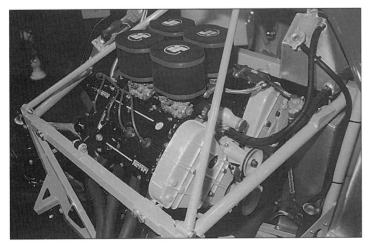

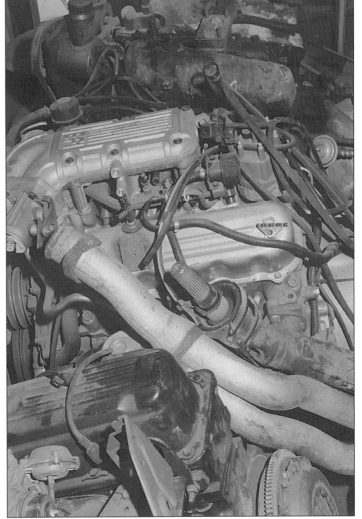

of the engine block, will come from a donor vehicle.

These mounts may incorporate rubber isolating bushes or the kit manufacturer may specify a different type of isolating bush. The design of these means that the engine itself is never 'solidly' connected to the chassis – all mounting contacts being through shock absorbing rubber bushes.

Make sure that you don't use cracked or perished bushes as these may well accentuate engine vibration through the chassis and could actually break, letting the engine sag or drop dangerously in its bay.

Typically, the isolastic mount will be a solid rubber oblong or cylindrical shape which might be permanently bonded to or simply bolted to the steel engine mount. It will also have an outboard bonded steel plate from which one or more threaded studs protrude, allowing the outboard side of the mount to be secured to the car's structure.

With the engine supported in position by a good quality rented engine hoist, it is a lot easier to make sure that the relevant studs and chassis apertures are aligned before the nuts are fully tightened. Remember to support the front and/or rear of the engine as it might pivot around its mounts until the gearbox and gearbox cross-member have been attached.

Running your engine with a decent air filter is vital for its long term health and will improve performance. There are many aftermarket filters to fit all manner of carburettor set-ups.

In some instances, the engine must be fitted only after the gearbox has been installed. This calls for proper support for the gearbox and careful manoeuvring of the engine so that the first motion shaft of the gearbox can be carefully inserted into the engine block as the mating faces of the bell-housing and block come together.

The *Haynes Workshop Manual* for your particular engine will have described just how to fit the flywheel/ring gear, clutch centre plate (friction plate) and the clutch cover (pressure plate). Again, don't skimp on new clutch assemblies as they can be a real problem to fit once the car has been completed. Even if your

donor clutch friction plate seems to have plenty of friction material left on it, and the cover isn't scored badly, it doesn't mean that the clutch is in good condition.

Previous owners of the donor vehicle may have economised by replacing only the friction plate while ignoring the cover and the clutch release bearing. This might have lead to cracks in the cover or weakness in its over-used spring tabs (tangs or fingers).

That can mean rough clutch response, clutch drag and even a collapsed clutch assembly with potentially life-threatening consequences. Shards of clutch blasting through the bell-housing and transmission tunnel are

more than an irritation. A worn clutch release bearing will start to squeak and rumble, producing a fearsome noise before eventually collapsing in a scatter of ball-bearings.

There could be excess wear in the pivot points of the clutch actuating lever or associated mechanisms. This might lead to a clutch drag that can't be adjusted out. All in all, it's worth getting a good quality complete clutch replacement kit and fitting it before the engine and box are hidden away in the chassis. Pay attention to associated levers and rods, looking for wear, cracks and bending. It's essential to have perfect clutch operation if you're going to enjoy driving the car.

The hit 'n' miss aspect comes in a bit later. The exact positioning of the engine and gearbox may seem very simple when the rolling chassis is bare but fitting subsequent items might require alteration in the engine and 'box positions. For instance, you might find that a tubular exhaust manifold or downpipe doesn't neatly align with the sidepipe or the rest of the exhaust system. Don't lever into place with an old crowbar.

To get them to line up properly might mean slotting out the gearbox cross-member mounts and adjusting alignment by moving the tail end of the gearbox slightly to one side. If

A good quality filter can often be cleaned and re-used. At worst it will have a throw away element. Don't ever run a carb without any filter at all, you may well damage valves and possibly worse.

Simple Halfords style aftermarket filter is usually worse than the original equipment fitted to the donor car. Avoid it at all costs. It will do you no favours whatsoever.

Bonnet bulges come in all shapes and sizes, with varying degrees of success. Above: Cobra bonnet vent looks terrific. Below: Eldon affair is plain ugly!

Above: This huge bonnet bulge on a Sylva Clubmans looks quite good on this serious racer. Below: Westfield didn't even bother to try and hide the huge filters needed for its psycho SEiGHT.

the height of the misaligned components is a problem, it is quite permissible to make up steel spacers that can be used either side of the engine mounts or mounting bushes to alter the angle (left to right lean) at which the engine sits.

Spacers might also be used to alter the front to rear (viewed from the side) angle of the engine by raising or lowering the gearbox at its cross-member. Remember that a propshaft must take a near-straight route to a differential or live axle when the car is at rest with a normal load. Similarly, half-shafts from a transaxle must also get a fairly straight run to the hubs when the vehicle is at rest on its own wheels.

More problems seem to arise with engines that sit too high and sumps that droop too low. Altering the position of the engine can sometimes lead to problems with bonnet and ground clearance. You don't want to be stuck with a tiny pancake air filter on your downdraft (or any) carburettor and you don't want to slice off the bottom of the sump on a slightly high manhole cover. The latter is a surefire way to wreck an engine unless you're very lucky.

If you can't move the engine and you don't want a huge hole or bulge in the bonnet, consult the manufacturer for alternatives. It is entirely plausible for sub-contract fabricators to cut and re-weld a steel (or even alloy) rocker or cam cover so that the oil filler neck is made shorter or moved to a more convenient location.

Replacement rocker/cam covers can be purchased off-the-shelf, as can shallow sumps with baffles and special oil pick-ups for a quick, bolt-on conversion. If your standard downdraft carburettor is too tall, your only option might be the fitment of a pair of sidedraft Webers or Dell'Ortos on a special manifold and throttle linkage.

Always use a quality (standard or after-market) air filter as large as you can fit. A pancake filter is probably worse than no filter at all. If you don't mind using a bonnet bulge, it's worth it for the sake of using a decent air filter and getting proper sump-to-ground clearance.

These options can be expensive and you should have established at the start whether a kit of your choice, built to these specifications, would need these modifications. If you want to change your mind as to engine and gearbox specifications part way through a build-up, these are the questions you should consider when pricing up the alternatives.

Even when you have the engine, gearbox, half-shafts/propshaft, exhaust, manifolds, carbs, air filter(s), oil filter, oil filler neck, sump, alternator, water pump, distributor, gear lever and other associated components all sorted in relation to each other, things might still have to change when the bodywork gets underway. That's what we'll be looking at in the next chapter.

Chapter 6
BODY WORK

Section 1
Body types

BEAUTY MAY ONLY BE SKIN deep, but there are no two ways about it, how your car looks now and how it will look in a few years time is of great importance. No, we're not talking about the styling but instead the quality of the bodywork and how it will withstand the rigors of sun, snow, ice, wind, water, stones, vandals, guano and the occupants of the vehicle. If there are design, manufacture or assembly faults in the bodywork, they will inevitably show up sooner or later and ruin the all-important look of your vehicle.

When visiting a manufacturer, you have to look carefully at the demo car's bodywork. As ever, the owners club will tell you what to look out for when considering the bodywork of that particular vehicle. There may have been

previous faults that have supposedly been "sorted out" by the manufacturer in current bodies – is there evidence of these in the company's latest demo car?

Look at points where it is attached to the chassis. Are there spacers there? Are the wheels symmetrically placed within their arches or are there different clearances? GRP, alloy and plywood are the principal body construction materials in the kit car trade. We'll be considering various points concerning their use here.

Unfortunately, some manufacturers have the knack of producing bodyshells that can appear great but are actually rubbish. The defunct Duttons and early Lamborghini Countach lookalikes proved this. Other exotic 'rip-offs' have fallen into the same trap. Just because it looks right, it doesn't mean that it will fit the chassis or last more than a few months

before rippling, cracking, changing colour and de-laminating.

Fitting together a multi-panel exotic has often proved to be a nightmare, especially when the bodyshell is a basic copy of a production car with a different kind of chassis. Even when a bodyshell has been moulded into just one or two main sections for simple attachment to a chassis, it may not fit any better than a shell made from many smaller panels.

industry has produced many excellent bodies made from separate panels. They are easier to manhandle and alter, even if you have to be a bit more careful with waterproofing techniques.

However, a main body tub will, if well moulded, drop into a self-locating position on its chassis and will rest down flush with all tabs and brackets to which it must be bolted. When it happens like this, you've saved a lot of time.

> ## THE WHICH KIT? TIP
> Return edges on any GRP panels are a sign that the manufacturer has taken time to get body panels to fit carefully. A return edge on a panel that butts up to another should mean you're in for all but zero trimming. No return edges on any panels is a sure sign of the opposite!

Don't presume that a single unitary tub is the easiest way out of body fitting. The kit car

Look closely at the company demo car and at club cars to see the body attachment points

Fibreglass bodies may come in a number of separate panels or in one major tub such as this Pilgrim Sumo. If made well the latter can greatly ease the way in which a kit goes together.

A multitude of separate panels, as with this Marlin Roadster, needn't necessarily mean a difficult build and may be better from a repair point of view should you have an accident.

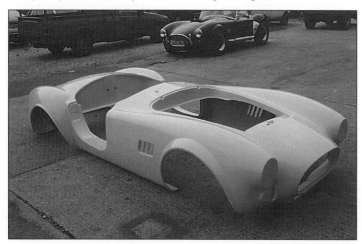

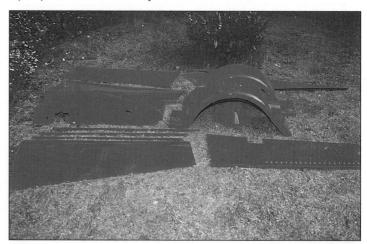

if it's a body tub. Are there spacers and washers between the mounting points and the chassis to fill a gap? Don't forget that sealant, chassis tape or rubber channel are legitimate shock absorbers/waterproofers often placed between the shell and the chassis.

If the body is made from separate panels, how well do these panels fit together? If a panel is supplied oversized, as they often are, it can be cut down accurately to fit. If it's undersized, though, you could have problems. Sections that are flat or single-curved can be easily replaced but large or compound-curved sections may not be. A quick search under the demo car can reveal much.

GRP is excellent for spanning compound curves but it's pretty bad at forming sharp edges, angles, and corners. The laminator can get the gelcoat into these odd places but the mat might not make it. In time, you might find cracks and splitting gelcoat coming away so the whole area looks awful. Flat or near-flat surfaces are also a problem for GRP, as it tends to flex too easily if there's no curve or reinforcement in the panel.

A traditional roadster body with integral body tub and full wings all supplied as a single unit is the result of some very complex mould-making. It can take a lot of work out of construction if it is accurate and strengthened at the right places.

Joins in the moulding must be smooth and progressive and not sharp and acute. When the full wings are forced up or down by wind at high speed, they can cause unsightly gelcoat cracks at the join lines. If you see unitary GRP wings 'flapping' on a test drive, presume that they are not very well designed/built and may well show gelcoat cracking quite soon.

Take a good look to see what wing or other panel attachments are used in the demo car. They may not be the same as those in the manufacturer's construction manual, so beware. Always realise that your kit car's bodyshell, apart from looking just how you want it to, must put up with all kinds of stresses and strains which can turn a flimsy product into an eyesore in a very short time.

A final coloured gelcoat finish is something which must be treated with respect. If you're unlucky and your laminator has used a duff batch of resin, your shell could get a distinct fade or colour change in a year or two. If you store a gelcoated body under a tarpaulin or plastic sheet, especially out in the sun, expect to get serious colour deterioration very quickly. Don't do it. It's better to keep GRP under shelter but even full exposure to the elements isn't a big problem.

It is best to prop up bodies and panels in storage so that they are evenly supported at centres and extremities. Flattish panels can be stored vertically. Large tubs with full wings should be supported very carefully until fitted to the chassis unit. The shell will still be curing for a while, so you can't risk letting it sag into the wrong shape.

Even an excellent gelcoat, like paint, won't last for ever. Many favour it to start with because it is a big time and money saving route when compared to paintwork. It can look every bit as good as a paint job when new but it will inevitably fade, crack or change colour. If you intend to keep the

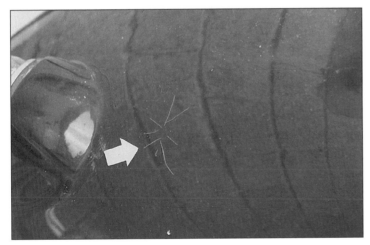

Above: Star cracks such as this are the results of stones flying off the tyre and hitting the underside of the wheelarch. Whilst not impossible, they are costly to put right. Below: Forget it!

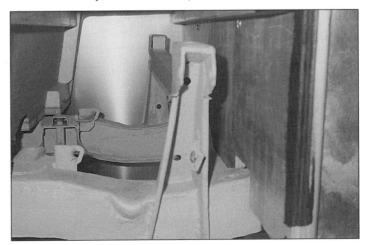

Above: Not all kits are made of fibreglass. This White Rose Midge is primarily made from exterior plywood and clad in very thin aluminium. Works well in conjunction with Triumph ladder chassis (below).

car for a good while, be prepared to fork out for a paint job eventually.

So, if you have taken delivery of a GRP-based body before you have completed the rolling chassis, take care where you put it while waiting to fit it. The loft is usually the destination of the smaller panels, or you can make up racks or cradles slung from the garage roof to store others.

If your kit uses a large one-piece tub and you really haven't got anywhere to store it safely, then preclude the problem by negotiating a later delivery date with the manufacturer. You'll have to guess when you'll be ready for it but you may be able to put it off a few times if you give sufficient notice.

Make sure that the workshop gets a good clean after the rolling chassis build. The worst of the mess will have been made while you were cleaning,

refurbishing and painting. However, assembling the whole lot will have involved the use of lubricants, paint, sealant and solvents. There will be traces of all of these on the floor and work surfaces, as well as selected samples of swarf, dust, engine grime and other nasties.

Try to roll the chassis out of the garage and use the opportunity to re-rack all tools and materials, sweep, de-grease and hoover the floor and work surfaces. If you have lino or hardboard available, re-line your worktops with these clean new surfaces. Get rid of grubby mechanical components that might be left over.

Clean up the rolling chassis itself to remove excess oil and grease that might contaminate bodywork. This is important if your shell is due for a paint finish. You will have to take serious precautions to make

sure that there isn't a trace of lubricant left on the shell prior to paint preparation. The best way is to ensure that none gets on there to start with.

Section 2
Alloy clad

IT WAS VERY COMMON, before steel and iron became cheap, for coachbuilders and the early vehicle manufacturers to clad structural wood chassis sections in thin steel sheet. Aluminium alloy also became popular for this. If the wood was properly preserved against damp and rot and the metal sheet was properly cut and bonded to it, then such a beam or member could last for a very long time.

The current availability of marine grade plywood and thin

alloy sheet, along with a host of super-efficient adhesives, makes this method even more viable today. Whereas some kits specify a body constructed wholly or partly from alloy-clad plywood, others are far more conservative with their use of ply, often not specifying alloy cladding at all.

If you want to embellish ply sections with alloy sheet, start by cutting out and 'dry' assembling the piece temporarily. Once the sheet of plywood (choose marine ply or water and boil-proof) has been covered with the alloy, which is wrapped around the edges like material, it will obviously be larger. Compensate for this by allowing the plywood section to fit a little loosely.

If you think that the alloy sheet will be difficult to bend over the edges of the wood

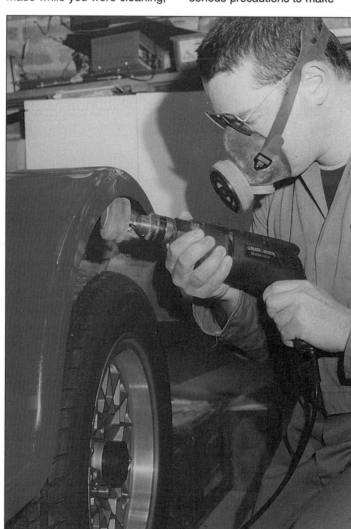

Left: When working with GRP a good nose/mouth mask and filter is essential. Top: Thin aluminium is ideal for cladding. Below: Always try to wear gloves when working with GRP.

panel, you should try it with a few scrap pieces first to see if you can manage. Cutting the corner pieces for a neat fold can be done with good tin snips. If you can't bend the alloy easily enough, try annealing the edges to be bent.

This is simply done by rubbing a normal bar of soap over one side of the alloy sheet. Heat the other side of the sheet slowly over a flame until the soap turns brown. Carry on along the edges like this. Once the alloy has cooled off, you'll find it much easier to bend. This is a safe process for non-structural alloy but don't do it to alloy brackets or other pieces which might have to withstand stresses or loads.

It is usually easier to glue the major flat surfaces of alloy and ply first and let them dry fully before turning the edges over. There is an array of glues which might be suitable. We have always had success with contact adhesives like Dunlop, Evo or Bostik. Make sure the work area is not humid and is relatively warm and well ventilated. Glue and its vapour are both flammable, so no flames in the area.

Most contact adhesives are used by coating both surfaces to be glued together and waiting until the adhesive is either tacky or touch dry before pressing the surfaces together. It is a good idea to coat the wood with a thin layer of the glue and leave it for a day before carrying out the standard gluing process.

Make sure that both surfaces are completely dust-free before joining together and that the glue isn't too wet or dry. Small particles under the alloy sheet will cause a very noticeable imperfection in the panel shape. Separating the sheets will probably lead to damaged ply or bent alloy.

Compress the glued panel between two other sheets of board or ply and place a heavy weight on top or clamp together with G-clamps and load-spreaders to prevent localised dents or depressions.

Once this has been left overnight, or at least a few hours, the alloy and ply edges can be glued up and stuck down. A rubber or hide mallet can be useful for bashing the alloy edges over neatly, with G-clamps and load spreaders holding it all in position afterwards. Small (rust-proofed) tacks or nails can be handy for holding edges down but watch their length.

If you prefer to use a non-contact adhesive, something like the two-part epoxy Araldite can be a strong alternative, if a bit expensive to use in quantity.

If the panel is expected to get wet regularly or to have very little access to ventilating air flow, it should be sealed against moisture. If it is to be a visible body panel, it is likely that you will deal with the alloy face using the general paint preparation techniques outlined in Chapter Nine.

Any invisible faces or edges can be treated with bathroom sealant at the alloy edges and then painted over with a primer

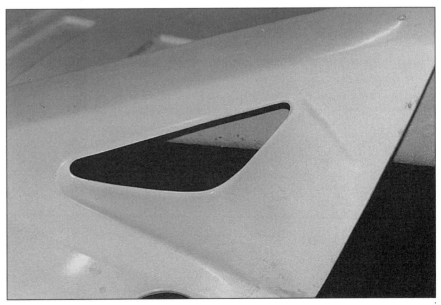

Above: Rough edges can then be gradually filed down. Work slowly and don't try to remove too much at one time. With care the result will be superb and require no further finishing.

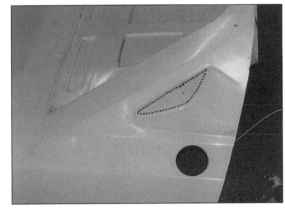

Cutting holes in GRP needn't involve expensive tools. Drill a series of holes just inside the desired area and remove centre section.

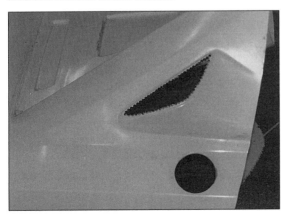

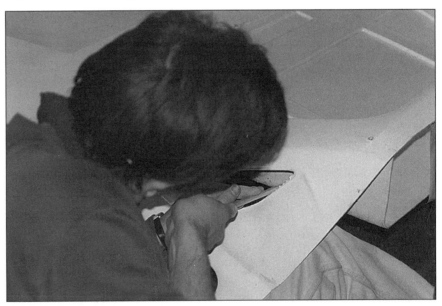

and an exterior gloss or one of the various underseal paints. If you started off with a good quality piece of ply and finished the proofing well, this panel will last for a long time indeed.

Section 3
Working with GRP

A FEW HINTS AND TIPS about working with grp might be of use here. Most hand-laminated GRP kit car bodies and panels aren't like normal moulded plastic panels you find in your car or home. They tend to be less flexible and one surface, usually the visible or outer surface, has been coated with a smooth gelcoat resin to hide the rough texture of the woven rovings or chopped strand mat underneath.

From the time you collect your kit, you'll be aware that non-gel-coated GRP tends to leave small, invisible splinters in your skin. You might not notice them initially but you will later on in bed that night. Use tough gloves and protective clothes when handling raw surfaces and edges.

Those same needles are produced in abundance whenever you drill, sand or cut GRP and they will damage your throat and lungs. Wear a good nose and mouth mask with replaceable filters. They are now available in many DIY shops.

You must exercise extreme caution when handling GRP panels, especially if the gelcoat is to be the final colour. It's like a thick layer of plastic paint on top of the GRP mat. It's flexible to a point but it is easily cracked by impact or excessive stress. Gel is particularly fallible where it has been applied too thickly or where there is an air space between it and the GRP mat below it.

Once it is cracked, it can be repaired. Your manufacturer should be able to supply you with a container of colour-matched gel and a catalyst. The repair process involves chipping and scraping the cracked gelcoat away from the affected area and 'filling' it with the new.

Once this has hardened off, it can be filed and/or sanded back down smooth using increasingly finer grades of wet and dry paper (the latter with water). The final shine can come from an abrasive chrome cleaner, T-Cut or specialised cutting compound recommended by the club or manufacturer.

If at all possible, do any drilling with a hand drill or electric drill with adjustable speed and drill from the gelcoat side. Most drills you use will have been designed for cutting wood or steel. Using the larger sized drills, 7mm and over, when they are very sharp, can cause jagged and rough cutting. Sometimes this can be reduced by drilling at higher speed with the big drills but there will usually be some damage.

Tape over the area to be drilled with one or two layers of masking tape. This stops the

Building up an edge isn't always ideal. Score the GRP first to give the filler/fibreglass paste a good keyed surface. Results can be good, as shown below left.

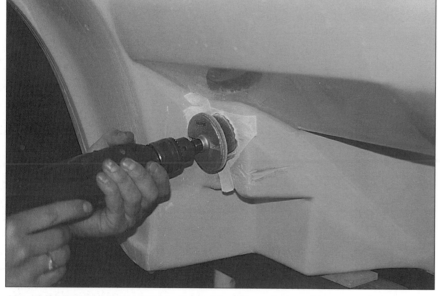

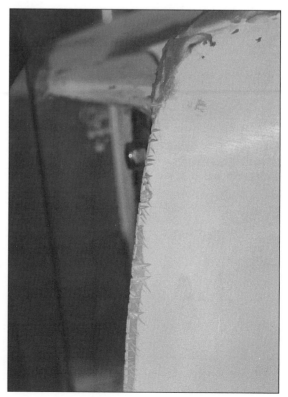

Above: Perfectly round holes can be made using a 'hole cutting saw'. Can give excellent results. Below: Adjusting shutlines is a careful business and may require lots of subtle fettling.

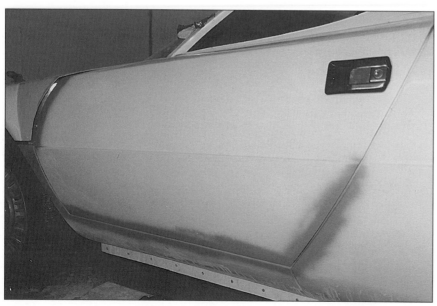

Above: A variable speed jigsaw with a fine-toothed blade is a good GRP cutter but cut well to the 'waste' side. Below: A good selection of different files is a must. Right: Don't use wood saws on GRP.

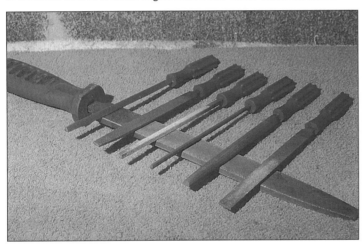

drill bit from drifting all over the surface before the hole cutting starts. A very blunt drill will make matters worse. Avoid pushing hard to compensate and, if necessary, drill a small pilot hole with a fine drill bit to help get a large drill started. Single or two-speed electric drills can cause problems as they don't permit you to start off slowly while the bit is still locating itself.

Using a countersink bit first can also be a help to prevent gel cracking and chipping. Having marked your hole centre on the masking tape, countersink the surface to just wider than the required hole diameter before using the drill bit.

If you have to drill from the mat side of the GRP through to the gel, the chances of splitting or flaking the gel increase greatly. You probably won't be able to countersink a hole into the gel exactly where your drill bit is expected to appear. If you can, then do.

If there's no way to get a drill in position on the gelcoat side of the hole, then carefully clamp a piece of timber to the gel surface so that the drill will go through the gel and immediately into the wood. This will reduce cracking as the bit penetrates the gel.

If you have to cut a hole of 15mm diameter or more, try to avoid using a huge drill bit just for this one job. It could well mangle the gelcoat and it will be expensive. A good DIY shop will have high quality drill-mounted hole-cutting saws with integral drill bits. Try to avoid the kind that offers you a huge selection of interchangeable blades which can be bayonet-mounted in a metal base piece.

We have found that inexpensive versions of these hole saw 'kits', £5-£10, don't allow for strong location of the base piece onto the drill bit supplied, nor do they score highly on concentric mounting of the hole saw in its base. The resulting hole can be a fair bit larger than you intended.

Spend out on higher quality options or use the old method of drilling a succession of small holes around the perimeter of a large hole and subsequently filing it out to the required size.

Small sized flap-wheel sanders can help to get a hole pretty round, even freehand.

Most kit car manufacturers and laminating shops use diamond cutting discs in compressed air or electric tools for cutting GRP. In the workshop, you'll probably be restricted to manual saws and electric jigsaws.

If you must use a manual saw for GRP, you'll probably get the tidiest results from a steel-

THE WHICH KIT? TIP
On larger holes that will be seen on the outside of a car, such as bonnet vents, grille apertures etc the most basic methods are usually the best. A hand held file can often give you the most control. Work lightly with it rather than trying to grind out huge swathes of GRP and always use the right file for the job - buy a decent set with proper handles

Separate alloy panels for the transmission tunnel top, sides and rear bulkhead. Don't forget that at some stage you may need to gain access to the propshaft etc through here. Therefore, rivets may not be ideal.

Typical modular floor, rear bulkhead, tunnel and wood footwell floor. All bolt to each other and to existing chassis rails. Seatbelt stalk bolts through into strengthened corner section.

cutting hacksaw blade. Wood-cutting blades will be far too coarse for GRP and will crack the gel ferociously. You can get manual hack and jig saws which allow you to change the angle of the blade. This can help to get a deeper cut in some panels but usually the saw shape will restrict the depth of cut.

This is where an electric jigsaw can come in handy. You guessed it, the variable speed versions are much more user-friendly than the rest. If you have to use a jigsaw to cut a GRP panel, you'll find that the return blade stroke will crack the gel. If possible, try to clamp wood firmly to the gel side of the GRP and cut carefully through the wood (do not use the wood-cutting blades though). As with drilling, cut from the gel side.

If this isn't possible, you'll have to try to isolate the gel at risk from the cut and minimise the quantity which will get damaged. Draw your exact cut line on the gelcoat side with a chinagraph pencil or similar and gently run a sharp Stanley knife along the cut line. Do this several times until you have cut through the gel and into the mat. You can then jigsaw just to the 'waste' side of the line, the knife cut preventing cracks from reaching through into the important gel surface.

If you are able to use a manual saw with a fine-toothed

metal-cutting blade, tape over the gel and scribe your cut line onto the masking tape. Work from the gel side, cutting only on the 'away' stroke and not on the return stroke. The return stroke will pull the gel away from the GRP.

If you want to be particularly cautious, cut well to the 'waste' side of the line and then use a flap wheel sander, sharp hand file, sanding block or electric sander to take off the excess GRP with minimal gel damage. This is time-consuming and produces more dust.

When doing any cutting and drilling of GRP, remember that it's very easy to cut off too much. It's a slow process to build up an under-sized GRP edge using makeshift alloy,

plastic or lino formers and extra mat and resin. When cutting away at a hole, stop often and check the size of the hole against the component to be mounted into it. When trimming down a panel, offer it up regularly to check for size.

Section 4
Multi-section bodies

MORE OFTEN THAN NOT, there will be a cross-over stage where some of the rolling chassis work will be intertwined with the early body assembly work. Typically, we find that pedal assemblies, handbrake levers, radiators, heaters, dashboards, fuel tanks, steering columns, engine ancillary parts

and the like can depend upon fitment to some part of the body.

Even if the above-mentioned parts are all fitted to the chassis, you must position them very carefully to allow clearances for the body panels. After-market radiators, exhausts and carburettors aren't always the same shape as original components. Even original equipment varies sometimes. Pre-punched mounting holes aren't always a guarantee of fit.

For the first-time builder, fitting important components such as brake pipes and hoses, the handbrake mechanism, pedals, steering column etc. can be a bit tense. Especially when the kit's construction manual doesn't give precise instructions and you have to put some relatively large holes in the bodywork. When there's a one-piece body or a large central unit, it can be even more dodgy to drill large holes in the wrong place.

Here's where the kit body supplied as many separate panels really comes in handy. If you're drilling the driver footwell or a tunnel side and you really stuff it up, there's always the option of getting another separate panel from the manufacturer as a direct replacement for the one you ruined.

Early body fitting often requires several attempts when something isn't quite right.

Underside of this Marlin shows a dropped floorpan to give occupants extra head height. Note no unsightly bolts in evidence. Everything kept neat and tidy.

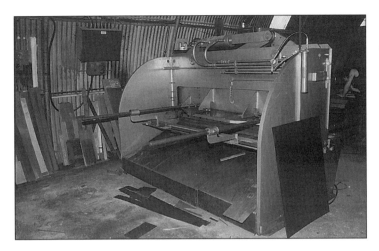

Manufacturers often leave some excess material so that there's no risk of a panel being undersized. This may prevent instant fitting of the body as something might stop the tub from sitting down squarely in its position on the chassis.

In the next section, we'll include more detail about the single-piece and/or central body tub. That group encompasses the Cobra lookalikes, many traditional roadsters, various utilities and exotic coupes.

In this section, we'll consider some aspects of the body which come as a combination of mouldings or basic panels. These include all manner of Lotus Seven-type roadsters, Marlin Roadster and Berlinetta, wood-panelled cars and various traditional roadsters.

Many newcomers to the kit car concept are daunted by the whole notion of body fitting. Does the body locate itself on the chassis? Do the separate panels have purpose-made brackets ready for them on the chassis? How is the whole lot aligned? How are body tubs and panels attached to the chassis? Will a body made from separate panels ever be waterproof?

Thankfully, a lot of kit manufacturers realise that this kind of thing does worry amateur kit builders who aren't specialist car craftspeople. The key to increasing sales has been better buildability. A good quality kit supplied with a clear and comprehensive build manual will attract buyers who don't have to be experts.

In the vast majority of kits, we find that the body panels and tubs are bolted to adjacent chassis brackets and tabs.

Many bodies/chassis already have holes punched through them and manufacturers' construction manuals offer guidelines on how many holes should be drilled and where.

It's likely that a rolling chassis to be fitted with panelled bodywork will have obvious flanges, tabs, ledges and brackets where the separate panels will fit. The builder will usually be instructed to start at the floor and tunnel sections and work outwards from there.

Plywood and aluminium alloy are the most common materials for panelling an interior. As far as flat panels go, plywood is by far the easiest material to work with. It's strong, relatively cheap and most tools will be capable of shaping or drilling it easily.

Alloy sheet comes in thicknesses measured as SWG (Standard Wire Gauge). 10 SWG sheet will be pretty thick and stiff whereas 20 SWG will be thin and more easily pliable. If alloy sheet contributes to chassis strength, it will usually be attached in advance by the manufacturer.

If you are working with alloy sheet, the main problem is accurately cutting long lengths of it. Jigsaws and other power tool blades can become badly clogged with alloy, making a long cut tedious and often erratic.

Very good tin snips can make the job easier if the sheet you are using is thin enough. Professionals will normally have a guillotine mechanism for making long cuts. The kit builder will have to employ patience instead and, if using an electric jigsaw, a few spare aluminium cutting blades.

Edge finishing for both wood

Top: Alloy chassis panelling will often be cut to size by the manufacturer using a large guillotine. Below: Solid timber may warp. Medium Density Fibreboard (right) is more manageable.

Above: A selection of GRP mouldings for a Rotrax. Large footwells in the foreground. Below: Trial fitting the panels according to instructions. (Continued overleaf).

and alloy panels is best done with a file and abrasive paper. Remove sharp corners and points where possible, being careful not to remove too much material from the panel. If all mounting holes are yet to be drilled in the panel and the chassis, check carefully where they will have to go before trimming the panel energetically.

An odd protrusion or spare edge might appear to be surplus but this could be essential for attaching another panel or component to the one you're working on. Don't lop it off without thinking ahead first.

The panels which support the seats are all-important. A quality steel chassis will provide steel brackets or cross-members through which the seats or seat runners will bolt. Some kits provide only a floor panel for seat attachment, so it's up to the builder to ensure that this is strong enough to do its job.

Not only does it have to support the weight of an adult thumping down into the seat but it has to hold the seat firm while the driver is braking hard, while the car is accelerating or cornering hard, during a collision from any direction or if the car runs over an obstruction which might bash the bottom of the cockpit hard.

Once you have finalised the hole positions for your seat

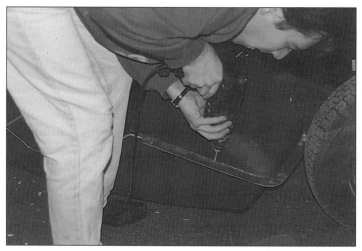

Rotrax panels have return edges for easier assembly. Here being bolted together. Without them assembly would be considerably more tricky.

mountings, you might reinforce that floor section by adding some steel bars (from an ironmonger or blacksmith) which can be bolted to the chassis, permitting the seat or runner bolts to go through them. The enterprising builder might even take a template of that floor panel and get a local engineer or garage to make a sheet steel equivalent.

If you're making a wood floor for the seat mounting sections, try to make it (no thinner than) 1/2" exterior plywood with large load-spreading washers against relevant nuts or bolts. Not chipboard or fibreboard etc. Avoid using alloy sheet as the seat supporting panel unless there are structural steel bars

doing the work. It would have to be very thick alloy to be strong enough.

At this stage, you will probably be dry fitting so that you can judge the size of the panels correctly and drill or cut all holes in the correct place. There is no need to undertake detailed finishing and smoothing work until you're sure that you have all the panels where they are meant to be. Use any handy nuts and bolts of the correct diameter at this stage.

When you come to finally fit the panels, you'll be more interested in getting the right rust-proof fasteners with the correct washers of the correct length. Use nyloc nuts if you can afford them but spring

washers and flat washers used with plain nuts are acceptable. Don't use plain nuts without shake-proof washers of some sort. It's inevitable that they'll let you down.

With the cockpit section trial-fitted, you can turn your attention to the front, rear and sides of the vehicle, depending upon the manufacturer's specific instructions. There will probably be a combination of alloy and GRP sections forming the visible outer panels of the car. Kits such as the excellent Teal Type 35 prove that you can still get compound curves in aluminium but this is the exception rather than the rule.

Usually, we find that the compound curves – the nosecone, radiator cowl, scuttle top, rear bodyshell, removable hardtop, wheel arches, wings etc. – are supplied in GRP. Many flat or single-curved panels – bonnet, engine bay sides, inner wheel arches, dashboard etc. – are in either alloy or GRP. Doors are usually GRP mouldings, some reinforced by steel frames.

Once they're on the chassis they will generally show you just how they are meant to fit and where. Even if complex mouldings don't instantly drop into position, you will be able to see just where they need to be trimmed and smoothed to get the clearance you need.

This Pilgrim door hinge clearly shows the slotted holes to facilitate adjustment of the door within the bodyshell to achieve an even shutline. This sort of thing makes a build so much easier.

This door weather seal is available in a variety of different thicknesses. Using one that is too thick may force the door to become proud of the main tub.

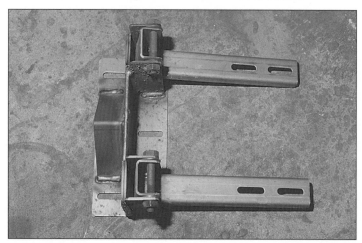

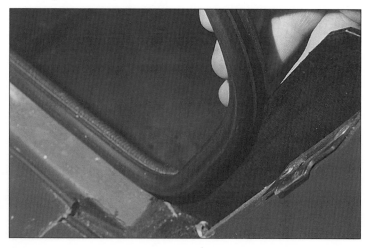

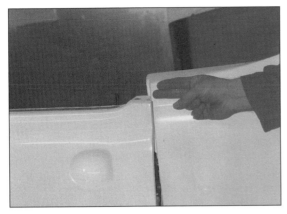

Above: Sometimes door shuts need a lot of adjustment! Below: Good results can usually be obtained with persistence or merely good fortune.

Above: Massive panels such as this GT40 rear engine cover have long shutlines that require very careful adjustment. Below: Sometimes gently heating a panel will help pull it into shape. Go carefully, though!

In the next section, which deals with unitary GRP tubs, we will mention the methods for dealing with warped or inaccurate GRP mouldings which fail to sit down flush against all the relevant chassis brackets intended for them.

This problem might arise if you're dealing with smaller mouldings as well. Don't be tempted to fill such gaps with spacers. The panel could well end up in the wrong position. You may need to gradually tighten it down into place with the mounting bolts so that it sits flush.

Failure to ensure that these mouldings are fitted properly may well compromise the fit of other more visible panels later on. Perhaps the door apertures or other shut lines depend on the fitment of cockpit or bulkhead sections?

If the gap between a moulding and the chassis is too great to be gradually bolted down, contact the manufacturer and state your difficulty. It might require a replacement panel to sort it out.

Once all of the inner panels (ie: all panels apart from the visible outer panels forming the body shape) are trial fitted, the builder can continue with the more exacting fitment of the outer body panels. These are the ones that you really have to get right because they are what all the bystanders will be looking at and judging.

This is where you might wish you'd purchased a kit with a unitary shell and tub. Then you wouldn't have all that hassle making the thing symmetrical and smooth. Not a bit of it. A shell in separate panels does take longer to complete and there are more separate jobs to be done but they aren't necessarily harder.

In a well-designed kit, the body panels will only fit in the correct positions, due to the provision of brackets or marked holes. Some trimming might be needed for a perfect fit.

If you are left with a lot of leeway when fitting external panels, you can end up with a fairly rough job if you're not patient and careful. Position the chassis level with the floor so that you can use some vertical measurements to aid alignments. The job must be seen as a

THE WHICH KIT? TIP
When you come to fitting the body, whether it be in one or several pieces, it's extremely difficult to line anything up when you are up close to the car in the typical confines of a garage. Roll the car outside and have a good look over it from several metres away. From here, your eyes will quickly pick out any irregularities

Self adhesive chassis sponge can be used between chassis and bodywork to stop squeaks etc. Below: Mastic does much the same thing.

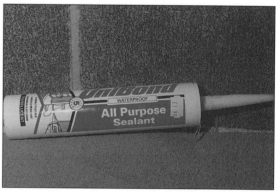

Above: Inner wheelarch panels will protect the outer bodywork from damage. These are Pilgrim Sumo panels. Below: Sumo body tub's lower edge can be bolted/sealed to the chassis.

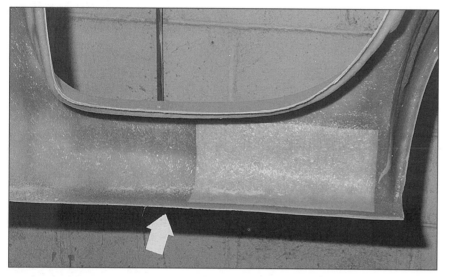

collection of panels together, not as one-at-a-time fitting.

A typical body assembly schedule, started by the completion of the floor and bulkhead areas, might then move on to the rear body section, the scuttle (that odd-shaped bit below the windscreen), the engine bay sides and the wings.

If there are doors to be fitted, the builder will be very concerned about the aperture for the door each side. A unitary bodyshell will have a fixed door aperture usually, with variations due to body twist or door twist being the main (and very considerable) problems. If you have to fit the bodywork below, behind and ahead of the

doors, you actually have a great deal of control over door fit.

Increasingly, quality conscious manufacturers are designing doors which have their own steel frames extending between hinge points and the latch. All hinging and latching relates to chassis-mounted components so that none of the GRP on the door or the body has to put up with these high-stress jobs. Gelcoat often cracks around the door hinges if they aren't properly chassis-mounted.

Trial fit doors using plasticene, Blu-Tak or simple wood wedges to hold them temporarily in position while checking for shut lines on the driver and passenger side

doors. Doors vary a lot in design. Some have extensive return edges which pretty much preclude any trimming down but allow you to build them up with extra filler or mat bonding.

Some have generous flanges around the edges which effectively hide the shut lines and therefore reduce the need to trim the door or its aperture. Some have narrow return edges and can be easily trimmed or built up to fit the aperture best.

If you find that the door is too large to fit in its aperture and does not allow you to trim it down easily, you may be able to shift the bodywork bordering the door in order to make more room.

If the door has a thick and trimmable flange, and it looks pretty impossible to alter the surrounding panel positions, you can carefully file, sand or cut away at the door edge, offering

it up to the aperture often to see if it fits. Better to remove too little than too much.

It's not altogether impossible to trim away part of the aperture edge if it is of a simple design but it's usually not feasible. Remember also that door apertures will often be fitted with rubber sealing strips as rain/wind guards. To check final fit, dry-fit the sealing channel to see if the door stands proud of the bodywork.

This door sealing channel, which usually includes a length of press-on edge trim with an integral rubber tube as the cushion and seal, does settle in with time and allows the door to sink deeper into its aperture. Don't go wild thinking of ways to make the door stand less proud straight away. You might just need to alter the type or size of sealing channel beading to allow for a better fit. There are several versions available from specialist kit build suppliers.

Whether you're bolting GRP doors to hinges or the rear bodywork to the chassis, use load-spreading penny washers against the GRP surface (usually out of sight against the mat face and not the external gelcoat).

You might want to reinforce the mounting faces of certain sections of the GRP, especially the wings or other surfaces which are wind-buffeted, with extra mat and resin. (See next section for technique).

Attach the subsequent panels in the specified order. You might just hold them in place with strong gaffer tape to start with. This will allow you to get a good overview of things so that you will know exactly what the effects of trimming certain panels will be. You'll also be able to tell if any panels threaten to foul other mechanical components when properly trimmed and fitted.

Gradually drill and dry fit all of the panels prior to dismantling for any paint preparation. The sealing mastic or chassis tape

strips will be added when the panels are finally assembled. Further mechanical work will probably depend upon body fitment and some of these jobs are dealt with below in Section 6.

Section 5
GRP tubs

WHERE THERE IS A complex central GRP tub, it will usually have only one place to go and the builder will be mainly concerned with assuring that the tub sits down freely and evenly against all of its chassis tabs.

Some mid-engined coupe kits feature what can be called a three-part body where the centre or cockpit section has to be carefully located relative to the front and rear panels. These are usually hinged and must abut neatly against the join with the centre.

Shut lines are all-important here and even if the main body centre has been fitted by the manufacturer, the builder may need to re-position it slightly to give the best overall fit with the other sections.

At least two pairs of hands are needed for lifting a centre tub on and off the chassis, especially if it sits well tucked in to locating chassis members and is a bit tight to start with. A common fitting problem is a slight twist in the moulding which prevents some surfaces from sitting flush against the chassis brackets to which they must be bolted.

Other problems might include excessive moulding width, so that the tub is too wide to drop down into the chassis, or insufficient moulding width, permitting the tub to slop about in its chassis 'cradle.'

A twist in the tub of more than

around 3/4" - 1" is worth mentioning to the manufacturer. If the centre tub has been thickly laminated, the removal of such a distortion will be difficult and even with the whole body warmed up to ease the stress, it might still be impossible to straighten the tub without instant or delayed stress cracking.

If the tub has not been distorted by thoughtless storage at your end, then the manufacturer is guilty of having either faulty moulds or of removing the mouldings before they have had a chance to cure properly in the mould.

Gaps below this width can usually be straightened out by a gradual and even tightening of the tub mounting bolts. Don't just put spacing washers or bushes where they're not meant to be as this will inevitably cause problems when trying to align other parts of the shell which

Above: Selective reinforcement of a GRP panel with coremat. It absorbs extra resin to stiffen flexible or flat panels. Below: Templates can be used for cutting reinforcing wood or extra GRP.

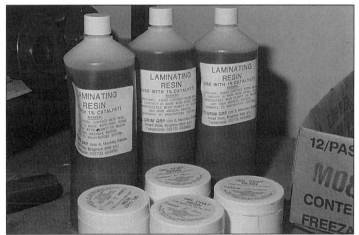

Above: The laminating resin (mixed with catalyst) is used to 'wet out' the mat. Gel resin is to colour and/or smooth the 'outer' surface. Below: Industrial quantities of final gel colours.

depend upon the correct fitment of the tub itself. Doors are a prime example of this and shut lines can be a mystery if the tub remains twisted.

If there is a manageable gap between the tub floor or sides and the chassis, it might help if you rest the tub in the chassis and fill it with heavy items to try and make the floor sit down flat where it's meant to. Increasing the temperature of the workshop to a hot room temperature should help the GRP to settle over a period of a day or two.

If the tub is physically a little wide to drop down into the chassis, always find out exactly where it is fouling and think carefully why. Are all the chassis members and mounting tabs where they are meant to be? Have a couple of them been accidentally bent over and are they causing the body

to sit too tightly against the chassis?

It might be permissible to grind away a small amount of steel from minor chassis tabs, brackets and members (contact the manufacturer if in doubt) but you might also need to remove some GRP from the body tub. If the tub sides are fouling the chassis, it will be inadvisable to sand them away until they are wafer thin just so that they clear the chassis.

It could well be a lot better to carefully cut away sections of the tub sides and bond them back into position using chopped strand mat with resin and hardener. Remember to contact your source at the owners club as well. If none of them has ever heard of your problem, it might be down to an overzealous laminator putting too much mat onto the tub. It might even be an inexperienced

or careless welder attaching a chassis member out of true or in a totally wrong position. Stranger things have happened!

You can cut the odd small hole in selected places to clear the chassis and then cover these holes with more mat or rubber grommets etc. Be careful that you don't do this where a gelcoat finish must remain visible nor if the manufacturer states that the body tub is in any way a structural part of the car. In most cases, the tub helps to stiffen the chassis incidentally but is not structural.

Do not be satisfied until the tub sits down into the chassis comfortably and easily. It shouldn't have to be a phenomenally tight fit - extra squeaks and rattles can be caused by this. No chassis are flex-proof and it is advisable to fit chassis tape, mastic sealant,

mastic adhesive or body caulking between the body and the chassis as a water and squeak-proofer.

Don't go ahead with the use of sealants until all body panels have been trial-fitted and/or painted up later. If the body must be dismantled to rectify a fault that is only apparent somewhere else down the line, you won't want to break an adhesive seal or to mess around with sticky mastic everywhere. Self-adhesive or plain waterproof chassis tape is pretty user-friendly and doesn't mean sticky dismantling.

Once you have the main tub bolted down correctly, check for flimsy or excessively flexible parts of the floor, footwells and bulkheads. Large and near-flat areas of GRP tend to suffer from flex more than compound curves, which are inherently

Above: Most kit car companies will be able to sell you chopped strand matt at reasonable prices. Below: Mat in a mould wetted out with a generous overlap to be trimmed back later.

Top: When drilling larger holes in GRP, use progressively bigger drill bits to avoid damaging the gelcoat finish. Below: Hacksaw blades make light work of fibreglass.

stiffer shapes. In certain areas, you may deem it necessary to bond in extra GRP mat (chopped strand mat or more expensive woven rovings).

If the area needs to be very stiff, bond in some thin exterior grade plywood. It doesn't really have to be more than 1/4" or 3/8" thick. Check with the kit manual that the area you want to reinforce won't need to remain thin for attaching various components. Does the pedal box bolt through it? What about the handbrake, seatbelt mounts, heater, gear lever aperture, body mounting bolts?

Rough up the area of GRP to receive the reinforcing with coarse abrasive paper. Remove all dust and clean with acetone. Acetone removes non-cured GRP resin and can be supplied by your GRP source as a brush cleaner etc. It also helps to remove any substances that will prevent your new resin and mat from bonding to the tub.

If you are simply adding GRP sheets, make a template of the area to be covered and cut this shape from the mat, using as many layers as you feel are necessary. Don't try to wet and bond large sheets of mat. Try sections around 1ft. square in area and overlap neighbouring pieces.

It's difficult to estimate just how much resin/gel mix you will need per square foot of GRP mat. If you're covering two flat floor sections, totalling six square feet, with one layer of mat, try mixing up about three quarters of a pint of resin with the hardener as instructed by the retailer or on the container. Have some spare resin and hardener available just in case.

Wet out (with resin and hardener) the area to be covered using a cheap, throw-away brush and lay down your mat in manageable sections. Wet out the top of the mat so that the GRP is just wet through. The professionals then use small rollers made of metal or wood etc. to roll the air bubbles out of the wet mat and to spread the resin evenly.

You don't want to drown the whole area in resin. There should be just enough to wet the GRP all the way through and no more, The combination of resin and GRP is very strong but resin on its own is very brittle and doesn't add to the strength of the layer.

If your resin starts to harden before you've properly finished wetting down the rest of the area and smoothing out the mat, concentrate on smoothing the area of mat which has already been wetted. If it hardens while shaped like the Himalayas, you'll have a very time-consuming job flatting the lot down. Use less hardener next time, when you're finishing off the rest of the job.

You can experiment with an offcut of mat to see just how long the resin takes to cure when mixed with the recommended proportion of hardener. If it's too short a time for you to finish all the bonding that has to be done, mix it with less hardener or mix smaller and more manageable

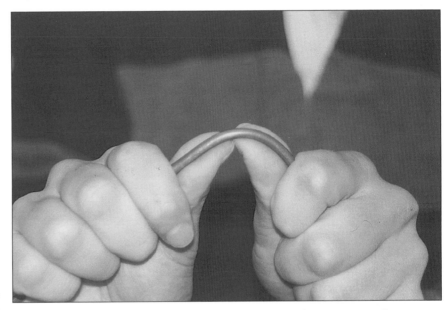

Above: Simple (and cheap) brake flaring tool works well when used with care. Below: A pipe bend like this could prove fatal.

Above: A brake pipe bending tool is cheap and effective but you can make perfectly tidy corners by using your fingers. Go steady and the results can be very good indeed (below).

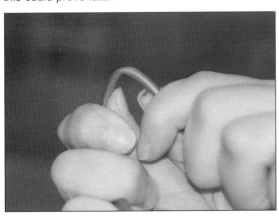

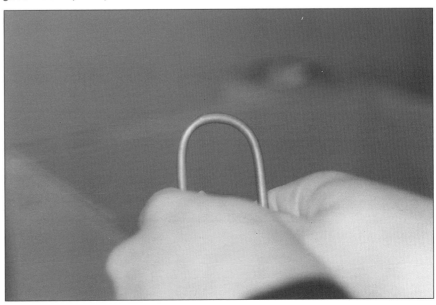

batches of resin. Curing times will vary with temperature and humidity of the workshop. That's why professional companies like to keep their laminating shops relatively warm and dry.

If you're bonding a sheet of ply, fibreboard or hardboard onto a GRP surface, make sure that the board and the recipient GRP surface are well roughed up, clean and dust free. If the board doesn't lie flat on the GRP surface, you'll need to fasten it there with screws, bolts or a good adhesive beforehand. Place heavy weights on the board to hold it down while gluing if possible. Clamps with load spreaders might also be appropriate. The board must be flush with the GRP below it.

Leave a clear margin of two or three inches all around the board to be bonded as the GRP mat you are using must overlap the board to hold it down properly. Cut strips of GRP mat in manageable lengths, which are at least 4" wide, to give a 2" overlap on the board and on the body surface you are reinforcing. Push the mat firmly up against all surfaces, along edges and into all corners. Exclude all air spaces and bubbles. You can cover the rest of the board with mat if you want.

Make sure that you keep the garage well ventilated. Your mask won't do a lot of good against the heavy vapour of the resin, so if you feel odd, walk away and get fresh air. It is true that a warm, dry atmosphere ameliorates the curing process but don't be tempted to close all the doors and switch on all the fan heaters. It's dangerous.

Keep the tub bolted into position while any reinforcing or repair patches are curing. If you remove the tub in less than a day, the resulting flex might crease, crack or dislodge your work.

If this body tub is also integral with an external bodyshell, you'll be keen to ensure that front and rear extremities of the shell are resting where they are meant to be. As ever, a well-designed kit will offer you a selection of chassis tabs against which the bodyshell will rest, albeit after some trimming.

If there are gaps and odd clearances between the shell and its designated mounts, check carefully before tightening bolts to pull the whole lot into shape. It's a good idea to fit the donor wheels (or even the kit's new wheels/tyres if you have them) to see how the wheel arch edges relate to the wheels/tyres. You might find that the front end of the body is slightly biased to the driver's side.

The net result of such a body distortion could be the use of packing spacers to keep the bodyshell straight vis a vis the wheels/tyres or it could mean bolting up firmly to eradicate gaps and thereby bring the bodyshell into line. This can be true of side to side adjustments as well as height adjustments.

Some bodyshells are notably higher at one wheel arch than at another. Sometimes it's due to the fact that most GRP moulds are asymmetrical to a greater or

Above: P-clips are the most common type of fixing for both fuel and brake pipework. They come in a variety of sizes, colours and can be plastic or metal. Below: Male and female brake pipe ends.

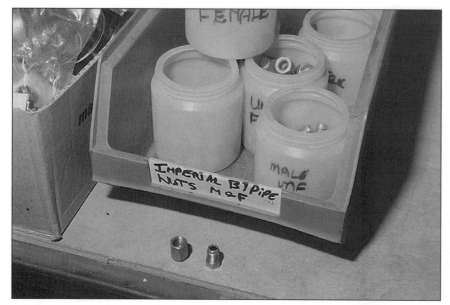

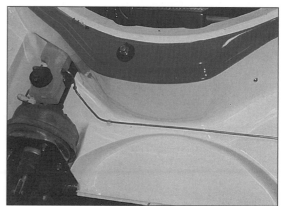

Above and below: Straight brake lines can make a great difference to the appearance of car. Results like this are easy.

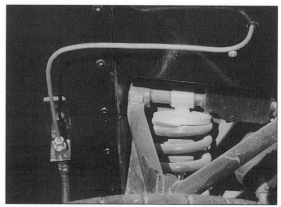

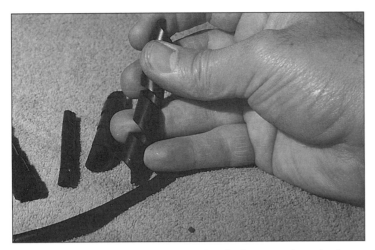

Above: Plastic Spirap is good protection for loom sections, brake and fuel lines. It can be retrospectively wrapped around or removed from a component.

Above and below: Fuel pipe diameters can vary between the tank, the pump and the carburettor. If you have different diameter components, in line fuel filters can be used as adaptors.

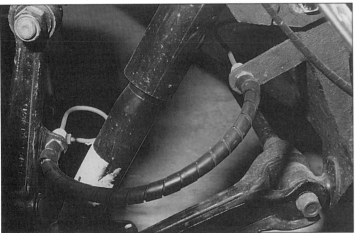

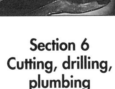

lesser extent, having been produced originally from a man-made buck. Even a moulding taken directly from a production car isn't necessarily symmetrical – ask the Countach counterfeiters.

Don't expect perfection. However, if you think that you have stored the shell, without permitting it to distort, and that there is a twist in it that prevents you from properly securing the shell against the chassis tabs and bringing the wheel arches or door apertures into proper alignment, take it up with the manufacturer as well as the club.

There might be a simple answer or you might be due a replacement shell. The industry's top mould and chassis makers produce kits whose bodies and chassis go together very easily indeed and with a minimum of asymmetry.

Section 6
Cutting, drilling, plumbing

WHEN MAKING APERTURES in the tub or cockpit panels, you'll find that the drill-mounted hole-saws and the electric jigsaw with a metal-cutting blade are the best tools. Try to avoid using a hacksaw blade hand-held as a slip can cut you very deeply and will put paid to your kit building abilities for a good long while.

A very small drill bit can come in handy if you must make a hole through the tub that allows components to align either side of the GRP. The steering column, for instance, must 'arrive' at the right place to support the steering wheel comfortably for the driver. It has to go through the front bulkhead at the right point so that it takes the straightest run to the steering

rack, via other universal joints if necessary.

The kit's own manual should give you guidance on cutting this hole. It's usually a matter of measuring from two or more reference points on the tub or chassis and drilling at that point. Use the very small drill first and get some stiff wire (like fencing wire) that can be straightened out and pushed through the hole. This will give you a good idea of what angle the steering column will sit at.

If you have to make a few attempts at drilling a pilot hole, the resulting grouping of holes should be removed when you eventually make the main cut for the column. If they aren't, they can be unobtrusively filled with Isopon or Plastic Padding.

The same principle of pilot hole cutting can come in handy when estimating the best position for the gear lever

aperture and also when you're not exactly sure where a hole drilled in a certain position will appear on the other side. Obviously, be very aware that you can damage fuel and brake lines and the wiring loom if they have already been fitted.

Quite often we find that the fuel and brake lines (or pipes) cannot be fitted before the bodywork in case they obstruct part of the shell or tub. Some of them are also secured to the bodywork. Once you have the relevant body sections in place and the fuel tank and all brake components have been carefully positioned, you can make the best judgments about the exact positions of these pipes.

Any decent kit manual will tell you in specific terms where the manufacturer recommends that these pipes be fitted. This usually won't be affected much by using a non-standard engine.

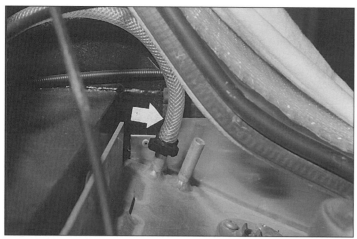

You can clearly see the braided reinforcement in this clear fuel line. Notice the neat snap together ratchet fixing to locate the pipe onto the fuel tank.

Cortina mechanical fuel pump is up near the carb – fuel pipe will be mostly low pressure.

It is customary for manufacturers to offer prepared brake pipe kits with all the specialised male/female connections already attached and pipe ends professionally finished.

These Kunifer or copper brake pipes, probably 3/16" or 1/4" diameter, will usually arrive coiled up and they must be straightened and finally bent to shape before fitting. Start off by using tape and stiff fence wire to check the exact route and shape of the brake pipe runs. Do the job very neatly with the wire, using a separate section where the manufacturer has supplied a separate section of brake pipe.

When you have taped the wire, cut it to length and remove it without altering its adopted shape. It can be used as a former or template for bending your brake or fuel pipes. We have found that some brake pipes supplied in kits are a little long for the task at hand and some curves must be slightly exaggerated to take up the excess pipe length. Slight re-routing can also help to lose an extra length. We've never found one to be too short.

Alternatively, you can produce your own brake pipes from a coil of Kunifer and a selection of male and female ends. Don't try this without a clear description of how to flare the brake pipe for the appropriate male or female end fittings to be used. Make sure that you have a high quality

flaring tool (in the region of £70-£100) if you intend to go it alone. It's more economical to get the manufacturer's kit-form pipe set.

Methods of attaching brake pipes vary depending upon what you're attaching them to. The best overall fasteners are stainless or galvanised P-clips with integral rubber sleeves. These insulate the brake pipe from destructive vibration and harmful electrolytic corrosion.

You can also get cheaper plastic P-clips and other combination clips which will hold the fuel line as well as the brake line. Make sure that they're a neat fit around the pipe. If possible, use rust-proof nuts and bolts to hold them in place – not self-tappers if you can avoid them.

Electric fuel pump is situated near to tank. Pipe will be under high pressure and can be more prone to leaks.

Most builders will rivet P-clips into the body or chassis. Obviously you should hold fire on this until you know whether the panel you're riveting into will have to be removed later for paint or to facilitate another fitting job. Sometimes it's not possible to use a nut and bolt and a rivet is the most realistic alternative. Perfectionists might tap a thread into a chassis member so that a bolt can be used. It will need thread-locking fluid to stop it coming loose.

Take the chance to mark holes for these P-clips now. The mounts for the solid brake pipes must be no more than 30cm apart along the length of the solid pipe. The pipe must not be allowed to touch any moving component at any suspension or

steering setting. It can't be allowed to rub against a sharp edge or rough surface.

If the pipe must be held against a surface, the live axle for instance, protect it at that point with some Spirap or a short length of flexible fuel hose sliced along its length, slipped over the brake pipe at the right point and held there with tape or small cable ties etc.

Be careful to keep the pipe out of the way of damage from road grit and it must not be allowed to protrude below the level of the chassis. If it does, it might be flattened by speed ramps or other obstacles.

Pipe bending must be done very carefully and preferably with the help of a proprietary pipe bending tool made for brake pipe. Bending copper or Kunifer pipes is quite feasible by hand but attempting to bend it around an extreme radius can cause it to flatten at the apex of the bend and hence restrict the internal diameter. If in doubt, buy some from a local motor spares shop and have a go at bending without flattening. A little practice makes perfect.

Use rounded formers to help create the curves that you need and use thumbs, a patient eye and a long, flat work top to get the main runs straight where appropriate. The annoying practice of supplying brake lines coiled up makes it practically impossible to get them dead

straight again, although there is a pipe straightening tool available from specialist suppliers.

Do not heat up brake pipes over a flame to get them to be more flexible. This will weaken them and might cause a pipe to split under heavy braking. Not very nice when it happens and liable to saddle you with an interesting court case even if you

diameter than the brake pipe (1/4", 5/16" or 3/8") and there will probably be only one main run – from a point near the fuel tank exit pipe to the carburettor fuel intake pipe.

It's essential that the main fuel pipe and all of the flexible fuel hoses you might use are no smaller in diameter than the fuel intake pipe of the carburettor(s). A common problem occurs when

fuel exit pipe on the petrol tank.

It's not too safe to join the Kunifer to the tank exit with an obliging section of flexible hose which can be coerced to fit over the odd-sized ends. It will split or leak sooner or later. One answer is to get one of the commonly available plastic canister-shaped in-line fuel filters.

These are supplied with stepped end nozzles that will accept two or three common fuel hose diameters. Use the correct diameter fuel hose from the tank to the filter and correct size from the filter to the Kunifer. This can also be the answer at the carburettor end if you have used Kunifer and hose matching the size of the fuel tank exit pipe and it is a different size to that of the carburettor intake.

P-clips are again the usual method of attaching the fuel pipe and you'll be applying the brake

pipe safety philosophy. Prevent any contact with moving parts or vulnerability to road grime or stone damage. In terms of safety and leak-proofing, it's better to have the fuel pump nearer the carburettor so that most of the fuel pipe length holds fuel at low pressure. The pipe and/or hose between the pump and the carburettor contains higher pressure fuel, more likely to force its way past a suspect join.

In the next chapter, we'll deal with cockpit equipment, dashboard, carpet and trim. These are jobs which can be done before you start to dismantle the panels or remove the shell from the chassis. Don't be daunted. It may seem like a nasty, fiddly and intricate job to come but it's not as bad as all that. The results can be very rewarding even if you're a total beginner.

THE WHICH KIT? TIP
We always bang on about making up neat brake lines during your build project, but they really do make all the difference to the appearance of your engine bay. Take your time and the results can be extremely rewarding

do survive.

Solid fuel pipe can also be fashioned from coiled Kunifer pipe. It's usually of a larger

you discover that even if your Kunifer pipe is the same diameter as the carburettor's intake pipe, it is smaller than the

Top: Large diameter fuel pipes. Make sure fuel hoses are correct type – not for water. Below: Use a clip closest to pipe size to avoid pinching. It will also look neater.

Above: Make sure all hoses etc are positioned well clear of any potential heat sourced such as an exhaust. Below: Heat can be a particular problem where the inlet manifold and exhaust are on the same side.

Chapter 7
INTERIOR DECOR

Section 1: Clear the decks
Section 2: Extremities
Section 3: Dashboard
Section 4: Carpet and trim

Section 5: Roof trim
Section 6: Interior hardware
Section 7: Soft tops

Section 1
Clear the decks

BY NOW YOUR PROJECT IS progressing well and there's a great temptation to begin thinking about when you'll get on the road. However, before then there's the rather daunting task of dealing with interior trim. The jobs involved here aren't always to everyone's taste and there's a lot of 'unknown' stuff which can cause apprehension and a distaste for the prospect of discovering how to do it. Sometimes, the kit will get finished off to an MoT standard and driven, with the cockpit furnishings given scant attention.

Because the car is so near to being driveable, it is tempting to say "I'll get it on the road and sort out the pretty stuff later." Try to avoid this. Take the view that a car with an incomplete interior is only 50% complete - not 90%. It's also worth noting

that trimming and fitting out a cockpit is more a case of meticulous than difficult. Although the mechanic-at-heart doesn't really have an advantage here, he or she is not at a disadvantage either.

It is a shame to trim a panel up nicely and then stain it with oil or grime that you didn't clear away beforehand, so one of the first jobs is to make sure the workshop gets spotless again. Yes, we've banged on about this in just about every chapter, but it really does make your life easier and more satisfying in the long run - take our word for it! You might layer your worktops with disposable sheets of lino or thin board which can be reversed and/or thrown away when grubby, to be replaced by new coverings.

Every kit builder will have an idea about the interior specification of their car. The manufacturers (intentionally or unintentionally) often leave a great deal of room for

manoeuvre. Personal improvisations can turn a standard car into a concours winner.

Many kits offer you a good choice of purpose-made or after-market seats, inertia reel or harness belts, donor or after-market instruments, leather or vinyl pre-cut trim kits, carpet colours, soft top and tonneau materials/colours and even choices of steering wheel, gear knob, door handles, locks and roll-over bar etc.

We must presume that you have made your own selections on these as it's such a subjective field. Generalised recommendations could be misleading. The order of fitment can also differ greatly between kits. Hopefully, we can help you in your choices by giving you some idea of the jobs, techniques, difficulties and other factors involved.

This chapter sets out to undertake a 'typical' cockpit finishing procedure which will

not, unfortunately, be applicable to each and every different type of kit. The principles we deal with, though, are there to help you to draw up your own schedule for a smooth job. Don't be taken by surprise. Your own kit's build manual may recommend radically different techniques and schedules and must be given precedence over this more generalised work.

Principles of cockpit trimming aren't complex even if there seems to be a bewildering array of jobs at hand. We've often found that it's best to start with the jobs that are easiest when the cockpit is empty and untrimmed/uncarpeted. It's like trying to avoid painting yourself into a corner.

You won't want to be doing too many dusty, cut-drill-saw-sand-glue-and-paint tasks just when the interior is beginning to look smart. You don't want to permanently fit a part only to discover that a different bit must

Go to just about any kit car show and you'll find suppliers of every type of trimming material. If nothing else, it's a great opportunity to simply find out just what exactly is available.

Slightly more specialist jobs such as edge trimming and sewing up gearlever and handbrake gaiters can often be left to the specialist suppliers.

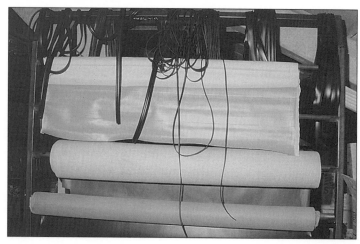

be fitted behind, beside or beneath it.

Lots of back-bending and low-level access work will be required here and it might well be a good idea to get the car back up on its stands again. If your back is liable to seizure, be careful and make sure someone knows where to look for you if you're not seen for the next week!

Protect the bodywork by taping cardboard or thick material to it at strategic points, especially at each corner or protrusion and at the main access points which will be extensively used for a while yet.

Useful tools will include the mobile light bulb with a hook or clip, a small mains or battery drill for reaching into restricted spaces, a sharp craft knife with a fairly narrow blade and a standard Stanley knife, hammer, copper and hide-faced mallet, centre-punch, straight edge or long ruler, tape measure, big scissors capable of cutting trim and carpet (unless you're buying them ready-made), various hack, jig, tenon, keyhole and wood saws for making trim panels out of lino, wood, hardboard, alloy, plastic etc., clamps, vice, pencils, rivet gun, durable dot (pop-stud) fasteners, tool/punch, hole-cutting saws and flap-wheel sanders for drill, sandpaper and

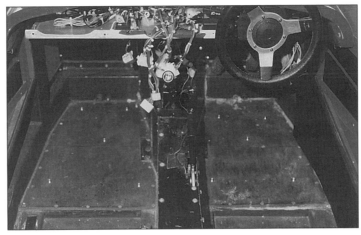

A typical bare interior awaiting your attention. Walking around the club stands at shows will give you lots of inspiration about exactly the type of interior trim you're after.

block (electric random orbital sander if available), various screwdrivers, junior and large hacksaws, paintbrushes old and new, glue spreaders, old hair drier, gaffer and masking tape, usual spanners/sockets (especially small sizes), domestic mastic gun etc. Got that lot handy? Then we shall begin!

This is the kind of equipment you're going to need if you intend to (or indeed have to) create your own dash, trim and carpet for the interior and boot. Some hardtop cars will need special tools for fitting windows or a sunroof and a variable speed (not single or two-speed) electric jigsaw with blades for wood and alloy is an invaluable addition to the armoury.

Section 2
Extremities

WHETHER YOUR CAR IS hard or soft top, we will presume the bodywork fitment, floor panels, doors, transmission tunnel and scuttle have been completed and the landscape in front of you takes the form of an interior which is empty apart from steering column, pedals, gear lever, handbrake lever and maybe a few wires or control cables which might have been fed through to the interior.

If you have an interior produced by the assembly of several different floor, bulkhead or side panels, Stage One will be initiated by checking that all

relevant panels have been fitted with the correct rustproof fasteners. Then decide which panels won't need removal in order to complete the car.

Ensure that these are properly sealed before the fasteners are tightened up. Sealing can be done via careful sandwiching of (adhesive or non-adhesive) foam or rubber chassis tape along joining flanges or by the application of a hardening or non-hardening mastic sealant.

Some builders swear by the adhesive properties of a sealant such as Sikaflex but a normal bathroom or exterior grade mastic can be just as effective and is more readily available in the high street. When choosing a sealant, decide whether the panels might need to be removed for regular servicing access. A hardening/adhesive sealant might be inappropriate for this.

Be choosy about the length of the bolts used. No point having rows of bolts an inch too long protruding through the floor and bulkheads. It's untidy, the threads will get clogged with dirt, the ground clearance of the car will be reduced and the MoT inspector will not like it.

Use nyloc nuts or spring washer between the nut and plain washer. In some instances, you'll also need wide 'penny' washers to spread the

As you'll be getting in and out of the interior a lot at this stage, make absolutely sure that you cannot damage external bodywork. Some form of protection may be necessary.

When you are bolting things like seat runners through the floor. Be very careful to use bolts the correct size. These ones stick out below the car just a bit too far. Possible MoT failure, too.

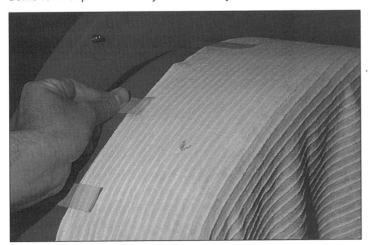

Above: Plain nuts will always need spring washers and plain washers while Nylocs (below) can be used with just plain washers.

Above: A small hand drill can sometimes offer more control in tight areas under the dash etc. This is also when cordless drills will come into their own, too. Below: If you're using the donor's column stalks make sure they all work smoothly.

load, especially in GRP panels that don't fit flush with the chassis, brackets or other panels. Make sure the washers are rustproof as well.

Panels which cannot be fitted permanently at this stage, ie: those which might have to come off for painting or for access to other parts, should now be fitted accurately but without adhesives or sealants.

Stage Two takes this 'dry' fitting just a bit further, as it is our plan to make all the holes, saw cuts, slots, extra panels for trim, dash, carpet templates etc. before the fragile and easily tarnished components and materials are finally fitted.

This can start with the real basics. If the kit doesn't come with a dashboard, make up your own mock dash from cardboard or similar and tape it into place. Put your chosen steering wheel on the column in its final position, with the correct boss or other spacers and column stalks if they are specified.

Both front seats should then be positioned (see Chapter 12) in the car either according to the kit's manual, to your own preference or to legroom/headroom requirements. The simple act of sitting in the driver's seat will tell you a lot about the way in which the cockpit build should progress.

Initially, your prime concerns will be good driver visibility all round, good view of the speedometer, sufficient legroom/headroom for the usual driver, easy and comfortable access to the most important controls (gear lever, switches, handbrake, door handles, window winders, stereo, seat adjusters and steering wheel), clearance for knees, elbows, head (don't forget the roll-over bar and weather gear if not yet fitted) and easy access to the inertia or harness seatbelts.

If you haven't sufficiently scrutinised the company demonstrator model, you might already have bought a steering wheel with too deep or shallow dish. The aftermarket seats might be too wide when in the right position for you; they might have excessively thick bases, reducing headroom; they might be too thin and need extra spacers or even angling with wedges to give a different rake.

The gear lever might be the wrong length or shape, it might foul the handbrake when second, fourth or reverse is selected. The seatbelt stalks might be too short for easy access. The steering column itself might be too low or high for comfort. The pedals might need bending, cutting and/or welding for perfect operation.

THE WHICH KIT? TIP
More and more kits use the column stalk controls from their respective donors. Older ones can sometimes feel a little vague or sticky in use but they should feel precise. Don't just fit them as they are. Some simple dismantling and cleaning/regreasing will do wonders and often make them work like new

Don't sigh with exasperation if things such as this need to be done. It's not often you get the chance to design and tailor-make your own car so it's worth spending some time and effort on getting it right. If you're disheartened enough to say 'Leave it - it'll do,' then we suggest that you pack up for the day and take another look when you are fresher and better motivated. Problems become much simpler with a new outlook.

Pay particular attention when designing the dashboard if the layout isn't pre-ordained. Kits such as Westfield, Caterham or Dax, which offer you one or several fixed dashboard displays can often take the headache out of this part. If you're going your own route, you have the leeway to be creative - but make it sensible.

It's far better to have the speedometer in your line of sight. That usually means viewed 'through' the steering wheel. Many kits do not allow for this due to the design of the scuttle and dash. You must therefore place the speedo, unobscured, as close to your line of sight as possible.

If controls have to be moved, take measurements, write notes and even draw little diagrams to help you remember where things have to be. Change any parts that need to be changed and do all the drilling and cutting before again removing the seats and all parts that will hinder trim, carpet and dashboard work.

Section 3
Dashboard

IN THIS SECTION, WE'LL BE dealing with the physical aspects of dashboard construction as the next step towards completing your cockpit (see Chapter Eight for wiring considerations). As we have mentioned, some kit builders will be lucky enough to be using a complete new pre-cut dash in wood, alloy or GRP supplied by the dealer, sometimes with instruments, switches and dash loom already fitted.

Others will be able to use all or most of a donor car's dashboard with its own instruments and associated loom. The most difficult option, also the option with the most flexibility, is to use after-market or donor gauges and clocks to be fitted into a totally self-designed dash blank with an unrelated donor loom.

In order to make up a dashboard from one or several flat panels, plywood or aluminium sheet are excellent materials. You will already have made up a cardboard dash blank to show where the instruments and switches must be. Tidy this up to give exact final dimensions, paying careful attention to where the mounting and support brackets will have to go.

A dashboard full of switches and instruments isn't lightweight. You may find it necessary to make up a selection of supporting brackets from wood or alloy and fit them in behind the dashboard.

Use your cardboard templates to mark a dashboard blank on a cheap piece of plywood up to around half an inch thick. You might, alternatively, use a single thick sheet of alloy or thin alloy glued to a plywood backing piece. The design of the car may dictate a dashboard design including two or three separate dash panels. The preparation principles are the same.

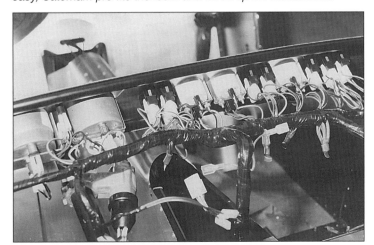

Above: Cortina MkV seat runner comes complete with seatbelt stalk. Granada seat belt stalk is separate. Below: To make things really easy, Caterham pre-fits the loom and wires up the instruments.

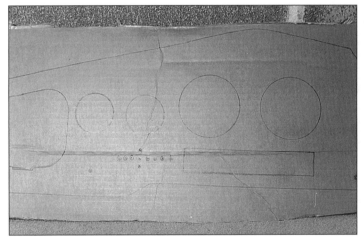

If you're starting from scratch, a cardboard dash template can help you plan where to put gauges and switches. Below: Quality plywood makes an excellent dash backing and is easy to trim.

Treat this first dashboard as an expendable prototype. Cutting the main instrument holes is the difficult bit. Most will simply drill a long line of smaller holes just within the required circumference of the cut and push or file out the disc of wood. The hole is then carefully shaped freehand using a flap wheel sander in a drill or a manual 'half-round' file. An electric wood router would make the job very quick for the all-wood dash blank.

For either wood or alloy, an electric jigsaw, especially a scrolling type jigsaw, with the correct type of blade and adjustable speed, will also be a help. The majority of modern after-market speedo and tacho gauges are around 80mm diameter.

Minor clocks are usually 52mm diameter and holes can be cut using a drill-mounted hole-cutting saw available from DIY shops. If you're using them for alloy, avoid those designed for wood. Various types of drill-mounted hole cutters are available for wood, steel and alloy. These can help when mounting larger round-bodied switches or warning lights. Otherwise, a selection of drill bits will suffice for the smaller apertures.

Small oblong or square holes in alloy or wood are a more time-consuming problem. It's unlikely that you'll know anyone with a fly-press and the right size of cutting bit. Start with a drill and then use a jig or keyhole saw, followed by manual filing. Always be careful not to cut out too much.

Remember that if you are going to trim the 'final' dash, have a go with the mock dash using material of equivalent thickness. Once it has been

glued back into the apertures for tidiness, you could find that your instruments no longer fit and the holes will have to be widened again to allow for the trim.

When you have all the necessary holes cut accurately, use your mock-up dash as a template for the final dashboard. It'll still be difficult to drill and cut out the holes correctly first time but an accurate guide is a great help.

If you are trying to keep to a neat wood-finish dashboard of ply and/or ply backed veneer, remember to use sharp saws and drills and only cut with the front (visible) face towards you. Use one or several layers of masking tape over the front face of the area to be cut as it helps to stop chipping and flaking. Hand drills generally give you more control over speed and accuracy.

All saw or file strokes should be 'away' from you, never towards you as it can lift or chip the visible wood surface. This pre-empts use of electric saws for the final dash unless you're going to trim it over with material.

Using solid wood alone for a dashboard is generally a bad risk. Unless it has a waterproof plywood backing piece bonded to it, it will probably split or warp badly in time. The appearance of a solid wood dash is usually given by using a high quality professional veneer on ply or by staining the top layer of a ply sheet.

Traditionally, exterior varnish is applied in several stages, starting with a large proportion of turps or white spirit to thin it and gradually increasing the proportion of varnish. Beware, not all varnishes use white spirit

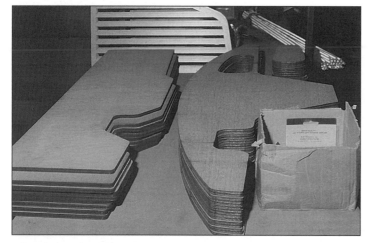

Many kit companies will supply you with a pre-cut blank like these from Pilgrim GRP. Below: These 52mm VDO instruments are typical of those readily available. Note simple clamping method.

Above: A hole saw is just the tool for cutting out holes for dash instruments. Below: Final adjustment can be made with a drill mounted flap wheel.

as a thinner and modern types require different methods of application. Interior or furniture varnish may fade – try to use yacht or special exterior quality varnish.

In a warm, dry and well-ventilated workplace, several coats of varnish should be applied straight away onto the whole of the dash. These first coats will be about 25% varnish and 75% white spirit (or relevant thinner) and they can be applied in quick succession, without waiting for the last to dry. Avoid runs and drips.

It is the purpose of this stage to reveal dust and loose wood on the dashboard. No matter how well you smoothed down the dash prior to the application of this thin varnish, it will still appear a bit rough after the varnish has dried. Do not try to accelerate drying by heating the dashboard. A dry atmosphere at room temperature is sufficient.

Use fine sandpaper to smooth down the dash yet again and apply two or three coats of varnish mixed 50% with white spirit. Let each coat dry fully before the next. When the last coat is dry, sand again with a very fine sandpaper. Some advocate the use of fine wet 'n' dry used wet but be sure that the plywood backing of your dash is waterproof and that you have properly sealed all of the dash with the previous coats of varnish.

Finally, thin the varnish with only 20%-25% white spirit and carefully apply the last two or three coats, allowing it to dry fully between coats. If there are still blemishes, use light sandpaper and start the last stage again, remembering to clean all dust from the dash and the bench before varnishing starts. The whole process could end up taking several days but be patient. Different varnish manufacturers give different instructions on this theme. Check carefully when choosing.

If you're fitting an alloy or alloy-faced dash which you intend to paint, refer to Chapter Nine for paintwork ideas. Remember that the wood backing behind an alloy dash needs protection also, even if it invisible. Make it out of exterior grade ply and finish it with varnish or exterior gloss. Don't be tempted to use something like Creosote for proofing cockpit wood fittings, the smell never leaves it – especially when the heater is turned on!

Alloy, wood and wood/alloy dashboards can all be upholstered and trimmed a lot more easily than you might think. Trimming and upholstering a flat panel, even if it is full of holes, isn't difficult. If you're using foam and vinyl for the job, they're cheap so it doesn't matter if you have to tear it all off and start again from scratch a few times.

The quickest and easiest way is to stick your vinyl (or even leather) straight to the surface of the dashboard. This will give it a totally plain surface, without that padded look, but some prefer it. Use a single piece of

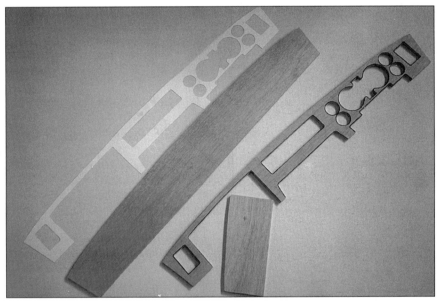

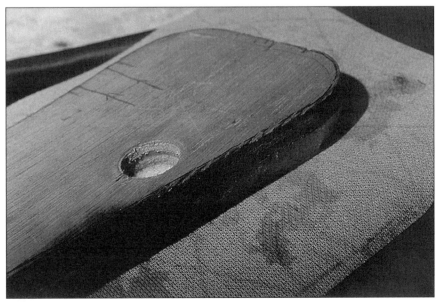

Above: If you're going to trim the dash with vinyl or leather, most apertures will need widening to allow for the material fold-overs. Below: Foam glued between glovebox door and vinyl sheet.

Above: Bonding veneer to ply is a specialist job. Tough Rustin's Plastic Coating, with hardener, is an alternative to varnish (below).

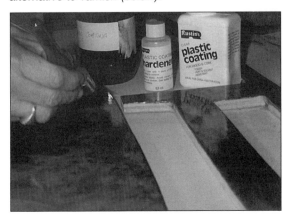

material big enough to cover the whole visible face of the dash leaving enough around the edges for a generous fold-over of about two inches all round the edge.

There's no need to pull the vinyl or leather very tightly across the dash face. If you use a glue which allows repositioning after contact (ie: not an impact or contact adhesive), then you can get wrinkles out easily enough. It makes it easier if the material is warm and/or sufficiently thin to be compliant with minimum effort. A clean towel spread out on the hard work surface helps to keep things smooth and scratch-free.

Once you've ascertained that the visible face of the material is smooth, let the glue dry fully before continuing. When you turn the dash over so that you are facing its back or hidden face, you'll notice that it's not simply a case of folding the excess material over the edges and gluing down. They make all kinds of creases, corners, folds and wrinkles.

You will need a good, sharp Stanley knife to cut strategic 'wedges' out of the vinyl or leather margin, especially where there is a corner or curve on the edge of the dashboard. If you cut right down to where the vinyl meets the visible face of the dash, there is a danger that the cut will be visible when you've finished. Cut just short of the front face of the dash to be sure.

This time, it's better to use a contact adhesive. The kind that you use to coat both surfaces, letting each dry off a while, before pressing them together for an unadjustable bond. In this way, you can tension the edges of the vinyl a little before sticking them down. This will help to avoid loose folds and corners peeping out at the edges of the dash.

When it comes to finishing the apertures for the instruments, switches, glove box, lights etc., don't simply cut the vinyl out using the edge of the hole as the template. Using a very sharp blade, cut the vinyl repeatedly from the centre of the hole out towards the edge.

If you temporarily mark dots around the edge of the hole at centimetre intervals and cut from the centre out towards each mark, (again remembering not to cut all the way to the edge) you'll end up with a load of triangular segments of vinyl.

You can then fold each segment back through the hole to stick it firmly to the invisible face of the dash with contact adhesive. A little tension when pulling the tabs back will help to smooth out creases at the edge. When a clock or switch is fitted, it will usually have a flange that usefully covers the edge of the aperture into which it is pushed.

One of the main problems of this method is that the triangular segments will leave gaps between each other on the edge of a hole through a thicker dashboard. That's OK when an instrument or switch then fills

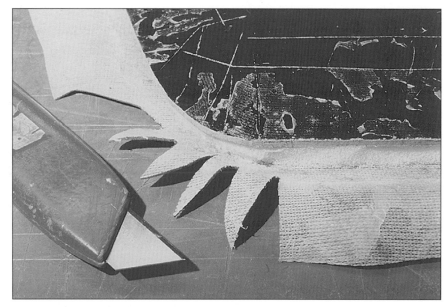

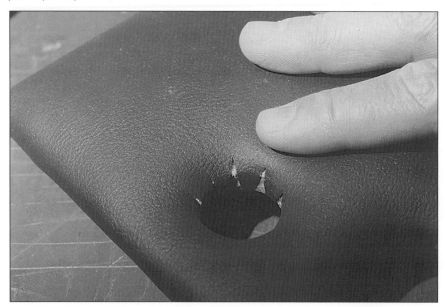

Above: You'll need to cut vinyl a bit like this to fold it over a curved edge. If you cut the 'wedges' too deep, they might be visible from the front face of the dash or panel (below).

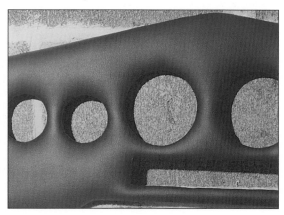

Above: Vinyl segments pulled back and glued in place on the back of the dash. Below: End result is smooth and tidy.

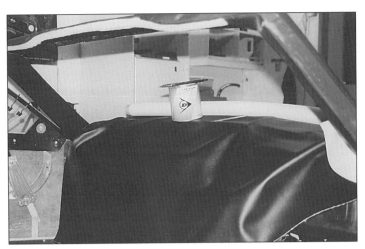

Above: Once the vinyl is in place, the holes should be a just the right size for the gauges. Below: Rear clamp holds gauge in place. Take care to get the face level when looking from the front.

This Midas Gold dash had several sections to it and many compound curves. We've found Dunlop 1358 to be an ideal trim adhesive. Below: Results can be extremely impressive.

the hole but a glove box lid will reveal these gaps whenever it is opened.

Circumvent the problem by narrowing (or sharpening) the edge of the dash around the glove box aperture (cutting and smoothing from the invisible side) so your triangular segments will fold back out of sight. You can create the same effect by cutting away the wood and by shaping the glovebox aperture itself from alloy sheet so that the material again folds back out of sight.

You could carefully glue an extra strip of vinyl around the edge of the glovebox aperture, if the door shut line allows clearance for this, or you could paint the face of the edge a dark colour so that details are less visible.

It's very much the same process when you're trimming a dash for a padded or upholstered look. One common misconception is that you need a thick layer of foam to give the dash that deep-padded look. Not true really. Half-inch thick is absolute maximum in most cases. It's much more common to use foam of around a quarter

allowing for the relevant thicknesses of vinyl or leather which might be folded in through them. Use a foam-friendly glue to hold a smooth sheet of foam to the front (visible) surface of the dash. A very sharp blade is used to cut

Use the same glue to stick an oversized sheet of vinyl to the foam and, when it's dry, carry on with the hole-cutting as described above. Using a contact adhesive for the triangular segments will help but be careful not to put too much tension on the fold-overs before gluing down. This can create stress creases in the face of the dash in time.

Some say that you're better off gluing down the vinyl around the outer edge of the dash panel and letting that set first. Then attack the various apertures and do all the tensioning of the material after it has dried. If you get the vinyl drum-tight, though, there's a chance that it might just rip right across when you start cutting for the holes. Be careful here.

At the end of this exercise, you should aim to complete the trimming of the dash, fitting the

THE WHICH KIT? TIP
For most trimming purposes we've always avoided using spray adhesives. Dunlop 1358 has proved extremely good in nearly all circumstances. However, when dealing with foam it is nearly impossible to paint on an even layer of glue with a paint brush or similar. This is where the spray glue comes into its own, giving an even layer of adhesive which dries quickly and easily

of an inch thick for a good effect.

Start with your dash blank plus all holes accurately cut –

the foam away from the apertures in the dash, keeping it flush with the edges.

Pop stud or 'durable dot' fasteners come in three pieces and will require a special punch. They give a smart finish to any trim panel you may wish to remove at a later stage.

Two sections of the pop stud are ocated onto the carpet and the third onto the floor/side panel.

instruments to it and supporting it properly in the scuttle area. As it's a fragile and easily damaged component now, store it away in a safe and dry place before continuing with the work on the car's interior.

Section 4
Carpet and trim

AS A GENERAL RULE, carpet and trim should be designed to be easily removable, especially in the floor areas if the car is a soft-top. It might not be possible when the kit is an exotic or other coupe type as the trim kit may need gluing down over compound curves or other complex shapes.

For the majority of open top roadsters and Jeep-like utility kits, though, where you expect the trim/carpet to need drying out or cleaning sometimes, quick removal is a real bonus.

Footwells are a prime example of a generally inaccessible area for trim and carpet jobs. An excellent place to start with. If you have any kind of boot space which is accessed from the interior of the car, it will also be a problem area once the furniture starts to arrive. Make these areas your first priority after the dash.

As ever, the kit builder who likes, and can afford, a manufacturer's pre-cut carpet

and trim set will save a lot of time and won't need much guidance from this section. If you're doing it all from scratch, though, be assured that the job may seem a lot more complex than it really is.

If the floor is relatively flat (often the case in front-drive cars and kits), you might be tempted to carpet the whole lot in one or two sections. Make sure that you can take out the floor coverings without having to unbolt the seats or seatbelts. It is a good idea to keep the front footwell floor carpets separate as they get the worst punishment of all.

Stiff card, lino or cardboard is again the right stuff for making panel templates. If you're not confident, don't try to trim or

Special centre punch is a must as it mushrooms out the central rivet section to hold the two parts of the 'dot' together (see opposite top left).

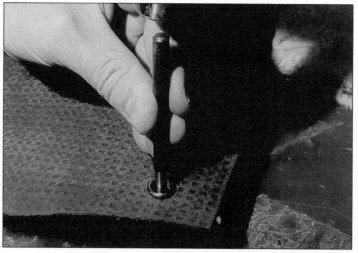

carpet large, oddly-shaped sections with one panel or sheet. It can end up a lot slower and less tidy than using several smaller panels.

First of all, decide which parts you'll be trimming and which are to be carpeted. Some builders choose to carpet the flat floor sections only, using vinyl for the tunnel, sides, dash and doors. Others bring the carpet half way up the cockpit sides, so that the tunnel sides and the lower half of each door are carpeted. If done carefully, it looks superb and helps to protect surfaces that are regularly scuffed by shoes.

Off-cuts of domestic quality carpets with a tough, thick pile can be a tempting bargain. It's

OK for covering flat expanses but try bending it around tighter corners and curves... Big problem there. Similarly, beefy, high quality vinyl or leather can seem just the job when you're browsing through the wares on offer at a kit car show but could also be too stiff.

What you should choose, especially if you're inexperienced at this kind of thing, is thinner and more pliable carpet and vinyl. They don't have to be cheap and nasty – trim and carpet suppliers to the kit car trade (Middleton, Woolies, etc.) offer huge variations on quality, colour, price and texture. It's best to get samples or see the stuff at shows rather than take a guess and mail order it 'blind.'

One of the better ways of making up trim and carpet panels for easy removal entails using simple Durable Dot (pop-stud) fasteners, female side on the panel and male side on the car. There are restrictions as to the thickness of a panel through which you can fasten the two halves of the female side of the popper. Buy some (along with relevant tooling) to check out the leeway available to you.

The other major question is what to use for backing any panels you want to make. Initially, you might find that the carpet doesn't need a backing panel at all. Once the shapes have been cut to the template

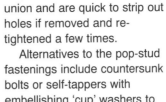

sizes and edge-trimmed (locally, or by one of the trade specialists advertising in *Which Kit?*), the addition of fasteners might be all that's needed to complete the job.

Separate panel backing material does comes in handy when making up trim panels in vinyl or leather. You might be after an upholstered look or just something to give a panel its own stiffness to cover a hole etc. Is the carpet you are using, with the pile face covered in vinyl, a good backing material for a trim panel?

If you want something tougher, but still not too thick, why not try different types of linoleum, basic hardboard or thin plywood (not very flexible and must be waterproofed), thick, plasticised kitchen/bathroom wallpaper, thin alloy sheet (can be bent around pretty severe angles) or

even heavy waxed cotton/canvas? Use your imagination here.

Having made your template, the process for making a plain or upholstered vinyl trim panel is very similar to that relating to the dashboard. You have to make sure that the template and the backing panel are cut to the right sizes and allow for any trim fold-overs around the edges or in the apertures.

Make sure you buy the appropriate punch and base tools for assembling the halves of the female part of the pop-stud. It's rather difficult to get around this and the tools are not expensive when the time saved is considered.

The male part of the pop-stud is a single piece and can be attached to the car body/chassis via a rivet, small bolt or self-tapper. Avoid using self-tapping screws into GRP as

they never create a very robust union and are quick to strip out holes if removed and re-tightened a few times.

Alternatives to the pop-stud fastenings include countersunk bolts or self-tappers with embellishing 'cup' washers to improve their appearance, velcro strips from material shops (use a generous quantity/width for a strong grip), special trim and carpet fasteners available from after-market kit-build suppliers, Dzus panel fixings from the same source and even the two-part plastic 'invisible' trim fixings used by production car manufacturers for door trims etc. Take a look next time you're in a scrap yard or at a kit car show and see how many different types there are.

If there is an unavoidable visible gap between two adjacent trim panels, through

which you can see the chassis or body, it can be camouflaged by gluing a strip of vinyl directly to the body/chassis there, with its edges hidden behind adjoining trim panels. You might also let the vinyl from the edge of one of the panels bridge the gap to hide behind the adjacent panel.

When you have finished cutting your carpet sections to size, send them off for edge-binding. This is the sewing process whereby the edges of each carpet piece are bound with strong loops of thread. You can order the binding in a contrasting colour and it is usually relatively cheap. Contact the trim and carpet suppliers who advertise in *Which Kit?*.

When they come back from the edge trimmers, check them all again for size and relative positions before attaching them

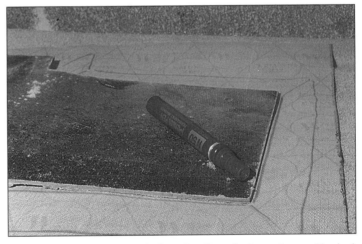

Above: Stiff trim panel made from hardboard, shown here with vinyl marked for cutting oversized to fold over. Below: Same trim panel being used as a template for cutting the foam.

Below: Cardboard templates are invaluable in ensuring you cut carpet or, in this case, a flexible lino trim backing board to the correct shape.

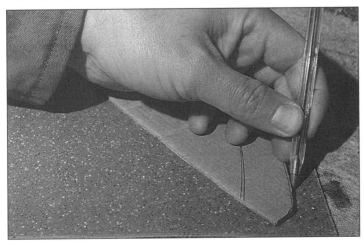

to their various backing panels. Unlike the more flexible vinyl or leather, you won't be folding the carpet back on to the rear face of the backing panels.

Use a strong contact adhesive or velcro to fasten the carpet to the panels and any of the methods described above to attach the whole lot to the body/chassis. If you are using carpets plus panels, you might put all relevant fastenings (pop-studs etc.) through the panel and then attach the carpet to it with velcro or glue, thus hiding the fixings.

Much the same process covers the boot area. Some manufacturers run out of design ideas in the boot. All too often we find that the body meets the chassis around the perimeter of the boot and there's no proper floor or lid to speak of. You might just find the fuel tank, rear wiring loom, some suspension components and various brake and fuel pipes and tubes, plus gaps through which the road is visible.

Even if the boot size (ie: available volume) is drastically reduced by flat panelling, it is an improvement in so far as the inner panels will protect the outer body from damage caused by any heavy boot contents shifting or rolling around. Try at least to have a strong boot floor and sides.

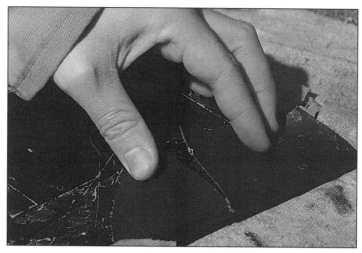

Vinyl flaps being glued down on the back of a hardboard panel. With foam underneath it, it will give the panel a smart and luxurious look which is perfect for something like a tradional tourer

Waterproof plywood and/or alloy sheet are inevitably good materials to use here.

Right-angled or triangular brackets used to fit each panel together can be well hidden on the 'blind' sides and by subsequent carpeting. Fixing the boot to the chassis can be a bit trickier and will probably involve using specially made brackets.

Don't be tempted to use suspension or other essential bolts and fasteners to 'double' as boot-mounting bolts. The compromise can leave the way open for dangerous free-play in these bolts after a short time.

Take care to support the boot floor and sides away from the fuel tank and fuel or brake lines. Any rubbing will soon lead to a

disaster or a breakdown. Ensure that the boot can be dismantled sufficiently for access to the fuel tank or any other parts that might need servicing.

One of the other advantages of panelling your own boot is that you can design a relatively secure lockable compartment if there isn't already one as part of the kit. Hidden hinges and a proper Yale or Chubb domestic front door lock are quite within the realms of possibility when you're designing from scratch.

With the main carpet and trim panels cut, assembled and fitted, the budding trimmer can then try the more intricate stuff. You might need access to a sewing machine (capable of sewing several thicknesses of

your vinyl) and someone skilled in its operation but the benefits are worth it.

Elasticated pockets are handy for the doors, seat backs or anywhere they might fit. They're simply made by folding the edge of a vinyl oblong (or other suitable shape) over a strip of strong elastic which has been half extended. Sew through the vinyl and the elastic so that when the elastic is released, it will wrinkle the vinyl to which it has been sewn.

Tidy up the ends of the elastic channel with fold-overs and cut, fold and sew the rest of the vinyl edge to give the final size and shape of the pocket you need. This pocket section can then be partially tensioned and sewn to another sheet of vinyl or to a backing panel which might become the trim panel for a door etc. Be careful to use strong elastic for a convincing and functional result.

Gaiters for gear and handbrake levers are usually sewn together from four or more separate sections of vinyl or leather. These sections are roughly triangular (isosceles type), and form the sides of a narrow four (or five, or six)-sided pyramid. Curving the upright edges might make for a more interesting gaiter shape. It is worthwhile to experiment with cheap material first.

Make sure that the

Door seal and other edge trimming is often used to hold edges of vinyl in place. Make sure you leave enough overlap of the material to allow for this.

This is a basic boot made in ply for a Marlin Roadster. Holes in the floor indicate access to vital suspension bolts etc. Trimming will be relatively straightforward.

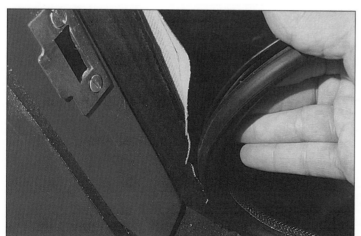

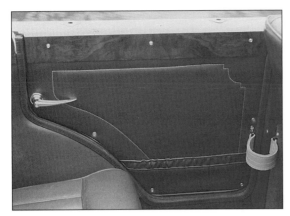

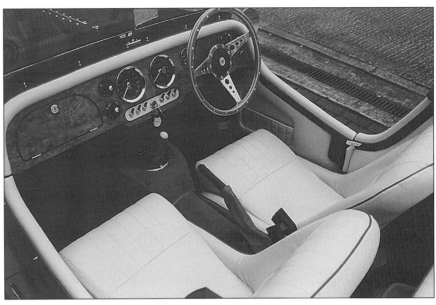

Above: Very tidy trim panel on a Beauford door. Note the screws with cup washers. Below: Velcro can sometimes be a handy for locating carpet.

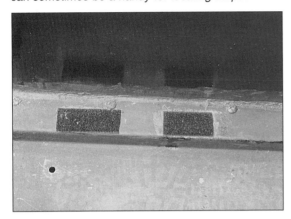

This terrific trim in an NG TF can be supplied as a kit by the manufacturer. When it's this good, why go elsewhere? Below: Simple door trim panel of a Domino HT retains all the standard Mini controls.

dimensions of the gaiter's base at least equate to the full movement of the base of the gear or handbrake lever. Sew the upright sides of each vinyl piece to the next so that only the 'back' of the vinyl remains visible. After sewing the last seam (fourth if using four pieces), turn the gaiter inside out to reveal the 'outer' vinyl face and hide the stitches.

The edge of the smaller top aperture can be tidied by folding over and gluing or stitching. The lower edge should be left with a generous excess flange of vinyl. When the gaiter is lowered down onto the gear or brake lever, the lower part can then be tucked under a carpet or trim panel and held in position with velcro or adhesive etc.

With practice, you can soon be very proficient at neat and precise trimming operations. If you know how to use a sewing machine, you can transform a drab standard interior into a plush and high quality environment which makes the car much more

pleasurable to drive.

Upholstered scuttle edge, cockpit edge and door cappings, trimmed oddments boxes, removable/ hinged trim panels hiding a fire extinguisher system, stereo or security cut-out switch, contrasting dash trim, carpet and edge binding colours and a matching boot area all add to the effect.

Section 5
Roof trim

THE GOOD THING ABOUT having a convertible is that you don't need to trim the hood! Those builders who choose a kit with a coupe body or a removable hard top will have a few days of extra work ahead of them if do not go for a factory

head-lining option.

Look very carefully at budgeting for a professional roof trimming option offered by the dealer. If the dealer doesn't offer one, get a quote from a professional properly set up to do the job. You guessed it. It ranks pretty low on the list of exciting and interesting kit building jobs.

Pop your head into many a production car at the breaker's yard and you'll see how it's meant to be done. Beautiful, upholstered look, intricate shapes and curves cut into the material, evenly tensioned outer skin, neat stitching – the works.

Look at the roof of your kit at home and find bare GRP chopped strand mat. If you're lucky, you might have been supplied with a roll of the appropriate material and instructions as to application.

When you're cutting your own material from scratch, it's difficult enough to apply vinyl or other head-lining material directly to the roof. Getting that deep, upholstered finish is, we fear, a job for the near-professional with lots of experience, equipment, aptitude or time and the patience for practice.

We would certainly recommend that the first-timer

Above: Cobra replica seats are available from several sources – they are all slightly different so shop around. Below: Simple seats in the Fisher Fury.

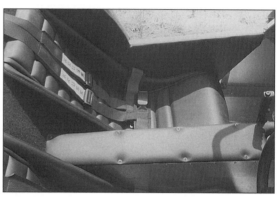

Above: There are a number of specialist seat suppliers who have good brochures to show you what's available. These are some upmarket Cobra items. Below: Some manufacturers make their own seats, such as these for the Deon Mirabeau.

should, if determined to go it alone, settle for affixing material directly to the surface of the inner shell. If the manufacturer can't recommend exactly what kind of material to use, go to a trim/carpet dealer or the relevant owners club. You'll probably find that the right kind of stuff appears similar to extremely thin carpet or specially patterned vinyl sheet.

When you stand back and consider the problem, you'll notice that the main difficulty areas lie in the various compound curves, as well as in the edges of any apertures. A lesser problem is deciding where and how the roof trim should finish at its lower extremity.

Simple card templates can be of use in some areas. Bear in mind that the pressure is on to successfully cut, trim and stick down relatively large areas of material, into compound curve areas. All this while avoiding obvious creases and joins. You'll need a good slow-acting adhesive which allows you to reposition material once contact has been made. It's a bit like wallpapering a ceiling.

Take the basic example of a simple oblong roof section with compound curve sections at each end. You might need an extra pair of hands and clever use of hard paint rollers (the sort you use for gloss paint) but sticking the material to the flat central

section will be relatively easy, even if it has a simple curve.

Try a 'dry' run on the compound curve sections by putting double-sided tape on the roof and then 'shaping' the lining material into the corners. Too much material for too small an area. The excess material will form into folds which can then be carefully marked and cut out using a sharp Stanley knife. Leaving little overlaps of material is better than cutting away too much. Leave visible edges pointing away from the vehicle's occupants. Keep hands clean and have extra material available, you might not get it right first time...

You might be able to do the main roof section with just one piece of material. When cutting extra material to trim the A, B or C posts and other parts of the upper vehicle sides, make sure

you leave enough spare so that their upper edges can be folded over for neatness and stuck down overlapping the edges of the main roof piece(s).

You may well find that the vehicle features a roll-over bar, roll cage, tubular windscreen frame reinforcement or other eyesores that should be hidden behind trim or head-lining panels. It's back to the template theory for this part.

If you absolutely need to drill holes into structural members for trim panel mountings or brackets, make sure that the holes are as small as possible for the job and are well away from welds, angles, joins, other holes or from any point where they might help to develop a stress crack or otherwise weaken the structure. If in doubt, contact the manufacturer or try to affix the panel without drilling.

If you have to glue your head-lining material right up to the edge of a window aperture, be careful to consider how this will affect window fitment. Most rear and side windows, as well as windscreens, are fitted by use of slotted rubber edge trims (looking like an H in cross-section) or by bonding the glass to a flat body flange with special mastic-style adhesive.

If your kit's windows are fitted with the rubber channels, check whether the rubber will push onto the edge of the bodyshell when the head-lining material is in place, folded over that edge.

If the material isn't to be folded over, it's useful to stick a length of robust, thin adhesive tape along the entire length of the edge first. This bonds the edge of the head-lining to the edge of the bodyshell aperture. The rubber strip doesn't push the lining material back as you push it onto the edge. It should be a pretty tight fit to be reliably waterproof.

If the windows are to be bonded to a bodyshell flange using adhesive, you might be able to fold it just over the edge and onto the window bonding face and glue it down firmly. It might not interfere with the window or windscreen sealant.

A thicker material folded over might compromise the screen sealant. All is not lost, though. Perusing a catalogue from a supplier such as Woolies, you'll find that there is a multitude of different rubber extrusions and edge trims. One or several of these can be glued to the inboard face of the window/windscreen mounting flange and form a nice camouflage for the edge of the head-lining if the latter could not be folded over and stuck down.

Section 6
Interior hardware

BEFORE YOU REMOVE items of demountable trim and carpet and send them for safe storage, you might take a while to consider what other parts and accessories you will need to complete the interior of the car. Some of them will involve the trim and carpet, as holes may need to be drilled or cut to fix new components to the wood, alloy or GRP backing behind the material.

For vehicles with doors, obvious add-ons include door check straps, door handles and even door-operated interior light or alarm switches. You might be contemplating a secondary dash console between the transmission tunnel and the main dash. Don't forget the rear view mirror – some mount theirs on the top of the scuttle to improve rear visibility with the weather gear in place. Loudspeakers for a stereo system can be mounted into doors, the boot, cockpit sides, footwells or rear bulkhead.

When you start making a list of interior equipment such as this, you might also be influenced by a need for that traditional look demanded by replicas, traditional roadsters and other lookalikes. It's up to you to decide whether the addition of a reproduction part is going to compromise comfort and safety.

We would always recommend a comprehensive array of steering column stalks to control lights, wipers and horn etc. rather than a selection of remote dash-mounted switches that you might be able to get new or from an auto-jumble. We must agree, though, that a set of Cortina stalks would ruin the look of a Cobra replica.

Such things as door handles and check straps are available in many sizes and types from the various retailers at kit car

Above: This NCF has an alloy body, with supporting steel roof members. Plenty of scope for attaching roof trim panels here. Below: Trim can be pressed and held in behind window edge.

Above: Complex areas like this might mean you'll have to trim the bodywork directly, too fiddly for a trim panel. Below: Special tool for inserting filler strip in window or windscreen seal.

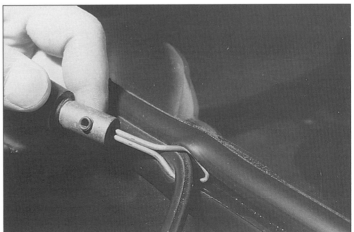

shows and through catalogues. Always sit in the car and find out where such things can be positioned without interfering with the occupants.

A check strap rubbing against your knee or a handle that you can't reach without leaning to one side are both a real pain. Once you've found out where such things can be sensibly fitted, you'll also have a clearer idea of the size and type of component that you should choose.

As a rule of thumb, try to make sure the components in the car's interior are well rounded. By that we mean that edges should have a minimum radius of around 3mm. Take a fresh look inside the standard interior of a modern production car. Type

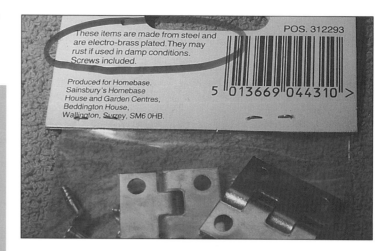

THE WHICH KIT? TIP
As with many parts of the build-up process, until you see the right bit for the job it is sometimes difficult to work out how certain things are fastened, where you can get the right bit of trim etc. There are many suppliers in the business specialising in exactly these weird and wonderful bits and bobs. Gather together a good selection of brochures from the likes of Europa, Woolies, Merlin Motorsport and others (see suppliers section at the end of this book)

Below: Selection of door, window and other edge trims available from trim specialist, Woolies. You have to go to kit car shows or to suppliers premises to properly examine this kind of gear.

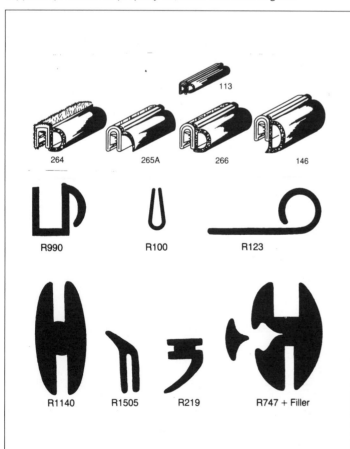

Approval requirements, which don't apply to home-built kit cars yet, state that all interior (and exterior) edges and corners must be rounded to certain minimum radii.

If you're really safety conscious in this respect, you will choose cockpit equipment, dash switches and other add-ons that don't threaten to pierce or cut on impact. Further safety ideas for the race enthusiast or for the very-road-safety-conscious can be found in Chapter Twelve.

Section 7
Soft tops

AMONG THE MOST DAUNTING tasks facing the kit builder is the fitment of soft-top weather gear. In fact, even the more experienced car builders tend to shiver a little at the memories they have. Unfortunately, the job can be made a lot more difficult by vague instructions from the kit manufacturer. Other owners of that kind of kit will be a great help in knowing what to look for specifically.

In general terms, soft-top hoods fall into two broad categories: those which can be folded down with a hinged or collapsible hood frame, allowing the car to be driven without stowing the whole lot away; and those which require complete removal of the hood and frame for safe open top driving. Some systems feature a frame which can be folded down onto the rear cockpit edge while the only the material must be stowed away.

In most instances, builders are supplied with a hood frame and body reference points

Top: Always make sure that a part that is going to get wet or just damp will not rust. Below: Door check straps such as this one need to be very securely located in order to be effective.

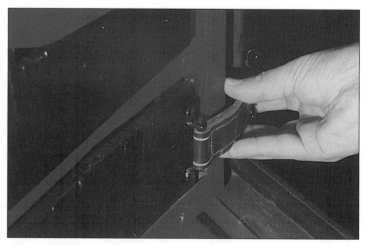

which permit accurate fitment of the frame to the body/chassis. Very little progress can be made until the frame has been finally fitted. Definitely a case of 'measure twice, drill once.'

You'll usually find that a pair of metal locating lugs has to be fitted into the edge of the cockpit and will either be inset into holes cut by the builder or will rest on a surface through which it is bolted.

If these lugs rest on GRP edges, make sure of the strength of the GRP supporting them, as a fairly hefty downward force will be exerted on the supporting GRP. Laminate extra GRP mat to the underside of the bodywork or use a load-spreading device – a shaped alloy plate for instance – between the frame mounts and the GRP body.

Obviously, it would be better if the hood frame was attached to the chassis or a steel subframe of some kind. However, we have noticed a pronounced lack of design

prowess when it comes to soft top hoods for many kit cars.

If your kit has a full windscreen, make sure you align the top of the hood frame with the top of the screen. If they are not parallel, you'll get a twist in the hood material between its frame and the screen frame.

Most hood frames have at least two top cross-pieces. If the front one is parallel with the screen frame top, then the rear one must be parallel with the rear edge of the bodywork to which the hood's trailing edge will be fastened in normal use. Obviously, if the rear body edge is curved, do the best you can to get the rear cross-piece in line with it.

Don't presume that you've finished with the hood frame yet. Even if you've had to file away at its

ends, joins and/or hinges to get the cross-pieces parallel to the relevant reference points, you may yet have to file it if the frame stands too tall for the hood.

Fitting the hood material is a very black art indeed. You will, in most cases be supplied with a pre-cut and fully stitched hood. Sidescreens will either hinge from the screen frame sides or zip into the hood.

Hood material is usually black vinyl but more expensive options can be made from 'double-duck' (or other canvas-like derivatives). Vinyl is

cheaper and benefits from a springier feel, which might help fitment and proper tensioning of the hood – especially when it's warm. The canvas type materials aren't as stretchy but offer greater strength at stress points where fasteners are attached. They have been criticised for 'loosening up' with age and starting to sag.

If your hood has been finally stitched along its front and rear edges, fitting is a matter of holding it tightly in place to get a sufficient overlap, at the screen frame top and at the rear body edge, for your choice of fasteners to be

This is a four-piece hood rail which makes it easier to dismantle and store in the car.

The frame on the left needs to be removed from the car when the hood isn't in use, but this Royale one (above) can be folded away on a cantilevering frame. Below: GRP moulding on this Marlin hood glues into the hood and grips onto screen frame.

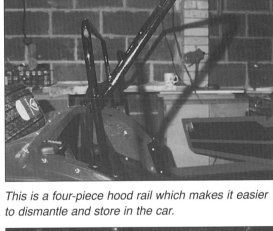

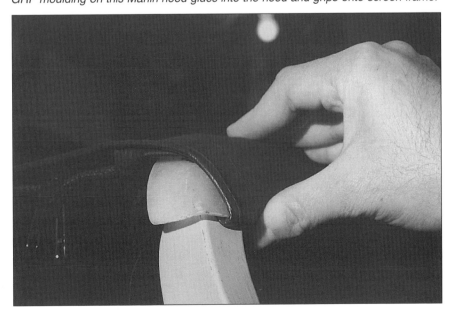

attached.

You might find that the leading edge of the hood has already been prepared for fitting to the screen frame top. The method of attachment might be a simple row of pop-studs, a clamped down GRP or metal former bonded to the hood or a long baton in the front edge of the hood which must be pushed up into a slot at the screen frame front face. In this instance, turn your attention to the rear edge fitment next.

There will usually be a rear bodywork surface, flange or rim designed to meet the hood at the same angle (viewed from the side elevation). If the rear edge of the hood sits parallel to the bodywork, then the fasteners can be well positioned to stay firm.

If the hood angles down to fasteners which are on a near-horizontal surface (like the Cobra lookalikes for instance), there is a greater chance that these fasteners will be pulled out of the hood or bodywork eventually.

Extra pairs of hands or a good quantity of strong gaffer tape can be used to tension the hood back towards its rear edge. Make sure that sidescreens are fitted so that you can see whether the hood needs to be pulled left or right to even out the sidescreen apertures. This whole job is best done at room temperature (20 deg. C.) or hotter so that the hood material is that bit more compliant.

Working in stages, starting with the relatively straight rear-most hood edge, mark the position of the fastener centres through the hood and into the bodywork without letting the hood budge an instant while you're doing it. A centre-punch can do this.

In this way, you'll know that holes made in the hood will relate exactly to holes made in the bodywork. You might want to make sure by fitting each fastener as you mark its position, then move on to the next.

Your choice of fastener will probably depend on your budget. Simple Durable Dot pop-studs seem to be the most popular and the cheapest. They leave a fairly innocuously shaped male half on the bodywork which isn't likely to harm anyone, spreads its load over a fairly wide area and is securely fastened through bodywork with a proper countersunk bolt. (Always avoid rivets and self-tappers – especially through GRP – on hood fittings. They're just not up to the job.)

Pop-studs aren't good at securing hoods when the material edge isn't lying nearly flat against the bodywork edge. If the material is being tensioned up and away from the bodywork, there's a good chance that it will release the pop-stud fastening.

The female side of the pop-stud is usually fitted into the hood. It can be attached through a pretty good thickness of material but tends to

Above: Webbing straps hold the Robin Hood frame in the right position to accept the hood material. Below: Taping hood and sidescreens in place before marking for fasteners.

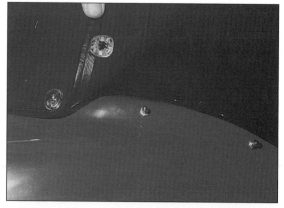

Lift-the-dot male pegs screw into the bodywork, femal tabs punched onto the hood.

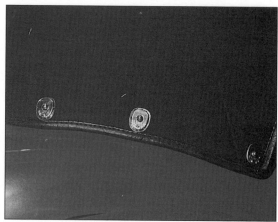

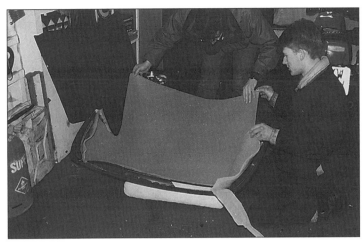

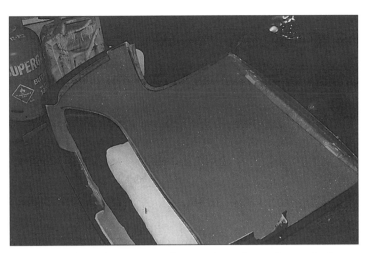

Successfully trimming a hardtop can be a real trial of your expertise and patience. We've found this is the one time when spray glues come into their own. An extra set of hands is vital.

Above: This foam has gone on in one-piece. It may be easier to use several different sections. Final headlining can look really quite impressive but will also let a car down if done badly.

concentrate its load through a fairly small central spindle which holds the two halves of the female portion together. This can initiate a rip, especially in vinyl, and cause the pop-stud to pull itself out of the vinyl.

Lift-the-Dot and Tenax fasteners are the more expensive alternatives and are much better at spreading loads where the female portions are attached to the hood material. They both operate on a similar male stud, like a rounded spike about half an inch long, which has a threaded or self-tapping end and may thus be tightened into the bodywork as a bolt or, less robustly, as a self-tapper.

One disadvantage is that the male end, in both cases, doesn't spread its load particularly well in the bodywork and can pull out or crack GRP in time. You need to fit load-spreading washers either side of the bodywork panel to be sure. That may then leave you with insufficient thread to tighten up on. When the hood is off, the male ends protrude in a rather menacing way. Certainly not recommended for fitment inside a cockpit or at the front of a car, even if the points are rounded off.

A big advantage of these fasteners is that they're both good at fastening the hood

material to the body when they do meet at odd angles. When properly fitted, they are much more secure under stress and less likely to pull apart than pop-studs. Tenax fasteners are release by pulling up on the rounded and sprung top of the female portion. Lift-the-Dots are released by raising the rounded end of the flat female portion.

If your hood has a finalised and stitched rear edge but there is spare material left on the front edge, it makes sense to fit the rear edge first, while making sure that there is sufficient material remaining to complete the front. This might entail gluing a GRP moulding into the front of the hood that will act as a capping piece on top of the screen frame.

It might simply be a question of cutting the front of the hood to the right length and folding it over for neatness by stitching or gluing. This would be followed up by fitment of front edge fasteners and maybe a rubber strip to interact with the screen top as a weather seal. Always beware of the sidescreens and their positions relative to the hood when fitting the hood.

Small G-clamps, with soft spacers, can come in very handy for holding the hood material/screen-top moulding in place. Best glue is impact adhesive. You don't get the chance to reposition the work

but it'll hold tight and not lose precious hood tension.

Hoods with a solid moulding cap at the front edge will subsequently be attached to the screen frame by hooking over a front edge or via over-centre catches. Some might have 'butterfly' bolts which screw into the screen frame via the hood moulding.

When cutting or drilling holes for bolts or catches, make sure that the relevant fastener will be positioned so that it pulls down firmly on the hood front. Some over-centre catches are adjustable for tension and they should be positioned so that they can gradually be tightened to take out any free-play that might occur as the assembly all beds-in with wear.

Remember that a windscreen frame made of simple alloy or brass channel is often fitted tight

up against the screen glass. Put a drill, screw, bolt, or pop rivet through in the wrong spot and you might well have a shattered windscreen to contend with.

If your budget can possibly stretch to the best quality fasteners, and, if necessary, a professional hood fitting exercise, it will certainly pay off for high performance cars. There are massive forces at work on a hood at high speed (ie: 70mph and above), especially when the sidescreens aren't in place. Feeble or insufficient fasteners, or weak areas where the fasteners are attached, will make it more likely that the hood will rip away.

The front edge is usually the first to go in this case, followed by the rear quarters and then the rear edge. Make the front edge bullet-proof as possible and you're well on the way to having

Chapter 8
LOOMING UP

Section 1: Think ahead.
Section 2: The easy way out

Section 3: Using donor looms
Section 4: Troubleshooting

Section 1
Think ahead

NOT EXACTLY A BIG favourite build area for most enthusiasts, wiring is often THE big problem area. If you don't have a knowledge or a 'feel' for the concept of auto-electrical work, then tread carefully indeed. If it is the builder who will sort out the kit's wiring all alone, then be sure that you can understand all the stages and techniques described in the kit's build manual before you choose your kit car. It's that important.

All too often, we find that the electrical systems of otherwise excellent kit cars let them down in the end. Anything from untidy wiring to downright dangerous, exposed wiring bodges.

At one end of the scale, you will find kit packages which boast their own special wiring looms, all tailor-made to fit a given set of instruments, connectors etc. Similarly, some kits will use a specific donor loom, along with the dedicated electrical parts, in its entirety or with a few length modifications only.

At the other end of the scale, you will find some kits which use engine, gearbox, instruments, electrical ancillaries etc. all from different sources. Instructions might say "use the engine loom from the engine donor and connect it to another donor's dash and lighting loom."

Don't be misled when you view the company demo car. If the manufacturer claims that the demo is simply "fitted with the donor's wiring loom," check the obvious signs carefully to see just how simple it all is. Is the donor instrument pod used intact? If it has been used but split up, was there originally a printed circuit board behind it and how has this been replaced? Always ask club members about their experiences here.

Are all of the original donor electrical components used? Did the donor have an alternator or dynamo? If it now has an alternator instead of a dynamo, how has the manufacturer changed the loom? Is the donor steering column used, with the ignition switch and all column stalks? Are the dash switches the same?

The kit's build manual should explain all if you need to undertake the jobs to get the kit built properly. Judge for yourself whether the system recommended to you by the manufacturer's manual and that fitted to the demo car are the same. Is the demo car a one-off for reasons of presentation or through necessity?

If you're given a precise and unambiguous set of instructions, that's fine, isn't it? If the instructions leave everything very generalised, then you have to decide whether you can handle it or not. Some may be lucky in knowing an electrical genius who has the time and the inclination to lend a hand when the time comes for the loom to be made or fitted and tested.

We have found, in our own experience, that there is a very wide difference in ability shown by amateur car builders when it comes to understanding the volt and the amp, let alone the Ohm or the Watt.

It's very different when you're tackling obvious mechanical and visual problems. A knackered ball-joint or a gelcoat crack can at least be easily spotted and recognised as 'wrong,' thereby initiating some sort of repair.

When the problem is invisible to many, the symptoms varied and inconsistent, the consequences include hours of testing and checking. An ability to assess abstract concepts and information appears to be a lot less commonplace than the ability to fix something tangible.

In this chapter, we have tried to set out priorities and techniques for the not-so-confident auto-electrician. It would require a hefty text book to try to turn the doubtful amateur

Disconnect the battery when you're working on your kit car's wiring loom. These clamps are too close to the terminal and could arc if moved. Put some tape on the terminals for extra safety.

A battery isolator switch, even in the off position, still has one live terminal. Always be careful when working with electrics. Whilst unlikely to do you serious harm, it can give you a big jolt!

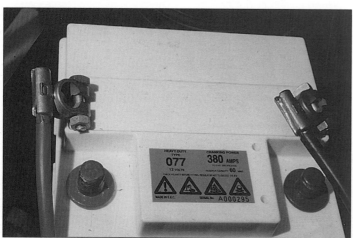

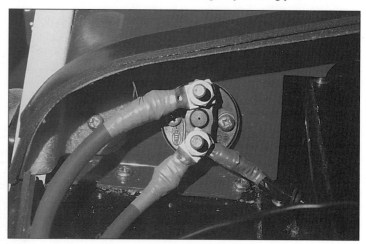

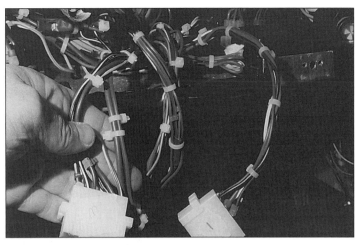

Some manufacturers offer full or part looms to suit their kits, when you use the recommended donor parts. Fit non 'standard' parts and you might have to make a few modifications.

Plugs like these can be purchased from kit build suppliers and are easily assembled into looms. Here they have been fitted behind the dash to allow easy removal of the whole dashboard.

car builder into a budding expert. We have come to the conclusion that if you approach the wiring loom in a very controlled, planned and thorough way, it is less likely that you will end up with problems.

Problem-spotting can be the cause of massive delays or even damage when you don't know a lot about wiring. This is especially the case when there isn't a wiring diagram or colour key available for the loom in question.

If you can be sure of certain routes, connections, earthing points and general principles, as well as safer methods of testing the loom, you will be well on your way to getting it all sorted without huge headaches.

Section 2
The easy way out

AN EASY WAY OUT ISN'T necessarily as dishonourable as it sounds. If the idea is to get the kit up to a good and reliable standard in a realistic time scale, then the easy way out can often be an assurance of success, even if it costs a bit more.

In the case of wiring looms, the easy way out is to get a specially made loom with the kit - along with all requisite instructions and terminal fittings to commission the loom. We are glad to say that there are more

and more kit car companies offering purpose-made looms and these are definitely a good thing.

A kit builder who wants to have total control over the type of alternator under the bonnet, the kind of instruments in the dash, the number of fuses used and the overall route of the loom in the body or chassis may well have to make a loom from scratch.

If you don't mind settling for the manufacturer's recommended engine, instruments, lights, fuse box and switches, then the time savings can be pretty impressive when you fit the tailor-made loom. It could knock months off the build schedule, especially if you only

have one or two days to work on the car every month. We strongly recommend this option for cautious first-time kit builders.

Typically, specialised wiring looms come with all relevant connectors, with some of them or with none of them. There can be legitimate reasons for these variations as donor components to which the loom must be connected can vary from year to year or model to model, even if they are all correct for the job. It might be left to the builder to identify which terminal connectors are needed for the donor in question.

A connector-less loom might also have been supplied oversized, so that the builder can trim the various wires down

Mid-engined cars with hinged front and rear body sections can benefit from pluggable loom sections such as these. They can also be perfect for racing kits where panels are often removed.

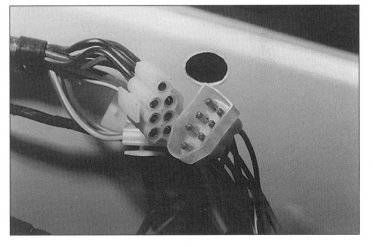

having trial-fitted the loom in a tidy position.

Be extremely disinclined to alter the positions of other components to suit the loom route or length. Instruments should be in line of sight or close as possible to it, not a few inches over to the nearside because the loom doesn't reach. Cable and connectors are relatively cheap. The loom should be made to reach all the electrical components comfortably after they have been positioned where they are meant to be.

The first step is to follow manufacturer's instructions as to where to route the loom. For a standard front-engined car, it is likely that there will be a two or three-piece loom. Broadly speaking, the front section will deal with the engine bay and front lights, the rear section with the dash area and rear lights. Sometimes, the rear lights loom is pluggable, making a third section.

If you have been given no guidance regarding loom routing, use strong gaffer tape to support the loom in various trial positions. Inevitably, the most concentrated part of any loom is the dash area. All of the switches, instruments and fuses tend to be concentrated in this area and the loom should 'start' from here on its journey forwards and rearwards.

Tape the loom into position

behind the dash, with all cables adjacent to the relevant terminals there. The rear section of the loom will probably be routed down towards the floor from either end of the dash or from the dash centre down one side of the transmission tunnel.

You will have to estimate which trim and carpet panels will best hide the presence of the rear loom on its journey toward the rear of the car. It's a good idea to keep the loom clear of the floor in case the vehicle gets wet occasionally. Some off-road vehicles have the main loom routed up into the A-pillars and along the roof to keep it dry.

Make sure that the loom will not be damaged by doors and door hinges, seats and runners, any moving components such as the handbrake, gear lever, foot pedals, pivoting seatbelt

mechanisms etc. Occupants' feet and heavy luggage can, after time cause insulation breaks or fatigue cracks in wire strands if the loom is constantly chafed.

As the loom enters the rear bodywork or boot area, try to keep it well away from the fuel tank filler, breather and fuel pipes/pump where practical. Run some spare cables between the dash and the rear of the car, in case of extra components later on, and a heavy duty black cable for earthing duties.

Much the same technique can be used to route the front portion of the loom if there is no printed wisdom on the subject. When considering where to feed the loom through from the dash area to the engine bay, you may well have to make a decision as to where to cut a hole (or two) and how large to make it.

Top: Whenever your wiring goes through a bulkhead you'll always need a rubber grommet to protect the cables. Below: One of these fans works automatically, the second is a manual back-up.

Bear in mind that the hole should be large enough to accommodate a rubber grommet which stops the loom from rubbing on an edge. Holes cut into horizontal surfaces, depressions, low down in the front bulkhead and directly below bonnet vents are all more likely to allow water back into the cockpit. A hole cut into a vertical or near-vertical surface, sheltered from water splash or drainage routes, is more likely to be dry.

Other hazards for this part of the loom are windscreen wiper mechanisms, especially the Ford lever-arm types, any heat sources such as exhaust proximity or convected heat, and wear from contact with moving parts or vibrating edges/surfaces. The fan belt, cooling fan, throttle or choke linkages, the engine itself, gear linkages (if applicable), bonnet hinges and

shutting edges etc. can all endanger the loom's insulation.

This is the most visible part of the loom and maximum attention should be given to the route. Many prefer to choose a route that hides the cables and connectors as much as possible. If they remain visible, run them neatly tucked away and parallel to adjacent edges or faces, with regular angles or corners and evenly spaced fasteners (more about these later). Look at yer average new Japanese car for engine loom tidying inspiration.

Where single cables leave the loom to reach engine block senders or a gearbox reverse light switch, make sure that there is sufficient slack in the branching wire to prevent over-tensioning of that wire when the engine rocks or moves on tickover or in torque reaction. Some of the 'taller' engines can

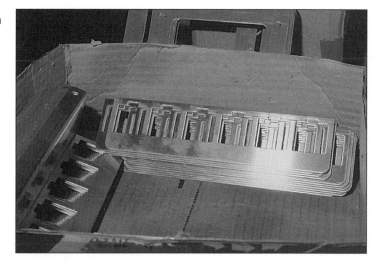

Above: Aftermarket switches can be mounted into special switch panels like these alloy ones. Below: It pays to label all wires, connections and components clearly when removing a donor loom.

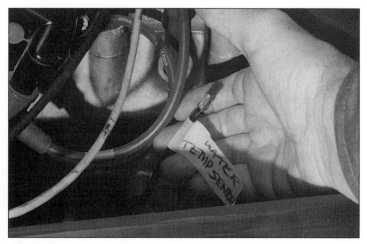

move a surprising amount in normal use.

If your kit is mid or rear-engined, the specified loom will be more complex at the rear end of the car. Much the same can be said in terms of caution when fitting the loom. Remember, however, that engine bays to the rear of the car can get a lot hotter than those at the front, especially if the radiators are there and the bay is badly designed in terms of air flow.

Parts of the wiring loom above the exhaust manifold and pipes may get too hot for safety and you should attempt to route them away from convected (rising) and radiated heat.

If the front or rear bodywork sections are designed for easy removal, it will be better to install multi-pin plugs, from the kit car after-market suppliers, so that any parts of the loom attached to the removable panels can be simply unplugged. This can also be handy for the dashboard and for the front and rear sections if you ever need to remove parts of the loom for repair, enlargement or re-routing.

Finally, even if your kit is not supplied with a dedicated wiring loom, there are a number of wiring specialists who will make up a custom loom to your own specifications regarding instruments, lights and layout etc. All of these things may cost a little more than making up your own loom, but if it's the difference between choosing one kit over another, completing a kit rather than giving up and selling it on, enjoying the build experience instead of hating it, then it's money well spent, isn't it?

Section 3
Using donor looms

IF YOU'RE NOT ABLE TO GET a complete new loom, the second best case is where the kit uses the engine, instruments, peripheral senders, column stalks and all switches from one donor vehicle. If this is the case, then all the connectors on the loom will match the relevant connectors on the components in question.

Third best case is where the kit uses the dash equipment (instruments and switches) from the loom donor, even if the peripheral parts are from different donors. You must be sure that there are senders available for the engine and fuel tank which will match the calibration of fuel, oil pressure, oil temperature, oil level, water temperature and other such gauges.

Worst case is where the engine, instruments, switches, senders, ignition switch and loom are from many different manufacturers. It can simplify matters if they are all Ford, for instance, but come from different models. If they are Ford, BL, Lancia and Jaguar all mixed up, though, it can be a circus.

Let's take the first scenario, with the loom and all equipment coming predominantly from one donor. It is pretty essential that the car builder lacking electrical confidence personally strips the wiring loom from the donor vehicle. First step should be battery removal, to avoid the chance of electrolyte spillage, a melt-down or fire.

Using pencil and paper, along with masking tape and a marker pen, it should be possible to make an accurate and totally unambiguous record of exactly what was connected to what and how. Mark any wires that seemed to be detached or tucked away as 'spares.' Many looms have spare wires and if you don't mark them as such, then you might try to connect them to something later!

Fold the masking tape over the end of a wire, having marked your own code on the tape, or a description of where the wire should go. If you find a group of wires going to a small selection of terminals close together, use the paper to draw a clear diagram of where each wire goes, along with a note of the colour of each wire. You can then tape off the group of wires and mark a reference to the drawing you have and/or the component to which they are attached.

Although most *Haynes Workshop Manuals* provide a wiring diagram for donor cars, many have found that their use can be limited because of minor or major variations in each model or year of car. Most of the diagrams also show the wires themselves in black,

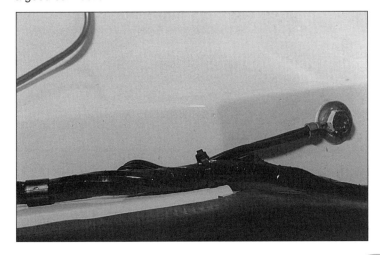

Earthing points may be scattered around the car. Always make sure the connections are clean. A painted chassis rail will not prove a good connection.

Top: A donor dash pod could be a simple plug-in part, particularly if you are retaining the original loom. Below: Local automotive suppliers will be best place to buy colour coded wiring.

with a separate colour code in a table. These are painfully slow to decipher, especially when the diagram itself bears little resemblance to the shape or route of the loom in the vehicle.

Make sure that your labels are securely attached to the loom and that the diagrams are kept safe. It may be some time before you can fit the loom to the kit and your memory of which wire goes where might be decidedly foggy by the time that you come to fit the loom. Never presume that you will remember where something is meant to go.

All you need is a few missing labels or lost diagrams to complete the confusion. If you can't understand your drawings and wording when it comes to the crunch, or if you can't remember the codings you used, things can get worse still. Try to do the job as if someone else will have to work from your instructions.

When you have finalised the positions of all the loom-related components in the kit, it's time to see just how much butchering will need to be done to get the animal to be the right shape and size. More often than not, donor looms are far too long in the rear section, short in places behind the dash and not so bad in the engine bay.

Even if the donor loom

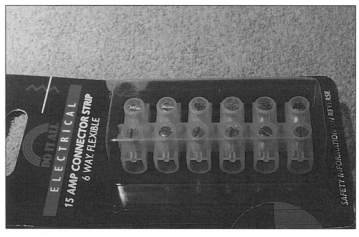

These cheap 'chocolate block' connectors may be adequate in the home, but they won't do in your car. Do not use them.

appears to be nearly the right shape, don't be tempted to fit it straight away and coerce the long and short bits into shape. You'll end up with all sorts of electrical anomalies in the future.

Make a large drawing of your car in plan view (from above) and mark down the positions of all things electrical. Use your judgement or the kit build manual to see where the main loom routes will be and measure the lengths of the resulting cable runs in the car with string and a tape measure. Note down the various dimensions on your diagram.

Here's the scary bit. This is where you will appreciate accurate and comprehensive loom labelling, coding and diagrams. Lay the donor loom

out flat on the ground and remove all the (usually black) loom binding tape from it. This will leave you with a collection of labelled, multi-coloured wires.

Making sure that all of the labels are still firmly attached and legible, carefully separate out the various groups of wires and lay them out on the ground or hang them up on nails or pegs against the garage wall. Some of the wires will be long, separate lengths and some will be joined by multi-pin connectors or earthing rings and tabs. A loom like the Marina's will usually be bound together with plastic heat-shrink wrap, which you shouldn't separate unless necessary.

Making the best use of the labels on the loom sections and the diagram of the car, with all

the relevant measurements of the new loom routes, lay the cables back out on the floor in the shape of the new loom for the kit.

If you have been diligent in marking the diagram with all the electrical components in your kit car, then most of the wires will be taken up in the new arrangement. Form temporary loops to take up excess cable and add new labels to identify parts of the old loom which need lengthening and how much by.

You may well end up with a few spare lengths of cable hanging on the wall. The labels on these may remind you of components that you have forgotten to include in the drawing or they might reveal that these wires won't be needed in the kit. Quite often, open top kit cars will dispense with courtesy door and boot lights etc.

Use short lengths of adhesive insulating tape or small cable ties to hold each branch of the loom together and to stop the new shape from unravelling. Don't pull the cable ties tight – just firm will do.

Are all wires the same? Which connectors are best for attaching new lengths of cable to parts of the loom that aren't already long enough? What special tools are needed? Valid questions all. To the newcomer, the size or diameter of a cable might seem a pretty esoteric

Solder bullets on the left are preferable to the crimping type connectors on the right. Always try to solder any wiring connections to avoid later trouble.

A cheap and cheerful volt/ohm meter is an invaluable purchase with even the most simple car wiring. It comes with comprehensive instructions and will be a good long term purchase.

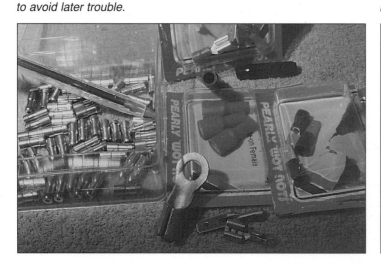

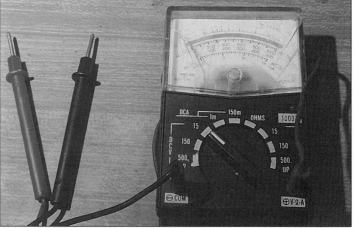

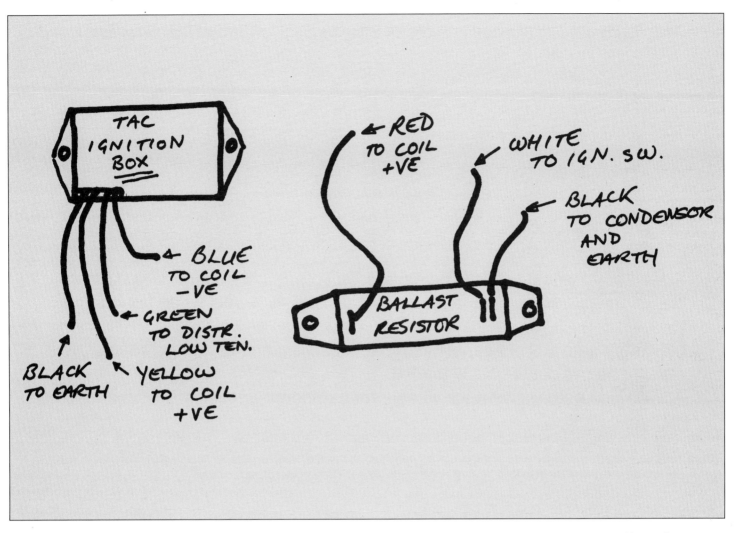

Simple diagrams like this, made while dismantling your donor's loom, can save a great deal of time and expense later. It's a nuisance to stop and make a sketch but you will find that details you think you'll remember soon become a distant and fading memory. Diagrams last slightly longer!

notion. Electricity runs along conductors and that's that, isn't it?

Nope. See the table in this section for cable sizes relating to loads. The capacity of a cable is measured by the number of strands of copper and the thickness of each strand. There will also be the problem of cable colour codings to match the existing loom.

If the cables you need to lengthen have special connectors or multi-pin plugs on the end, you'll need to make a cut somewhere back along the length of the cable and insert a new section of wire to get the overall length you need.

If the cable in question ends simply in a spade-end (Lucar) or solder bullet connector, you should be able to produce a

new section of cable extension that plugs straight into the end of the old but has the same kind of connector at the other end.

If you are using spade-end (Lucar) terminals, they are designed to hold both the bare end of the cable and the end of the insulation by crimping different metal tabs across them. Some builders prefer to follow this up by soldering the

crimped connection just to make sure.

Avoid soldering the bare cable ends before crimping as this can reduce the contact area, increasing the chance of an intermittent or 'hot' connection. Some spade-ends come with full insulating sleeves, some with part-sleeves and some come bare of all insulation. Choose carefully.

Solder bullets are, as the name suggests, small cylindrical connectors. The male connector looks like a small torpedo and the female is a cylindrical receptor. The bare wire goes into the back of each of these so that the insulator pushes up against the connector and there's no bare wire visible. Some solder bullets come with insulating sleeves, some are bare.

The male or female parts are heated with a soldering iron and the bare wires are soldered to the inside of the bullets. Some prefer to 'pre-load' the bullets with solder and then push the wires into the solder, which must be re-melted for this.

If you have had to cut the existing cable to insert an extension piece, take it to your

THE WHICH KIT? TIP
When you're buying any type of spade connector, P-clip, cable tie etc always try and buy in bulk rather than boxes of five or ten like you might find in Halfords. You're bound to use quite a number and they become very cheap when bought in larger quantities. See our suppliers listing at the back of this book

Max. Current Load (Amps)	No. of Strands	Strand Diameter(mm.)
5.50	9	0.3
8.75	14	0.3
17.50	28	0.3
25.50	44	0.3
35.00	65	0.3
42.00	84	0.3
50.00	97	0.3
60.00	120	0.3
170.00	37	0.9

Sizes above would typically be expressed as 9/0.3, 84/0.3 or 37/0.9 etc.
Maximum safe current capacity for all cables is 40% less when bound in a loom.
Maximum safe current capacity for cables 28/0.3 and bigger is reduced by 40% if cable is continuously loaded.
Always use automotive quality cable for car looms - never use household cables.

This table shows a selection of cable sizes and the relevant maximum intermitted loads permissible (in amps). An automotive cable is normally measured in terms of the number of strands within the cable and the diameter of each strand.

local motor factor or auto-electrical shop to buy the same size (or thicker) colour-coded cable. Do not use narrower cable as this could lead to overheating, melting and maybe fire.

If you cannot find cable of the right colour(s), then some electrical suppliers can sell you cable sleeves or collars which can be used to identify the cable by colour and/or number codes. Make a note of any colour variations you have to make or it could be a real headache for future work.

Insulate the new connections in the loom, if the connectors you have used are not already fully insulated. This is best done by using fully sleeved bullets or Lucars in the first place or by buying special heat-shrink insulating sleeves.

A length of this can be slid over the join and shrink-wrapped into place using heat from a hair-drier, hot-air paint stripper or convected heat from

a small flame or powerful soldering iron. Avoid using adhesive insulating tape for permanent insulating jobs.

If you have to lengthen a bunch of cables, take extreme care to find new cable of the right thickness or greater than necessary. Multi-pin connectors are available from a selection of after-market sources advertising in the kit car magazines or in the high street. Choose well insulated varieties.

Do not use those 'chocolate block' connectors which employ screws to fasten the cable ends in place. They may be OK for household or dry and vibration-free applications but are not OK for automotive use.

Scotchlok connectors, which sandwich wires together and connect them by piercing the insulation, should also be avoided as anything other than a short-term measure. They are convenient but prone to intermittent connections, high

resistance and broken cable strands.

You can also solder cable ends together to extend the part of the loom in question but you must make sure that you use a tight-fitting insulating sleeve to protect this join. Smooth off any sharp ends of solder or wire which might puncture the insulation and any neighbouring wires – with dire effect. Don't just twist wires together and tape over them. This really is a bodge.

You'll be using the same techniques to insert connectors or solder joins where cables are being shortened to fit. Needless to say, the new loom should be laid in place, as per the preceding section on ready-made looms, to see if it actually is the right size and shape for the kit. There's no point having an unpluggable dashboard if there isn't enough free cable to give access for a hand reached behind the dash to unplug it!

No cutting should be done

until exactly the right lengths have been decided. Obviously, some slack will be needed to make sure that the loom can be routed neatly, not just straight to the relevant components. If, for instance, a component such as a switch or a gauge has spade end terminals or a block connector behind it, you'll want the relevant wires to reach these terminals from a point somewhere directly behind them.

If the wires immediately take a right or left turn from the terminals, there will be a certain tension pulling them to that side all the time. This could dislodge a block connector or cause stress cracks in copper wire strands. It could also help to dislodge connectors if helped by vibration. That's why loom lengths should be carefully considered.

When you have reached a final decision, go ahead and modify the donor loom length to suit your purposes. Final tidying of the loom should be done with the non-adhesive type of black loom tape. This can be anchored at each end with adhesive tape but when tensioned it generally does a pretty good job of staying put. Problems arise when you bind too loosely.

Spirap is now becoming very popular as a loom-tidying product. It's just a length of tough and non-adhesive plastic strip shaped in a spiral. This can be wrapped around the loom and although it doesn't cover 100% of the cable surface, it is very tough and permits you to let wires branch out from the main loom. It comes in different sizes to cope with all shrouding jobs from looms to wires to brake hoses and fuel pipes etc.

How are the main loom runs fastened to the body/chassis? Simple, really. In the engine bay

and at the rear of the car, it's probably best to use various sizes of rubber insulated or plastic P-clips, bolted or riveted at even intervals (of about six to nine inches) to the bodywork or chassis.

They should grip the loom only loosely so that you can run extra wires through them later, if necessary, without having to unbolt them from their mounts. There might already be handy body-fitting bolts along your chosen route.

Second best are cable ties, those strips which use a kind of ratchet system to fasten like a belt. They can be used to support the loom from suitable points. You can also get small base brackets which fasten to the chassis or panels specifically to locate cable ties. Small P-clips can also be used as anchors for cable ties.

The main loom running front to rear, usually behind the trim and carpet, can be simply held in place using generous strips of strong gaffer tape. This kind of attachment helps to keep the loom unobtrusive as there isn't a

thick parts of the loom when P-clips cannot.

Odd cases can be solved by walking around the electrical and plumbing departments of DIY shops to see the huge variety of plastic, steel and

> ## THE WHICH KIT? TIP
> When using a cable tie remember to cut off the excess cabling when it's tightened. Not only that, you can usually push the more unsightly 'ratchet' part of the tie out of sight under what ever it is you have located the wiring to, such as a chassis rail. This really helps to keep everything looking tidy

set of regular lumps denoting clips under the carpet.

In the dash and front bulkhead area, the massed wires can get very bulky and you might find that larger cable ties will have to be used to reach around

copper brackets available for fastening conduit, central heating pipes etc.

Special tools and materials for the realistic wiring jobs aren't expensive. An auto-electrical crimping set is essential (the

Earth connections. A for rear light clusters. B for fuel tank. C for electric fuel pump. D for rear screen demist. E for gearbox (usually a braided strap). F for instrument pod. G for wiper motor. H for main engine block (usually strap). I for electronic ignition. J for battery negative terminal. K for front lights. L is solid connection between alternator and block.

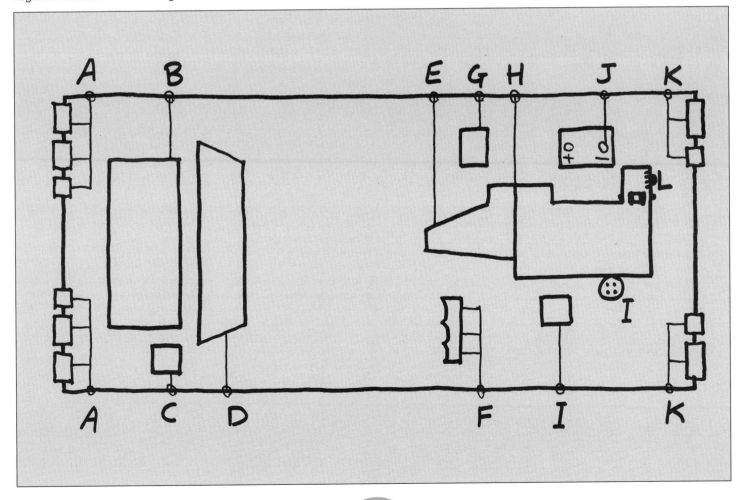

quality of these varies greatly) and will probably include wire stripping, cutting and crimping pliers (all in one), a selection of terminals and connectors and some insulating sleeves. Buy the best you can afford.

Add to this a good set of side cutters (cutting pliers), a good mains soldering iron, a roll of multi-core solder with integral flux, heat-shrink sleeving and a suitable heat source for it, extra male and female Lucars, single, twinned or triple solder bullets, multi-pin connectors, cable ties of different sizes, P-clips, adhesive insulating tape, non-adhesive loom tape etc.

Section 4
Trouble-shooting

HOW DO YOU TAKE THE necessary steps to check whether the loom you have fitted

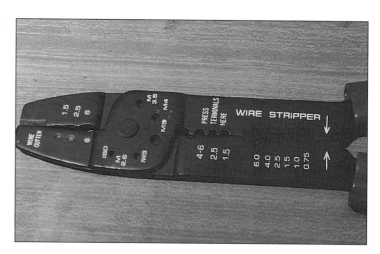

or created can have the full force of the battery unleashed upon it? What are the more common faults when fitting a loom?

All of the principles and concepts behind even a simple car wiring loom are fantastic to behold. Even qualified domestic electricians can be totally mystified by some of the shortcuts and sophistications employed by the car loom designer.

In general terms, many amateur car builders understand the notion of positive and negative, live and earth. 99% of kit cars will have a negative earth electrical system, meaning that the chassis, body or other earthing points are all connected to the negative battery terminal.

A loose or exposed live wire from the positive terminal touching against the earthed components will cause a short circuit, probably with an audible

and visible spark. It can also cause a fire – even if the fuse box is properly sorted. If a live is connected to earth via a functional electrical component, it will not cause a short circuit.

By far the most common problem is sorting out bad earths. This is closely followed up by difficulty in understanding how to find faults in the 'route' that current takes from the battery positive terminal, through switches and components, to earth and back to the negative terminal of the battery.

The donor car loom will probably be interspersed with earthing points everywhere. The benefits of a steel bodyshell include a great variety of earthing possibilities adjacent to most components. A GRP-bodied kit car doesn't offer as many, even if it does have a steel chassis and a new and heavy-duty general

earth 'ring' wire run in with the loom to pick up stray earth wires from it.

Many mistakes are made when connecting earth tabs and terminals to the steel chassis, usually via handy bolts that have other primary functions. You must make sure that the connector itself is new and properly crimped or soldered to the earthing wire or braided strap. It must be strongly fixed, directly against the chassis, with a clean and large as possible metal to metal contact.

This connection can be painted or undersealed or Vaselined after it has been firmly secured. Any insulators such as paint interfering with the contact area will either reduce the capacity of or will isolate the earthing connector.

More often than not, it's a partly-functional earth connection

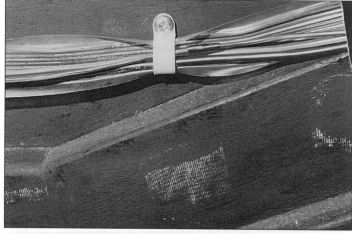

Above: P-clips can be attached to body panel bolts etc. to support the loom. Below: Typical 5-pin switching relays, probably for the low-high beam. They have their own metal brackets.

Top: An automotive crimping tool usually comes boxed with a few terminals. Below: (from left) Engineer's pliers, wire stripper, side cutter and pin-nose pliers - all useful purchases.

that causes consternation. Slow engine cranking, dim lights, flashing tail and brake lights, burning shell! The connection will get hot as it can't handle the current passing to earth from the component.

A simple continuity test across this earth point might yield a good result, with the problems arising only when a high current component is engaged. The dodgy connection will limit the component's function and will tend to get hot. (A hot cable means that the cable size is insufficient for the current it has to carry). Deal with these promptly.

Checking separate circuits before connecting up the 12-volt car battery and doing some real damage isn't all that difficult. It can be helpful to remove all the fuses but the ones you need for the circuits you're testing. You should invest in a good test meter for 12-volt circuits.

This must include an ohmmeter, voltmeter, and can even include engine tuning functions such as dwell etc. The Gunsons Testune is a commonly available and very handy meter.

It is also handy to have several varied lengths of strong insulated cable, each with a powerful crocodile clip at one end. The test meter itself should have some cables with probes or clips but these are sometimes too short.

When testing for continuity from the dash to a distant part of the loom, you can use these long leads to reach the relevant connectors on the meter. The meter will be switched to Ohms or resistance for a continuity check.

If you want to safely check which wires become live when the battery is connected and when the ignition switch is moved to different positions, use one small disposable 6-volt battery in place of the car battery.

For a 12-volt, low-power check, use two of these batteries connected in series or a very run down car battery which only just shows 12 volts on the voltmeter and has insufficient power to run the headlamps brightly or to operate the starter motor properly.

The 6-volt check is a handy way to look for obvious short circuits (is there a current between the main negative lead and the battery when everything is meant to be switched off?). The 12-volt check can be handy where 6 volts weren't enough to get the relays operating. A fully-charged battery packs a lot of power, usually indicated by its amp/hour rating, and may cause a burn up if there is a serious short-circuit.

Understanding the complexities of positive feed and negative earth can be helped by understanding simple car switch circuits. Several switches are constantly operated by the driver to make the car work properly. Usually, a car loom will include switch circuits connecting positive feed - to switch - to component - to earth. Some may be alternatively wired positive feed - to component - to switch - to earth.

In the former case, the component (such as a headlamp bulb) is permanently earthed

Simple operation of a points ignition system. A: when the points are opened by the distributor cam, the low tension (LT) voltage across the coil primary windings is broken, resulting in a spark at the plug electrodes. B: when the points are shut again, the LT voltage resumes, building up a magnetic field in the coil. Points must be shut for the right length of time - dwell angle.

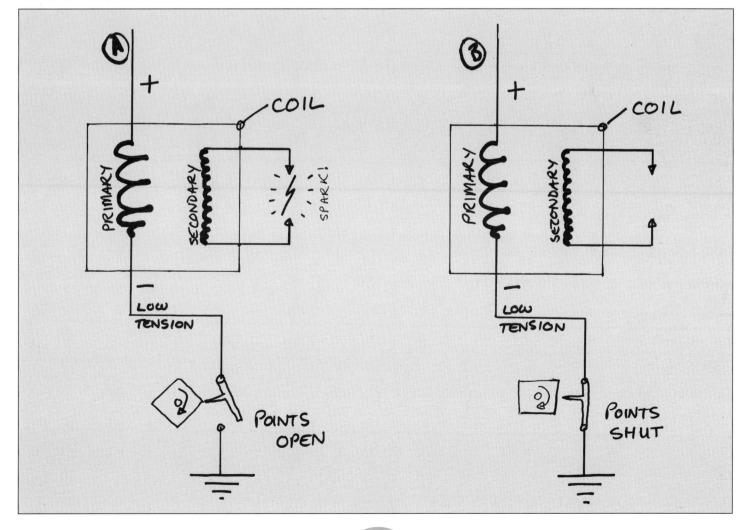

and the switch provides it with the positive feed when operated. In the latter, components (such as courtesy lights) will have a permanent live feed and the switch provides the necessary earthing contact when operated.

Increasingly these days, although less common in most popular donor vehicles, driver-operated switches merely operate relays. Relays are themselves switches but are capable of resisting damage when operating a relatively power-hungry component such as a rear screen demister, headlamp bulbs or wiper motor.

By operating a switch, the driver energises an electro-magnetic switch in the relay box which, in turn, operates the heavy-duty contacts of the relay.

Therefore, a basic relay (which probably takes the form of a plastic or metal box sprouting male spade-end-like connectors) usually has four terminals.

Two of the connectors relate to the low power switch operated by the driver, energising the electromagnetic coils switch in the relay. The other two relate to the high power current from the battery to the main component concerned, via the main relay switch.

Switching relays add extra confusion to the scene. Instead of turning a component on and off by means of a heavy duty internal switch, they simply divert current away from one component and towards another.

This is exemplified by the low beam/high beam headlamp relay (although not every vehicle uses this system). In addition to a normal relay switching the headlamp power on or off, there may be a switching relay which diverts current from high beam to low beam circuits and vice versa.

This will typically be a five-pin relay. Two pins for the electromagnetic coil mechanism, a pin for the high current feed from the battery positive and two other pins which alternately send the high current to the low or high beam filaments.

When the low power electromagnetic switch is off, the relevant steering column stalk switch will probably be in the low beam position. When it is on, it diverts or switches power away

from the low beam filament to the high beam filament.

Obviously, there are many more electrical problems to be found in any car, be it a kit or a production car. Automotive electrical systems have been the inspiration behind several very good text books, including a *Haynes Workshop Manual*, and they can be very helpful to the beginner about to embark on a project.

When it comes to the crunch, though, you should always get knowledgeable help in this department when in difficulty. If you take on a difficult electrical set-up without recourse to club, manufacturer or professional assistance, be prepared for long hours of blind testing and maybe some expensive mistakes.

1: Lamps A, B and C are all vehicle rear lamps. When lamps A are switched on, current goes across each filament to earth each side of car. 2: When the left earth contact is broken, current from left side bulb A earths back to the right of the vehicle through all filament B and C. Lamps A, B and C may all illuminate as a result. Left lamp A may go out or shine dimly etc. etc.

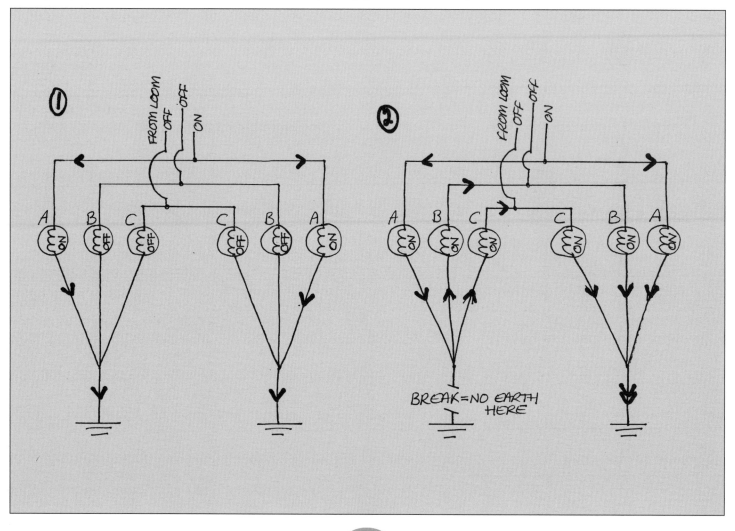

Chapter 9
DETAILING

Section 1: Userfriendliness
Section 2: Bay watching
Section 3: The underworld

Section 4: Rolling stock
Section 5: Glossing over

Section 1
Userfriendliness

ONCE ALL THE WIRING HAS been fully sorted and the cable runs have been thought out, the builder can get on with job of finishing nagging detail jobs around the car. For simplicity's sake, we've decided to focus our attention initially on the interior and boot areas of the kit.

As you gradually replace the trim and carpet, you'll be able to tell just where the loom is best positioned. Keep the main loom runs inside the vehicle and above floor level where possible. Certainly avoid running the main loom underneath the car, vulnerable to road grit etc. Some will choose to tidy the main loom in Spirap spiral plastic binding from the kit parts suppliers or in non-adhesive loom tape. Special looms will already be taped.

With the trim and carpet and all equipment replaced in the car's interior and boot, you can start to assess the whole job for necessary detail work. If the car's body has a final gelcoat which needs no more attention, then this could be regarded as the final fitment of the interior equipment before the car is pressed into service.

Take a pencil and note pad and sit in each of the car's seats in turn and have a good think. The driver might need a stereo or even some small padded trim panels where knees are adjacent to the dash centre or other bodywork. There might be a need for special heel stops in the driver and passenger footwells. Door handles might be wrongly positioned or might feel too weak or small.

Other occupants might notice GRP mat or raw edges sinfully visible. There might be sunlight showing through some GRP panels. Are there sufficient hand-holds for easy entry and exit? Does the car need interior lighting front, rear or in the boot? Are there unprotected 'scuffing points' which get scratched by occupants entering or leaving the vehicle?

Do a basic weatherproofing check on a soft top or hard top car by getting inside and checking carefully for leaks as someone sprinkles water all over the car. Is the floor a water trap? Put in discreet drain holes to stop the floor area filling up.

Obviously a pressure hose pointed into all the joins and aperture edges will force the water in. At this stage, you'll just be checking for the equivalent of rain ingress when the car is outside.

The best kind of stereo is usually the sort that can be removed and taken away easily by the driver when the car is left (relatively inexpensive speakers left in the car). No point having a superb system in an open top car. They're easy enough to nick from a production car.

You can place the mounting brackets up under the dash, in the glove box, in a special housing on the transmission tunnel or even under an accommodating driver's seat. It must be protected from rain in an open car. Don't be too secretive if you want to reach it safely while driving along!

Speakers can go in all sorts of places but they're best mounted on vertical faces in an open car to minimise rain damage. As we mentioned in Chapter Seven, the boot lid can be an excellent prospect if the boot is accessed from the interior of the car. Doors, rear bulkhead, footwell sides are all possibilities. A hard top car offers much more scope.

If you haven't managed to clear up all the visible GRP mat surfaces, it can be done with more trim material stuck into the right places or even with a dab of paint a similar colour to the adjacent trim or carpet.

You should combine user-friendliness with presentability. It is a merciless irritation when the throttle pedal ends up buried in the carpet (right). An alloy bracket can be made of thick sheet (left). Long bolt plus locknuts form the positive pedal stop.

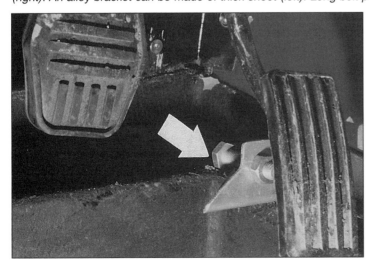 

It takes a while to find the right sources, but there is an endless supply of neat finishing pieces for your car. Extensive use of different edging strips has made for a neat finish here.

More often than not, using the right finishing parts can often result in a practical improvement to the car. These tread strips look great but have the practical function of protecting the paint.

Trim retailers also sell a large range of push-on edging strips to disguise raw GRP edges, a very simple job although the ends of these edge strips might need clever little alloy capping pieces shaped to hide them and riveted or bolted into place.

GRP panels can let sunlight through and this gives the impression of flimsiness. If the offending area of GRP has a hidden face, a good coat of mastic underseal on that face is an effective remedy. If both surfaces of the offending panel are normally visible, then any final paint process may have to suffice. If it's a final gelcoated body and light is visible from the interior, more trim may be called for.

Where occupants exit or enter the car, you're bound to get areas that will be scratched. For running boards on a traditional roadster, there is a multitude of different alloy/rubber strips which can be attached as scuff protection.

Alternatively, properly shaped and rounded alloy or stainless sheet can be glued, bolted or riveted down - watch out for protruding sharp edges. Lower edges of the door apertures can be protected from scratches in this way, as can rear wheel arch front faces from stone chips.

We've never found a soft top to be 100% waterproof. That goes for production cars as well

THE WHICH KIT? TIP
Putting the finishing touches to your kit makes all the difference. Go to some kit car shows and look over other privately built kit cars to see how their builders have overcome similar problems - they don't necessarily have to be the same type of kit as yours. Some builders are incredibly inventive, so why not borrow/pinch some of their ideas?

as kit cars. Needless to say, the low-tech hoods of some kit cars are the worst offenders. However, you should go to pains to avoid leaks which are manifest when the car is left standing, otherwise it'll have to be garaged or covered to avoid it deteriorating quickly.

Over-centre catches can be used for many different applications (here to locate the external spare wheel on a Beauford). Cheap ones can sometimes come undone. Better ones lock in position.

Main leak areas for soft tops (when stationary) are windows/sidescreens where they meet the hood, rear hood edge and the stitching on the top of the hood if the cut of the material allows water to puddle there.

Hoods should feature a pair of flaps along the entire edge of

their contact with the sidescreen or door window. If the outer flap is too small to overlap and protect the edge of the glass or sidescreen, then you should get extra material sewn onto the outer flap by someone with the appropriate machinery.

Check if altering the position of the sidescreen or the angle of the glass channel(s) will solve the problem first.

Trim dealers will usually supply a selection of waterproof beadings which can be sewn onto the edge of a hood, clear of the fasteners, to act as a sealing strip between the hood and the rear bodywork or top windscreen edge. There may be a way of attaching a strip with a similar purpose to the bodywork or screen top without compromising the look of your car.

A hood with a sagging top is a real problem. You might be able to re-tension the material by re-positioning the rear edge fasteners in the bodywork and hood, repairing the holes left by the previous set.

Tensioning straps running under the hood from the screen frame top, over the hood frame and down to the rear bodywork can be made from old seatbelts. They might be attached by pop-studs or wide metal 'hooks' at each and tensioned by velcro strips, a strong elastic section sewn into their length

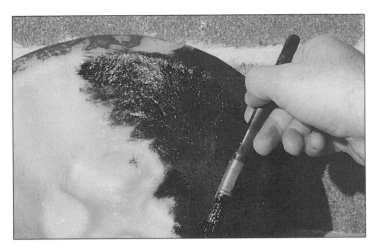

somewhere or by a belt buckle arrangement suitable for a strap of that width.

Don't tighten them so much that the screen gets cracked! Don't stitch through the strap to fasten it to the hood itself as the stitching may create extra leaks. For the non-vinyl hoods, you can buy extra waterproofing liquid to bolster performance.

There's such a wide variety of kit cars on the market that you'll have to sit there and use your imagination when finalising interior detail work. Obviously, you might think of things later but you aren't setting out to get it all right first time.

The main task is to eliminate as many jobs as possible in advance. More work might become necessary after the car has been used for a while, so don't think that the first battle is the last!

Section 2
Bay watching

DETAIL FINISHING IS ALSO applicable to the engine compartment area. If the last of the wiring work enabled you to get the engine up and running, now is a good time to sit and contemplate anything that you might need to do here.

Remove the bonnet or engine cover to give you better access to all areas of the engine bay. How does it look? Clean engine, bay and ancillaries for a start, we would hope. Before firing up the engine or running it for any length of time, a simple visual check can save a lot of heartache. Look for any ways in which a running engine might damage any components near to it.

Is there any wiring, as yet

untidied, close to the exhaust (especially above it in the path of convected heat), are all fuel, brake and electrical components well away from the exhaust, electric or mechanical fan, fan belt, cam belt, pulleys and anything that might be rubbing against them consistently? Are there any fuel, oil, coolant or brake fluid leaks? Is the exhaust too close to a GRP or other flammable surface?

Have a decent (petroleum fires type) fire extinguisher ready and don't run the engine in the workshop. Take the car outside and stay upwind of the exhaust fumes if you're going to be a while searching around the engine bay. Don't wear a tie, scarf or other loose clothing which can be caught in the moving parts of the engine.

Any of the problems listed above can be cured by relatively simple re-routing, trimming and

even by the application of special heat-resistant alloy/asbestos sheet available from kit car parts suppliers. Be patient. Even though the car is close to roadworthiness, don't expect it to drive reliably until you've been through these areas with a fine-toothed comb.

Nasty aspects of engine bays we have noticed in ill-prepared demo or amateur built cars include haphazard routing of wires and fluid pipes. Try to keep the (well insulated) loom out of sight as far as possible and run the fuel and brake lines in neat, straight runs with regular corners, parallel to adjacent bodywork or other lines etc. Don't just run them straight to their destinations or it'll appear chaotic.

Another commonly found fault is roughly hewn holes through the bulkhead for control or speedo cables and loom

Top: Painting the underside of wheelarches to stop light penetration. Below: A simple engine bay is the result of very careful installation. Right: Sometimes it's impossible to keep tidy.

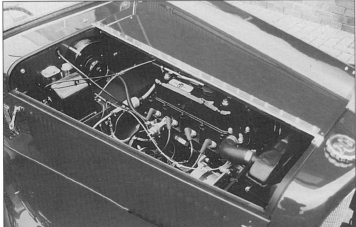

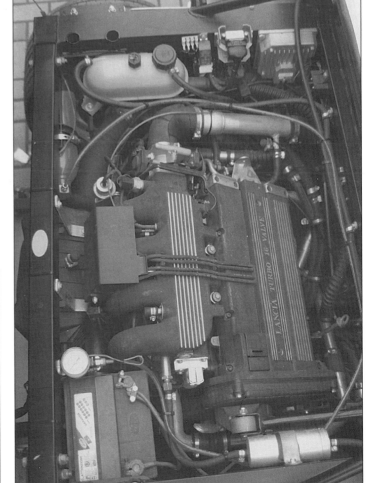

sections. Try to rationalise your hole-cutting so that various pipes and cables can use the same hole. Try to fit a panel grommet in each hole to make it weatherproof.

Never choose a kit or an engine option that requires use of no air filter or a tiny pancake air filter squashed up against the bonnet or the engine bay sides. It's very naff and can lead to extremes of lean or rich fuel mixture at high engine speed even if the carb has been re-jetted or if it seems OK on tickover.

If you can't use the engine donor's standard air filter, then use the largest possible K&N or other quality after-market filter available. If the filter protrudes through the bonnet, it'll need rain protection by a bonnet bulge panel or by an integral or hand made waterproof top.

Other uglies include nasty thin aftermarket HT leads (go for the thickly insulated and suppressed type like NGK - long spark plug caps are essential), a grubby mechanical cooling fan too far from the radiator to do any good (use an electric fan and thermostatic sender in unit with the radiator), any inelegant makeshift brackets and supports (round off all corners and paint for maximum discretion), coolant drying marks and other evidence of overheating around the coolant cap.

Overheating might simply be due to incorrect bleeding of the cooling system, wrong settings on a cooling fan thermostatic switch, pressure loss in the cooling system due to a leak or bad cap, incorrect engine or carburettor settings, jammed coolant thermostat, a clogged second hand radiator and even a lack of anti-freeze in the coolant. If all else is in order, then it may be that the radiator itself is too small. What was fitted to the company demo car? Did it work well?

If there are problems here, the manufacturer and the owners club are your best sources of information again. Fear not. Someone will know a better radiator that can be fitted and nationwide companies like Serck Marston can build you a custom radiator at a surprisingly reasonable charge.

Again, logic must prevail in tidying an engine bay. Hopefully, you will have spotted the problem areas and rectified them at the mechanical and body fitting stage. Some faults will only become evident after use but we still see others that defy belief. No access to fluid reservoirs, parts of the exhaust, engine, rocker cover or oil filler neck rubbing against the bonnet or other bodywork, no coolant expansion bottle, horribly low and exposed sump etc.

A lot of these can be avoided with careful study of the company demo car and other amateur built examples using the same engine as yours. Once you have read these warnings, make sure you ask the relevant questions, especially if you're thinking of fitting a non-standard engine or gearbox and don't know of anyone who has done it before.

Section 3
The underworld

SOME OF THE TASKS LISTED in the preceding sections are far from simple, last minute adjustments. Don't think that the difficult jobs are over just because the kit is nearly finished. Granted, the better sorted kits with the better build manuals will leave fewer surprises for the builder. Last-minute horrors can also be predicted in advance when talking to the manufacturer or club members.

Keep yourself in an objective mode, as if you were a vehicle inspector or other kit car enthusiast with high critical standards, and get the car firmly supported on its axle stands/wheel ramps again. Take a last look underneath for anything that might need tidying.

Remember that the nuts and bolts relating to suspension parts equipped with rubber bushes should not be tightened at all until the vehicle is resting on its wheels under its full weight. It is, however, worth checking other fasteners for tightness in case you forgot them earlier. Make a

Top: One-off bonnet bulge seen from underside of bonnet helps hide SU carb on a Rover V8. This air filter will be doing more harm than good. Below: Some decent ITG air filters.

It doesn't matter how big the radiator, air must also be able to escape from the engine bay. Side panel vents such as these on a Marlin Roadster work very well.

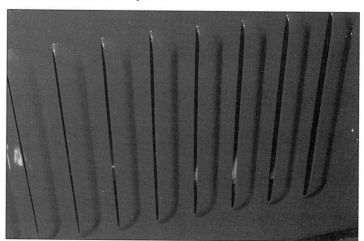

comprehensive written list, with diagrams if necessary, of all the bolts that will need last minute tightening.

Other things you're looking for, as we have mentioned before, are floor or other panel mounting bolts which are too long and protrude more than a few threads out past the nut. Replace them with screws or bolts of the right length. Sharp self-tappers protruding anywhere are a complete no-no. Similarly, you should replace bolts that are too short to reach through the nut.

Can you see a component or pipe which might be affected by a suspension component or axle with the suspension at full bump? Remember that the car's suspension can become fully compressed at just one corner, at one side or all round. Suspensions at full bump should come up against proper bump stops before hitting anything else. Brake pipes and other cables can be sandwiched by compressed coil springs.

Full bump can be approximated by removing coil springs, coil-over shock units or torsion bar springs. You'll need to estimate where a leaf-sprung axle will end up on full bump. Full droop happens when the kit is supported on axle stands placed at suitably strong points on the monocoque or chassis.

Are all solid and flexible

If you're making up your own brake lines it's very important to cut the pipes correctly. A hacksaw may leave swarf in the pipe. Special tool is not expensive and cuts cleanly and squarely.

brake lines clear of the wheels, suspension, tyres and bodywork at full suspension bump, droop and from lock to lock at the front wheels? Are the flexi pipes a little too long or short to cover the full range of wheel movement?

Goodridge Aeroquip braided brake flexi pipes can be made to order by companies such as BGC who advertise in *Which Kit?* The club or the manufacturer might be able to tell you the part number of a production car brake hose that will suit your needs at a relatively small cost. After-market suppliers can sell you the tools and materials to make up your own kunifer solid brake lines with the appropriate

threaded connectors each end.

A handful of tough tiewrap plastic strips can cure a dangling handbrake cable, overflow pipe, fuel tank breather, speedo or clutch cable. Don't tighten them so much that the operation of the supported component is affected adversely.

Even if you have painted or undersealed the lower body surfaces and the chassis, there's a good case for repainting any corners or patches that might have been missed or scratched during the build.

Some builders recommend that you use non-hardening sealant along the edges where the chassis meets the body or

at panel joins, so that water can't find its way in and start a rust problem. Be careful not to paint or seal over threads, screw or bolt heads that you can reasonably expect to use in the foreseeable future.

Check the entire exhaust system for proximity to GRP or other flammable material. This is particularly important if you have a catalytic converter fitted. Don't hesitate to stick asbestos/alloy mat onto nearby surfaces to shield them. Your DIY shop should be able to recommend a fire-proof glue to use.

If the car has already been road tested for a few miles, you can look out for any scuffing or rubbing. This might be found to the side of or above the propshaft of a live axled car, on the bottom of a low sump and adjacent to any of the tyres.

A propshaft/live axle showing evidence of excessive side to side play might be the result of worn leaf springs and/or worn metalastic bushes. Remember that live axles with leaf springs do move sideways a lot even when new, (it's more a question of the car chassis/body moving in relation to the axle) unless located by extra arms such as a Panhard rod.

If you've fitted the correct prop and there's only a half inch clearance between the rear propshaft flange and the tunnel,

As we've shown earlier, you can bend brake pipes by hand but a special tool isn't expensive and can guarantee (almost!) good results every time.

Cutting around suspension, exhaust or anything else that protrudes from the bodywork needs careful and accurate preparations. Always take off too little first if in doubt.

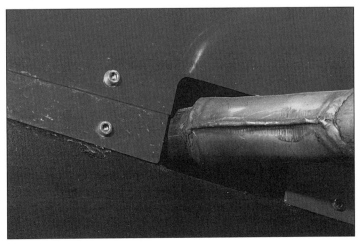

Above: Propshaft flange in a live axle car may cause side-to-side clearance problems if axle is located by leaf springs and space is tight. Below: A rough and ready wheel back-depth measurement.

Above: R-rated radial tyre, 195mm wide, section height 60% of width, 14" internal diameter. Below: Arches must cover tread. Watch for rubbing on full lock/bump.

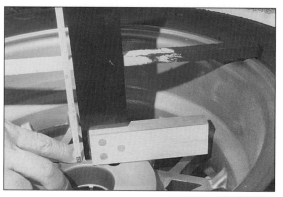

it could be bad kit design or a poorly fitted body. It's likely that you'll need firm axle location aids to stop the sideways shift or a re-make of the tunnel section. The kit manufacturer might offer a Panhard rod kit or the club might know a way around the problem.

Propshaft rubbing at the top extreme of movement is likely to be an indication of poor design, worn springs, worn bushes, wrong spring rate, ineffective bump stop rubbers or a combination of these. Obviously, beefier bump stops might be the cheapest way out of this one.

If it's the sump that's rubbing

after only a few miles of experimental use, expect it to become a big problem as the suspension all settles into place. If the sump gets punctured by a manhole cover etc., you could have a seized engine in no time flat.

Unless an off-the-shelf baffled shallow sump conversion exists, you might have to settle for a steel sump guard welded or bolted into place. Be careful that it leaves you service and engine removal access if it's a permanent fixture.

It should be angled (viewed from vehicle side elevation),

sloping down from the front of the car to just lower than the lower front edge of the sump. In this way it can slide over obstacles without stopping you dead and it doesn't drastically reduce ground clearance.

The meticulous kit builder will want the underside of the vehicle to look clean, simple and functional. Some even go to the extent of covering it with alloy sheet for a clean underbelly.

A messy, multicoloured jumble of odd nuts, bolts, self-tappers and dripping mastic won't do you any favours with the MoT tester. Because you are an amateur, the onus is on you to show just how well you can do the job. Don't forget to tighten last suspension bolts to the recommended torque

settings when the vehicle has settled on its wheels.

Section 4
Rolling stock

A GOOD KIT MANUFACTURER will give you precise information about wheels and tyres. Don't be tempted to go for maximum wheel width just because it makes the vehicle look good. If the manufacturer has worked it all out properly, then there will be an approved selection of wheels with the correct diameter, rim width and offset. Suitable tyre sizes should also be supplied.

These statistics should enable you to purchase a set of specially made wheels if the manufacturer doesn't supply wheels to your liking. Never use wheels of incorrect specification to enhance a vehicle's look. Incorrect wheel/tyre fitments can ruin a car and cause a road hazard.

Wheel and tyre specifications

Above: Correct offset is vital but excess tyre width can still foul obstructions from lock to lock or bump to droop. Below: 3-piece wheel gives a choice of bolt-on rim widths to alter offset.

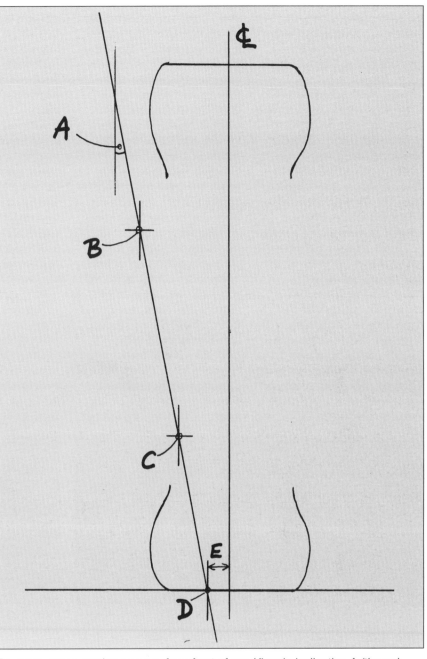

Front tyre cross-section as seen from front of car. Kingpin inclination A (through ball joint B and C) hits road at D. Distance E, to wheel/tyre centreline, is (positive) offset.

are closely linked with steering geometry, so it would be true to say that wheel sizes and offsets are a little less critical at the back end of the car. At the front, the designer or kit manufacturer must have done some homework to get the geometry right or within safe limits.

Wheel rim and tyre widths must be finalised with relation to the space available in the wheel arches, especially at the front where the wheels steer from lock to lock. Widths must be calculated so that when the vehicle body/chassis is in roll or pitch, when any suspension assembly is at full droop or bump or when the steering is at full lock, the wheels or tyres do not foul any part of the vehicle.

Overall diameter of the wheel/tyre combination, decided by the diameter of the wheel and by the profile (aspect ratio) of the tyre, must also be sufficiently small to allow for clearances within the wheel arches, especially on full bump and full lock.

It must also provide the vehicle with suitable drive gearing when the specified gearbox and differential are fitted. Some kits suffer from under-gearing due to insufficient wheel/tyre diameter. This means that your car is quick off the mark but the engine is screaming away at a mere 70mph.

Unfortunately, there aren't always alternative gearboxes and diffs available to sort the problem out. Find out what gearbox, diff. ratio, wheels and tyres the company demo car uses. Hardly any kit cars suffer from under-gearing.

With the steering straight ahead, none of the tyre tread should be visible protruding beyond the wheel arches. Preferably, no part of the wheel or tyre should protrude beyond

THE WHICH KIT? TIP
More often than not, a manufacturer may recommend two different sizes of wheel/tyre combinations. A 15" alloy with a medium profile tyre may be the standard while a 16" alloy with ultra low profile tyre may be the more expensive and fancy option. Both may work quite admirably, but expect the lower profile option to give the car a firmer ride. Do you really want that for a touring car? Probably not. Think carefully before you plump for looks over practicality

the arches. This is primarily so that debris thrown up by the tyre will normally hit the arches or mudflaps and not other road users. They are also mostly shielded from contact with the tyres of other vehicles in the case of collision.

The most complex aspect of wheel/tyre specification relates to something called wheel offset. (See diagram in this section for further detail). If you view a wheel from the vehicle dead ahead position (wheel standing vertical), imagine a vertical line or plane through the centre of the wheel. Call this the centreline.

If that wheel is actually transparent, you can see the edge of the inner mounting face. This is the surface of the wheel which is pushed flush against the vehicle's hub or brake drum when the wheel nuts are tightened up. Imagine a vertical line or plane level with this surface.

If the plane or line extended up and down from the wheel mounting surface is 'inboard' of the centreline, the horizontal distance between the centreline and the mounting surface is called the wheel (positive) offset. If the mounting surface is 'outboard' of the centreline, the distance between them is called the wheel negative offset (or inset). The latter is prevalent on front or four wheel drive cars, the former on rear drive cars.

If you tell your chosen kit manufacturer that you want to get some after-market wheels made up especially for your kit, you should be furnished with the relevant information as to wheel width, offset/inset, tyre width, speed rating and profile.

Offset can also be described by stating the rim width and the subsequent back depth. Back depth is the horizontal distance measured between the vertical

plane of the wheel mounting face and the vertical plane through the inboard rim. If the back depth is smaller than half the wheel rim width, the wheel has a positive offset and vice versa.

Offset and inset are designed into a steering geometry in order to ameliorate steering characteristics such as self-centering (directional stability) and lightness of steering feel when stationary and at low speed. Excessive positive offset could mean that the steering will pull strongly to one side if a front wheel is punctured or if braking on a slippery surface.

Needless to say that if none of the manufacturer's staff can give you specific measurements for the (real or theoretical) wheels that you want to order, think carefully about how well the kit has been designed. Just because the kit uses one or two

complete donor subframes, it shouldn't necessarily adopt the donor wheel offset and diameter. What is fitted to the company's demo car?

Section 5
Glossing over

ONLY WHEN YOU ARE SURE that the vast majority of the interior, wiring and mechanical work is complete should you start to initiate the final body finishing process. From now on, you shouldn't be expecting to drill or cut more holes in or near the body.

If your bodyshell has a de-flashed final gel colour, protective sheets should have left you with just a touch of polishing to do for the final look. Light scratches can be removed by using very fine wet 'n' dry abrasive paper, used wet,

Above: Alloys can certainly lift the look of your car, but their specification is vital. Below: We'd advise you always take your kit manufacturer's advice on wheel/tyre sizes.

Above: A laminator carefully paints gel colour resin into a body mould prior to the matting. Good quality moulds will give you a great finish without the need for painting.

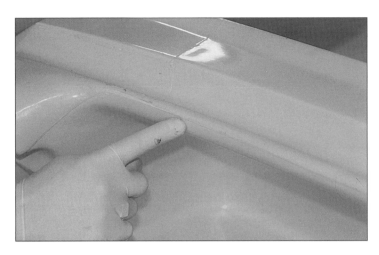

followed by a slightly abrasive polish like chrome cleaner and then T-Cut for the final shine.

Avoid using power tools for this job as it is possible to damage the gel with friction. Tackle small areas at a time, removing polish or T-Cut with cotton cloth. Retired bed sheets are good for this.

Flash lines are thin flanges of gelcoat which have seeped into the joins between mould sections. In the knowledge that you'll be trimming these away and smoothing them flush with the adjacent bodywork, the good laminator will have left a slightly thicker gel coat layer under the flash line to compensate for minor mistakes you might make.

You need to be more careful when removing flashlines and other moulding marks from a final gelcoat. If the gel is destined for a paint finish, a few stray scratches and blemishes can be made good with paste or spray filler.

Initially, flash lines can be reduced in size by scraping with a very sharp Stanley knife held across the line and perpendicular to the body surface. Keeping the blade clear of the rest of the gelcoat, you will be able to gradually scrape away at the thicker base of the flash line until there's too much risk of scraping the adjacent gel surfaces or of scraping too much gel away under the flash line. A sharp, flat file can also help in some areas.

Laminators par excellence Pilgrim Cars of Small Dole, near Brighton, recommend that you finish off by using 1200-grit wet and dry on a sanding block and then Farecla G7 and G3 cutting compounds. It takes one of their trained staff members, using all the correct materials and tools, two days to completely de-flash a Sumo bodyshell!

While de-flashing or polishing a gel finish body, you might uncover certain small pinholes and hidden air pockets or accidentally damage and chip the gelcoat. Get some colour-matched gel resin from the manufacturer. Used with a hardener, this thick liquid can be used to fill up holes in the gelcoat.

If necessary, 'dig out' pinholes or air pockets to make sure you've revealed the whole lot and to make the filling job a bit easier. Any surface abnormalities can then be smoothed down in the same manner as de-flashing. If the body is to be painted, then you can be a bit more abrupt and fill holes with a standard flexible body filler like Plastic Padding or Isopon.

A professional paint job, using modern two-pack acrylic paint, seems to be in the region of £1000 for GRP, alloy, steel or combination bodies. You can buy and rent sufficient equipment to do this in your own workshop and take a few goes at getting it right with cellulose paint for this kind of money but it is time-consuming.

If you're going to go it alone, you must embark on yet another workshop clean-up, especially if you're painting a whole body tub instead of a collection of panels. You need room to walk around the work. There must be nearly zero dust when spraying, even though there's plenty of sanding to be done.

Remove the bodyshell or dismantle it into separate panels if at all possible and put the rolling chassis under cover outside the workshop. This can save a lot of masking effort and

Top: These are typical flash lines on a GTM K3 centre tub. Below: Removal can innitially be done with a file but go very steadily and, if in doubt, move on to wet-n-dry paper.

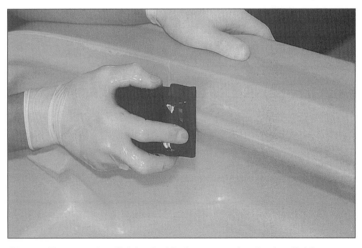

Above: Once you've finished with the wet-n-dry, final polishing can be done with special cutting compounds. Below: A paint job on something like this Mirage Countach replica can cost £2000+.

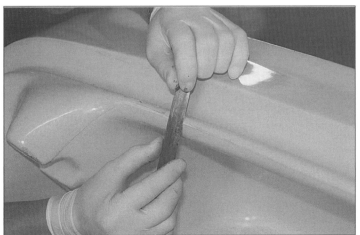

means no accidental overspray on engine or interior equipment.

If the shell, or part of it, must stay on the chassis, you must mask and cover every surface that you don't want to paint. This stuff will get everywhere. It's better to use proper masking tape and thick brown paper from a roll or special masking paper, not newspaper as it can leave marks.

First priority is to key all surfaces to be painted and make sure that they are free of contamination. Use 600 grit wet 'n' dry, with a water and detergent mix, over every surface (but keep wood dry).

You can get sponge-backed sanding blocks of varying coarseness which are particularly handy to use with water/detergent. Using the wet 'n' dry with water and soap keeps down the dust in the workshop.

After thorough keying up, rinse away the detergent. When the panels are dry, a quick wipe over with cellulose thinners or white spirit should get rid of any

remaining nasties. Keep the workshop well ventilated at this stage and remember that solvent/paint is highly flammable and can cause explosion in vapour form.

Home paint jobs are most often done using cellulose paint products. This stuff is none too friendly but it's apparently a lot better than modern two-pack acrylic paints which have a cyanide content. The safety equipment required to spray two-pack is beyond the reach of most amateur sprayers.

Locate a knowledgeable automotive paint supplier for guidance on quantities and prices. Typically, you'll need a high quality anti-bloom thinners, acid etch primer (probably yellow), high-build primer/filler (probably grey), your final gloss colour and a few aerosols of cellulose gloss

Special paint schemes can be difficult to map out and visualise on a car. Painting a scale model can really help (if such a thing exists).

(probably white or black). A quantity of cheap thinners might also be handy for the repeated cleaning of the spraygun.

Calibrated disposable paint mixing containers are good for getting the right ratio of thinners to paint. Large quarter or half sheet sanding blocks are useful for rubbing down and you'll need a selection of wet 'n' dry grades from 400 grit to a finishing 1200 grit. These are better when cloth-backed as opposed to paper-backed.

Your paint supplier or local hire shop should rent you an electric compressor and matched spray gun with an

output of at least 45psi. Get clear instructions as to the operation, dismantling and cleaning of the spray gun and make sure they know it's for cellulose car spraying. Don't use cheap electric 'airless' spray guns or any which can't output 45psi. Aerosols are right out of the question for large jobs.

Major setbacks can be caused by humidity, cold, dust or swift temperature changes on all or part of the paintwork. It's better to do the job in a well ventilated workshop over several hot summer days.

If you have to do it in the winter, a good workshop set-up

Above: Accidents will happen! Repairing GRP panels can be done at home, even when the damage looks severe. Below: Having cleaned up the torn edges, the torn off parts can be taped into place.

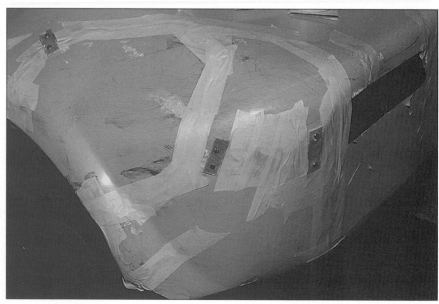

might include a powerful electric fan heater, with an uninhibited source of intake air, and a good extractor fan at the other end of the garage. Both of these will be positioned high to avoid disturbing floor dust. Bottled gas heaters produce moisture and flame.

Mask and seal off any doors into the house and cover anything in the workshop that you don't want to paint. Don't park the family car near the extractor outlet or it'll suffer too.

Equip yourself with a full boiler suit, preferably a disposable sprayer's suit with hood, gloves and overboots. Avoid getting any paint on your skin. Use your nose/mouth air filter mask and goggles, you might even put barrier cream on the exposed parts of your face. Design useful props, hooks and supports for the separate panels so that they can be sprayed from all sides and moved while still wet.

It can get highly unpleasant in a hot, dry spray room so drink water beforehand. If the fumes are making you light-headed, there is insufficient ventilation. Walk out into the open until you feel better and then tackle the ventilation problem. These vapours can be highly damaging to brain tissue. If you get any kind of allergic reaction that might be attributable to the paint or thinners, see your doctor immediately.

Acid etch primer is recommended for alloy surfaces but there's no harm in putting it onto GRP as well. It should be thinned as per instructions and only one or two coats are needed. When it is dry apply up to three coats of primer filler, thinned as specified by the paint

manufacturer/supplier, and allow to dry off. With an aerosol of any vividly contrasting cellulose paint, spray over the whole body or the panels.

When dry again, use a large sanding block (wherever possible) with 400-600 grit wet 'n' dry used wet. Sand lightly over all the surfaces and you'll see that the block removes the aerosol colour and some primer from any high points but leaves them intact in the low points.

Be careful but it doesn't matter if you get down to the etch primer or body surface in places. Leave the low points alone once they have been

revealed by the sanding block. Rinse off any residue and allow to dry.

Keep applying two or three extra coats of the thinned primer filler, followed by the aerosol colour and wet sanding with the block and 400-600 grit. Remember to clean up the spraygun immediately after each spray session is complete. Once the paint dries inside it, you've got big trouble.

This painting and sanding technique will build the low points up level with the high points. Your sanding block and 400 grit will eventually remove all of the aerosol colour evenly

Above: Cover the whole repair area with a layer of mat and resin. Below: Grind off any rough edges and rub whole lot down with 40 grade production paper. It's hard work!

Above: Once the under-surface has been cleaned, 4" wide strips of mat can be applied to the underside of the cracks along with the resin. Below: With tape removed, clean up the outer surface so that only solid material remains.

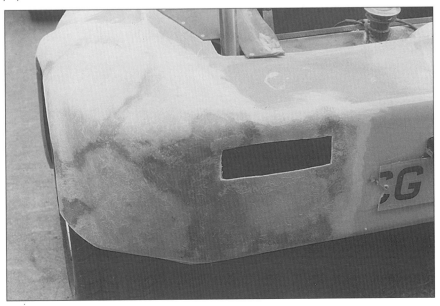

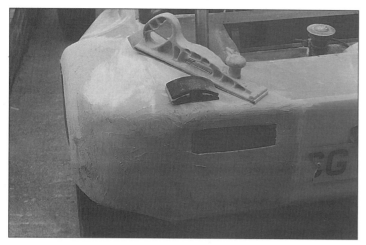

Above: A final layer of filler will help to smooth out any high and low spots. Below: An orbital sander can be a boon but pure hard graft works just as well.

Above: Final smoothing down should be done with wet 'n' dry paper. Below: A decent paint supplier should be able to colour match paint and then it's just a matter of spraying it on! Simple.

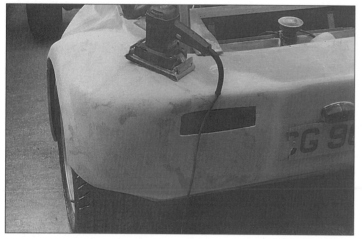

with light sanding and you will no longer be revealing the surface or etch primer. Don't attempt to fill 'huge' body panel depressions in this way, you'll need body filling paste to get them near smooth.

When you are satisfied with the levelness of the body or panels, finish off with a few more coats of primer filler. Don't sand after these. You may end up taking several days to complete this stage and may apply many coats, so it's difficult to know how much of the stuff to buy beforehand.

Be patient, you need to get the primer coat nice and even for the top coat. It's like providing a good foundation for a house. High gloss surfaces will show off any ripples, dips and bumps with merciless detail. Don't be fooled by the apparent smoothness of the mat-finish primer.

You will probably have thinned your etch primer and primer filler with around 50% thinners. Much the same applies for the top coat gloss cellulose but defer to the supplier's or manufacturer's recommendations. Having left the last primer coat to dry for a few days, apply four or five gloss coats, allowing the paint to dry between each.

How does it look? Blemishes, dust, lumps? (Expect the orange peel effect, though). Sand it down wet with some very fine paper, cure the dust problem in the garage and apply another four or five coats. If it's still OK, apply another four to five coats, allowing it to dry between each. Some sprayers say that a final two coats can be applied with 60% thinners to improve smoothness.

Leave the whole lot a few days to dry off properly before attempting to cut and polish the surface. This should be done with very fine wet 'n' dry used with a strong detergent solution to keep the abrasive unclogged. It's best to do this manually and very gently. Power tools are still inappropriate. Avoid excess heat due to friction.

Having sanded it all with very fine paper, rinse off the residue, allow to dry and finish off with T-Cut and plenty of fresh non-abrasive polishing cloth. Tackle small areas at a time. A special slow-speed random orbital sanding machine with sheepskin polishing bonnets is handy for this but again be careful of overheating the paint. Leave this newly 'cut' surface for at least a week or two before polishing and don't polish in direct sunlight.

It might look superb but you haven't won yet. Once the paint is exposed to direct sunlight, any moisture trapped below the surface will happily bubble up and cause blistering that can be widespread. Your paint shop atmosphere wasn't dry enough. Sand down and try the top coats again.

Moisture can also cause a 'bloom' or odd contours like small explosions or 'splats'. Sand down a bit and try again, maybe when the weather is hotter or if you can organise some serious de-humidifiers in the workshop.

Reassembling your panels or bodyshell onto the chassis and refitting all other components should be done with extreme care and there should be little or no further work to be done on the kit that involves activity close to the paintwork. From the minute the painting is complete, it will inevitably start getting scratched. That's life.

Chapter 10

PAPERWORK

Introduction

REGISTERING YOUR KIT PRIOR TO SVA
Section 1: MoT
Section 2: Registration
Section 3: Construction and Use

REGISTERING YOUR KIT AFTER SVA IMPLEMENTATION
Section 1: Revised registration procedures
Section 2: What is SVA?
Section 3: SVA basics
Section 4: SVA tests outlined

Introduction

AS WE GO TO PRESS, THE way in which you can register your completed kit car for the road is in the process of changing. Single Vehicle Approval looks set to take over where considerably more flexible and simple registration processes are in place today. At the time of writing it appears that traditional methods of making your kit road legal have just months to run, but new regulations have a habit of getting delayed and Single Vehicle Approval has been threatening for a number of years.

As such, this chapter really has to be divided into two sections: The regulations as they stand today (the latter part of 1996) and the proposals for Single Vehicle Approval. The official 'launch' date for SVA is April 1997, but none of us would be too surprised if it took longer.

Equally important for you to bear in mind when reading this chapter is that we have only been able to work from draft proposals for the SVA and some areas may change as the documents progress towards becoming law. We don't expect many alterations, but you should certainly check it out nearer the time your kit approaches the registration process. Which Kit? magazine should keep you up to date with progress.

REGISTERING YOUR KIT PRIOR TO SVA

Section 1
MoT

A CHASSIS OR VEHICLE Identification Number must be permanently affixed to the car chassis or body in at least one visible spot under the bonnet or at the front of the vehicle. MoT inspectors will need to find it easily, as will the staff of the Vehicle Registration Office when it comes to registration for the car.

If there is no chassis number supplied by the manufacturer, then you should certainly phone up and ask for a VIN or chassis number plate to be sent to you, free of charge, by the manufacturer. Some builders in this situation have ended up devising a chassis number of their own but many will ask the local VRO to supply one. An MoT will be impossible without it.

It is usually far easier to buy insurance from the specialist companies advertising in Which Kit?. Your local high street broker will rarely be conversant in the ways of kit car policies but will probably quote you an outrageous price.

Specialist kit car insurers will be more sympathetic to the bureaucratic delays suffered by the car builder waiting to register a newly built kit car. As it happens, insurers' willingness to cover a kit on the strength of its chassis number is absolutely essential, as this is the first major step in getting the car registered.

Amateur builders, acting on advice from their local VRO, the kit manufacturer or friends or the club, will set about registering their kit cars in different ways. When your car is, to the best of your knowledge, finished and ready for the road, even for a short journey, then you can think seriously about registering it for the road. Once you've got the valid insurance cover note, you are legally permitted to drive the car to a pre-booked MoT in the local area.

The wise kit builder will have conspired to get a copy of the MoT tester's standard failure slip. This will give you an excellent idea of what the car will be tested for. If you're not totally familiar with the MoT requirements, you

Because this Quantum retains its donor registration you can see that the MoT certificate has the original Fiesta's registration in place along with Quantum's own chassis number. Vehicle name is also put as 'Quantum'. If it had read simply 'Fiesta XR2' that would not have been good enough and the Police would not be amused!

The motor vehicle of which the Registration Mark	D 734 XCF.

QH 0904761

having been examined under section 45 of the Road Traffic Act 1988, it is hereby certified that at the date of the examination thereof the statutory requirements prescribed by Regulations made under the said section 45 were complied with in relation to the vehicle.

Vehicle identification or chassis number   Q139

Vehicle Testing Station Number   O212B5   Vehicle colour   BLUE

Whatever kit you are building, you'll need a chassis plate clearly positioned somewhere in the engine bay and firmly attached to the body/chassis. This Caterham chassis plate has all manner of details included on it beyond the chassis number.

may omit an essential feature from your vehicle. You can't always presume that manufacturers' build manuals are always right up to date.

When you think that your car is ready, phone around the local MoT stations to see which of them has most experience of kit cars and modified cars. There have been so many kit car sales that it's more than likely one of them will have experience of the hitherto 'unknown.' Other local owners might give you guidance here.

If you have managed to get an insurance cover note, book the test and drive carefully to the MoT centre. It'll probably be your first drive of any length in the car and it feels glorious, although most builders are a little nervous as to whether it'll all work or not.

Go easy because you will still need to get the tracking properly sorted, the engine accurately tuned, headlamps properly

aligned and, in the case of adjustable suspensions, you might need to change the castor, camber, spring and damping rates.

There's a chance that the MoT garage will be able to do a pre-MoT inspection and give you some warning of things that your vehicle might fail on. They might also be able to adjust the suspension settings to the manufacturer's specifications etc. You will be able to decide whether to get the car home and sort potential MoT problems yourself before re-booking the test proper.

Bear in mind that if you go straight for the MoT test, it is theoretically not permissible to drive the car home if it fails. It must be transported home or repaired in situ at the garage premises.

Assuming your car will be registered using a Q-plate, the current emission test requires

only a visual smoke test but if you are able and intend to use the donor car's registration then the emissions test will relate to the donor car's year of manufacture.

If all the mechanical parts used to build your kit are brand new and you intend to get a current prefix registration, the MoT tester will have to give you an emissions test relating to the age and type of the engine fitted. You may be penalised for fitting non-standard fuel or induction/aspiration systems to a new engine designed with a different set-up.

MoTs are becoming tougher all the time and much more pressure is being put on MoT stations to be ever vigilant and strict. They are usually particularly strict in the kit car department because an inept amateur car builder might be trying to put something lethal on the road, in ignorance.

You shouldn't let the car get as far as the MoT station if the tyres

rub on anything at full lock, if the exhaust blows or leaks anywhere, if there is a brake fluid (or any) leak, if the lights, wipers, washers, seatbelts, doors, seat mounts, ignition switch and other obvious functions are less than perfect. You'll be wasting your money and you won't be able to argue a valid defence.

Eventually, you'll get a pass. This doesn't mean that you can drive all over the world with a 'number-plate applied for' sticker front and rear. You are allowed to drive straight home and that's all. The MoT station will write down your vehicle's chassis number on the certificate, as there is still no registration mark.

Section 2
Registration

NOW'S THE TIME TO SET about getting a registration document, registration mark and

The first side of the V55/5 looks pretty complex but your kit's manufacturer or club associates will tell you just what to fill in and where. Information such as chassis number and vehicle weight must come from the manufacturer. Phone VRO if in doubt.

Department of Transport

Please do not write above this line

Application for a First Licence for a Motor Vehicle and Declaration for Registration

S ☐   **3070990**   **V55/5** Rev. Aug. 92

* See note at foot of page

1 Registration Mark
2 Taxation Class
3 Period of Licence Applied for — MONTHS ☐ WEEKS
4 Duty payable £
5 Make
6 Model
7 Type of Body/Vehicle
8 Wheelplan
9 Colour(s)
10 *Hackney Class Only* Seating Capacity (Exclusive of driver)

Official Use Only — Receipt Number — 3 / 4 / 5 / 9 / 11 / 13 / 15 / 17 / 19

Important *In your own interests, before completing this form, please read the booklet V355 The First Licensing and Registration of Motor Vehicles. Please complete the form in black ball-point pen or typewriter and in BLOCK LETTERS.*

11 Date from which Licence is to run (and Date of Registration) — Day / Month / Year — 7 — Official Use Only 8
12 Type of Fuel — 10
13 V.I.N./Chassis/Frame No. (IN FULL) — 12
14 Engine Number — 14
15 Cylinder Capacity (in cc) — 16
16 Gross Weight — Tons / Kg — 18
17 Unladen Weight — Tons / cwt / lbs / Kg — 20

110 | 111 | Used | Re-reg. | Export | Captive | Private | B'ness | Fleet
| | U | R | E | C | P | B | F

Original Dealer Code | Original Dealer (Name, Address and Postcode) | Selling Dealer Code | Selling Dealer (Name, Address and Postcode)

This box must be completed ▶ Type Approval — 113
Official Use Only — AB 21 / WC 22 / SN 23 / SPMK 24
Date of first registration abroad

17a Is the vehicle new? **In either case, please write the last 2 digits of the year of the vehicle's manufacture in this box.** NOTE: If it is new, evidence of newness must be supplied in the form of a statement of vehicle particulars from the manufacturer/importer. If it **is not** new, **attach an explanation of why it has not previously been registered.** — 19 ☐ 25 — Answer YES or NO.........

18 If the vehicle is constructed or adapted for the carriage of goods (this includes dual-purpose vehicles of the estate car type) will it be used at any time to carry goods or burden (including samples) for or in connection with a trade or business or for hire or reward?. — Answer YES or NO.........

19 Will the vehicle be used with a detachable container for carrying goods etc? — Answer YES or NO.........

20 Will the vehicle be used to draw a trailer (including a caravan)? If the answer is YES will the trailer be used to carry goods or burden (including samples) for or in connection with a trade or business or for hire or reward? — Answer YES or NO......... — Answer YES or NO.........

21 Have any alterations been made of the kind mentioned in the note on this question in the booklet 'Notes on Completion of Vehicle Registration Forms'? — Answer YES or NO.........
If the answer is YES were these changes made after the vehicle came into your possession? — Answer YES or NO.........

tax disc for your vehicle. This is simpler than you might think and has been helped recently by some far clearer guidelines being issued by the DVLA regarding whether a car can retain the donor's registration mark or whether it will end up with a Q-plate.

Directory enquiries, your phone book or the Post Office will supply the phone number of your nearest Vehicle Registration Office (formerly the Local Vehicle Licensing Office). You might be midway between two areas and have the choice.

Give them a quick phone call to explain that you want to register a newly constructed kit car (now officially known as a 'kit conversion' unless absolutely all of the parts are supplied by the kit manufacturer). You'll need form V55/5 from the VRO and any associated forms or instructions.

While you're on the phone, enquire about the current waiting lists for home vehicle inspections and VRO site inspections. There might be a big difference between the two and this may encourage you to get the car inspected sooner at the VRO's premises or chosen test centre.

You were allowed to drive an insured kit car to the MoT, and from it when it passed. You apparently are not permitted to drive the same car to be inspected at the VRO test centre. It must be transported there on a car trailer or similar. As such, many enthusiasts go for a home inspection.

This involves the VRO sending a roving inspector to look at your car wherever you're keeping it. They usually can't be specific about when they're turning up, so you'll have to be sure that you have the whole day available to show them the car.

When you get your V55/5, it will probably come with a host of other documentation. Don't be alarmed, it's not all that complicated. There's usually a very copious set of notes describing how to fill it in. There's the V55/5 itself and also another vehicle report form asking for

details of the donor, new or special parts you used for the build-up of your kit car.

If your manufacturer has done the necessary homework, then the kit's build manual will include all the details you need to complete the V55/5 accurately. If there are no guidelines at all, then telephone the manufacturer or a club member for more details. You will notice that the V55/5 is a very wide-ranging form and many of the sections will not apply to your vehicle.

Any questions about the make and model of the car must be answered with the kit manufacturer's company name and kit model. You'll be lying if you try to register a Cobra lookalike as a rebodied Jaguar 4.2 or as a Ford Granada 2.8.

The main reason for registering your kit with its own correct make and model names is to keep you out of trouble with the police. If you zoom past a police car in your newly-built V8 Pramhood LX, and the police officer checks your registration mark, he or she will be rather bemused to find that this open two-seater bristling with bell-mouths is registered as a rebodied Renault 4. Certain misunderstandings could then follow.

As we have mentioned, cars which have been made using the engine, gearbox and some suspension/brake parts from one donor stand a good chance of getting that donor's registration mark. According to the DVLA's most recent info on the subject, *'The Registration of Rebuilt or Radically Altered Vehicles and Kit Cars'*, different parts of a donor car are awarded points, and the kit builder has to use enough of these parts to assemble a points score of eight or above. The points system is below:

Donor chassis or both subframes	2 points
Suspension	2 points
Axles	2 points
Transmission	2 points
Steering assembly	2 points
Engine	1 point

The other way of legally avoiding a Q-plate is to build a kit car using all-new parts and register it as a current prefix vehicle. You need absolutely all the receipts and a certificate of newness to be supplied by the kit manufacturer. Some kit manufacturers will not issue a certificate of newness unless they sold you all the relevant parts. Check beforehand if you're taking this route.

You guessed it, once a Q-plate, always a Q-plate. You can't change it once your vehicle has it, although we have heard that it's possible if you export the vehicle, register it somewhere abroad for a while and import it again! Probably a dubious practice, that. Sounds expensive and involved, anyway.

If you are trying to register a vehicle as an all-new car for current prefix plates or to get the donor plates, as a car using the majority of parts from a single donor, make sure that you tell the VRO (politely) what you would prefer. They may make a special effort in your case instead of dishing out a (usually) irreplaceable Q-plate.

On the relevant additional form, include details about all of the components you used from the donor vehicle or from elsewhere. The VRO will need to know part numbers and the registration mark of the donor vehicle if there is any chance of getting the donor's registration mark. It's far better to have the registration document relating to the donor or at least a bill of sale stating where you got the car.

We have found the VRO to be very helpful in terms of telephone advice and vehicle inspections. Keep in touch to see when you should expect a visit. They will also tell you how much it will cost to register the vehicle. This is traditionally included in the price of a six or twelve-month tax disc, which the VRO also supplies, having registered your car.

It is most likely that the VRO will ask you to post them the cheque and the V55/5, along with all receipts relevant to the kit

build, the registration document(s) for the donor vehicle(s), the MoT certificate, the insurance cover note or certificate and any other appointment forms they have asked you to complete.

They will need time to peruse these various forms before the inspection, so that they know what they're looking for when they see your car. In general, the inspector is trying to verify that the details you have given concerning the car are correct and that this is the vehicle you have described to them in the V55/5. They will need to see the chassis number or VIN plate firmly attached or stamped permanently in place.

They may look at the engine number and various other identification numbers but they won't be testing the car's features or roadworthiness. They won't need to listen to the engine (at least we've never heard of this) and they won't need to be driven in the car.

Eventually, the VRO will return your receipts, along with a new registration document, a tax disc, the MoT certificate (modified to show your registration mark) and your insurance certificate. Check the registration document and tax disc carefully to see if all the descriptions and numbers relate to your car and contact the VRO straight away if they have wrongly described the car as a Hackney/Invalid/Mowing/Tracked/Agricultural-vehicle-and-sidecar with a design speed of less than 20 mph.

Now you can attach the tax disc to the screen, get a set of number plates made up, bolt them on and start testing your vehicle properly for its intended use. At this stage, certain cautionary rules apply and you should refer to Chapter 11 and to any such points described in the kit's build manual. As we have mentioned, certain manufacturers offer free check-ups for their customers, even if you have to get the car there yourself. Take up this offer because the experienced manufacturer may well spot faults you have missed.

Only the top half of page 2 is relevant to most kit builders and is self explanatory. There's usually a third page asking for general 'car owner' information and you don't have to fill in that bit. A handy instruction booklet is often sent with the V55/5 document.

Please complete in **BLACK INK** and **BLOCK LETTERS** or typewriter.

23 Name and Address of Vehicle Keeper
Please tick box to indicate Mr. Mrs. Miss or state other title in section below:

*Unincorporated Bodies
If registration is in business or association name, please also give full name of person responsible for vehicle.

Title	Mr	1	Mrs	2	Miss	3

Other Title or Company name

Christian or other names (in full) — **26**

Surname — **27**

Address — **28**

Post Town — **29**

Postcode — (Your Registration Document may be delayed if the postcode is not entered in full) **30**

Official Use Only

	Day	Month	Year		CD		CTRM		VC		Trailer Weight	
CRED				**31**		**32**		**33**		**34**		**35**

DECLARATION To be completed in all cases.

I declare that I have checked the information given in this form and that to the best of my knowledge it is correct.

I enclose the duty payable (where appropriate)
a valid certificate of insurance (not the policy, receipt or schedule) or security in respect of liabilities to third parties which provides insurance cover for the named keeper of the vehicle
suitable evidence of unladen weight (where appropriate);
a Form DLA404, MY182, MPB1266 or MHS330 (Disabled tax class only)

Signature .... **Date**..................................

In the case of a partnership, limited company or other legal entity, state capacity in which signed ....

In the case of signature by a duly authorised agent, state full name and address ....
....
....

ADDITIONAL DECLARATION To be signed and completed as appropriate if the vehicle is to be licensed as FARMER'S GOODS, GENERAL HAULAGE, SHOWMAN'S TRACTOR or SHOWMAN'S GOODS or RECOVERY VEHICLE.

FARMER'S GOODS VEHICLE **I declare** that I am a person engaged in agriculture of the following type ....

and that the land I occupy is at ....

Signature..

GENERAL HAULAGE TRACTOR **I declare** that the vehicle is constructed for haulage solely and not for the purpose of carrying or having superimposed upon it any load except such as is necessary for its propulsion or equipment.

Signature..

SHOWMAN'S HAULAGE TRACTOR **I declare**
(a) that I am a person following the business of a travelling showman;
(b) that the vehicle is constructed for haulage solely and not for the purpose of carrying or having superimposed upon it any load except such as is necessary for its propulsion or equipment

Signature..

SHOWMAN'S GOODS VEHICLE **I declare**
(a) that I am a person following the business of a travelling showman;
* (b) that the vehicle is a goods vehicle permanently fitted with a living van;
* (c) that the vehicle is a goods vehicle permanently fitted with a special type of body or super-structure forming part of the equipment of my show.

*(delete either (b) or (c) as appropriate)

Signature..

RECOVERY VEHICLE **I declare**
(a) that the vehicle is constructed or permanently adapted for the purposes of lifting and towing a disabled vehicle or for any one or

Section 3
Construction and Use

CONSTRUCTION AND USE Regulations apply to amateur-built kit cars even though full Type Approval Regulations don't. We all have cause to be very wary of C&U Regulations because they are primarily written to control the design of production vehicles made by the multi-national corporations. However, their wording often is generalised to include all cars built or first used in a designated time frame.

The Specialist Transport Advisory and Testing Utility Society (STATUS) of the Manchester Metropolitan University appears to be the kit car industry's main contact with the Department of Transport and they keep their members up to date with all the latest C&U requirements which can affect kit cars.

We have consulted the experts at STATUS on a number of occasions, to find out just how the complex Regulations affect the amateur kit car builder. Note that these Regulations put the onus of responsibility on the vehicle's constructor as well as its user. Arguably, in terms of a kit car, that's you on both counts. Even if the kit manufacturer has built design faults into the car, you could be answerable for them.

What kind of things are specified by the C&U Regulations and which of them affect kit cars? It's a complex question, made even more shady by the fact that there's very little machinery to enforce the C&U Regulations in the current MoT test. Even the traffic police seem to tread very carefully in terms of the less clear C&U Regulations, and there are plenty of those.

The obvious set of C&U-related Regulations refers to vehicle lighting. Poorly positioned lights can be a road hazard and can soon get you into trouble with the police and other road users, let alone the MoT tester. Main offences include head and tail lamps below minimum heights,

necessary lamps missing, lamps fully or partly occluded by bodywork or accessories etc. and essential lamps positioned badly.

Shouldn't the whole lot go together correctly if you follow the kit build-up manual? Unfortunately, this isn't always the case. STATUS has certainly improved things by increasing manufacturers' awareness but there is still some way to go before amateur builders can presume that their kit definitely complies because it's been built 'by the book.'

Fortunately, advance warning of the lighting Regulations will enable most builders to devote fruitful attention to the number and position of lights. There's no excuse for being caught out here, especially as the buck stops at you. See the table printed later in this chapter for the facts.

A kit car which has received a donor registration mark and not a Q-plate will have to comply with the lighting and C&U Regulations pertaining to a vehicle of the donor's age. It will also have to undergo the appropriate emissions testing for a vehicle of that age.

A kit car which receives a Q-prefix plate will have to comply with all of the latest C&U Regulations in force at the time of the kit's registration. It will only need a visual smoke test in the MoT and no other emissions test.

Construction and Use Regulations go much further than just lights and emissions. Windscreens and side windows must be manufactured from approved safety glass but soft-top sidescreens are not considered to be part of the car but instead part of the weather equipment.

Rearward-hinged doors are OK, as are single-position non-burst-proof locks. There is no specific C&U clause that says that wheels and tyres must not protrude beyond wheel arches and wings. Wings must be designed to prevent the wheels from throwing up debris into the air and from creating excessive spray in wet conditions. Guidelines also exist for noise

emissions and external protrusions.

Tyres fitted must be suitable for the maximum loads and speeds of which your vehicle is capable. This last point can be forcibly imposed by insurance companies who might object to a client fitting antique-style crossply tyres to a 400bhp D-Type lookalike! Who could blame them?

Pub philosophers, the fount of all tall car stories, tend to confuse the Construction and Use requirements with the Full or Low Volume Type Approval rules which are applicable to the production car trade. Full Type Approval testing has become so expensive that it is often beyond the scope of British kit car manufacturers. Ginetta was the last specialist to get full Type Approval for its G32 mid-engined model.

Low Volume Type Approval, for limited production runs of cars, has permitted the top kit car manufacturers such as Westfield Sports Cars to enter the production car fray, but it's still rather too expensive for most manufacturers and Single Vehicle Approval may well negate the need for a more complex approval anyway.

We would certainly say that there's a moral onus upon the kit car designer and manufacturer to produce a kit, and a relevant construction manual, which would enable the amateur builder to make a car bang up to date with all of the most recent C&U Regulations. This would alleviate any problems caused by having to guess which registration mark your car will receive and which parts to use as a consequence of that.

Until all kit car manufacturers are brought into line either by government or market pressure, the prospective customer must ask the right questions. Is this emblem or mascot OK? Is this edge too sharp? Are these tyres good enough? Are the lights right? A manufacturer must be able to point to the relevant parts of the printed C&U and Lighting

Regulations and show you that the kit complies. It doesn't necessarily have to be tested in order to comply.

REGISTERING YOUR KIT AFTER SVA IMPLEMENTATION

Section 1
Revised registration procedures

IF YOU STILL INTEND TO retain your donor car's registration details then your kit will not have to undergo Single Vehicle Approval. SVA only pertains to cars which will receive a current or Q-prefix number (ie. are having their first registration). Be aware when you retain the donor's registration mark that the new registration document for your kit *must* state the kit manufacturer's name alongside any reference to the original donor car. For example, an MGB based NGTF roadster kit car which is retaining the donor's registration number may be called 'MGB NGTF open-top' in your new registration document. Simply 'MGB' will not do.

However, retaining your donor car's registration details may not be quite as simple as before. The VRO is very keen that any car which has had major changes to its design/structure should not simply be allowed to change its registration document details without some check on the work done. This area of new legislation is particularly vague at present but it seems likely that such cars may have to undergo what might be called a 'Super-MoT'.

This will be carried out at the approved HGV SVA testing stations but exactly what and how much of the car will be tested is still a little hazy. Check the details with your nearest Vehicle Registration Office nearer the time and keep an

This form is usually sent to you with the V55/5 and we have compressed it here (it's a double-sided sheet). Make sure that you give serial numbers and not part numbers for all components listed (if possible). Kit cars are officially known as kit conversions.

Built Up Vehicle Inspection Report

V627/1
Rev May 90

For completion by Applicant

Name and Address

_____

_____

_____

_____

Telephone No. _____

Daytime Telephone No. _____

Present Registration Mark [   ]

Make _____

Model _____

Colour _____

Taxation Class _____

Year of Manufacture _____

Currently Licensed   Yes [ ]   No [ ]

Principal Parts (delete as appropriate)	Serial/ID number	Origin (Reg Mark or New)	Make of Vehicle Component	Receipts *Yes/No
Chassis { Sub Frame / Frame (bicycle)				
Body/Body Shell				
Prop shaft/ Rear Axle				
Drive shaft/Universals				
Gear Box				
Steering Unit				
Wheels				
Suspension (Front and Back)				
Engine				
Front Forks				
Handlebars				
Seat				
Tank				

A. Original parts not used (state below how disposed)

* *Failure to produce Receipts or appropriate Registration Documents may cause delay*

B. Any other Information/Additional Documents produced
(Retention of original Registration Mark may be considered but only if the details of the vehicle prior to alteration are held at DVLA.)

Signature_____ **Date** _____

The particulars given above are believed to be correct to the best of my knowledge.

Year in which rebuild was completed _____

Was the vehicle rebuilt by you ? _____

If not, who carried out the rebuild ? _____

Additional notes or comments
(Please include any background information and further details which you consider relevant)

Place of Inspection, if different from overleaf

Address _____

eye on *Which Kit?* magazine for any updates.

If you are going the Q-plate route then the first point to make clear is that Single Vehicle Approval forms only part of the new registration process. In the most simple terms, SVA takes the place of the first MoT, and so you'll still need to be thinking about road tax and filling out various other forms.

When your kit reaches the point when it is complete, you'll need to get hold of an application form to request an SVA test. This you'll be able to get from various sources — the nearest Vehicle Inspectorate Office, Vehicle Registration Office or a HGV testing station. You must fill this out and return it to the Vehicle Inspectorate central office at Swansea (The Vehicle Certification Authority (VCA) deals with LVTA and EC Whole

Vehicle Type Approval, but the Vehicle Inspectorate deals with SVA).

Once the Vehicle Inspectorate has checked that your car is eligible for SVA it will pass the details onto your nearest approved HGV testing station who will issue you with a SVA test appointment. Once your car has passed the SVA test you will be issued with a Minister's Approval Certificate (MAC) in much the same way you receive an MoT certificate after your MoT.

You will then get a new form from your nearest VRO and make a normal registration application in much the same way as you did before SVA came into force – sending in a cheque for your road tax along with evidence of insurance and your newly acquired MAC. As before, you'll then be issued with a tax disc, registration number and new

registration document.

One of the major objectives of the new system is to speed up the process by which you actually receive a registration number and it seems likely that eventually this may be allocated to you immediately after the SVA test. As such it is hoped that you'll be able to drive away from the HGV testing station with a registration number, tax disc, insurance etc, etc. Not surprisingly, the VRO will not be sending an inspector out to look at your kit because the car has already been inspected during its Single Vehicle Approval test.

Whilst the background workings of the new registration system still seem a little vague as we go to press, the test itself is well documented and outlined in Section 4. But what is Single Vehicle Approval and why is it necessary?

Section 2
What is SVA?

SINGLE VEHICLE APPROVAL has been in the offing since 1992. Since then a number of launch dates for this ambitious scheme have come and gone but the most recent paperwork would suggest kick-off in April 1997.

But what do we mean when we talk about Full Type Approval, Low Volume Type Approval and, most recently, Single Vehicle Approval? How and why do they exist? Prior to 1992, European countries each set their own standards for Type Approving cars, so one country enforced one standard while another ignored it or made it even more strict. With the increase in European unity it made a lot of sense for there to be an agreed European

If you intend to retain the donor car's number plate and registration details, it's going to be extremely important that the registration document describes the car correctly. 'Ford Escort' would not do for this Autotune Gemini! It seems likely that this sort of car will still have to undergo a more in-depth 'super MoT' after the implementation of SVA.

standard whereby cars produced in one country would automatically meet the requirements of another.

So, in early 1993, a 45 test approval system was agreed with the proviso that it should be fully implemented by 1/1/96.

But, and here's the important part, from the very outset it was understood and agreed upon that member countries could choose a different level of approval where the volume of sales was particularly low. In the UK that has resulted in a three tiered system: At the top is EC Whole Vehicle Type Approval which is specifically aimed at high volume manufacturers such as Ford. Next you'll probably be familiar with Low Volume Type Approval aimed at companies wishing to produce fully built cars but not exceeding 500 a year. The likes of Westfield, Caterham and Marcos have this system of approval. Finally, and most

importantly for all of us, will be the implementation of Single Vehicle Approval (SVA).

So, SVA is an officially recognised Type Approval test aimed squarely at very low volume car manufacturers and cars built at home.

Section 3
SVA basics

SO WHO WILL HAVE TO comply? Currently, anyone building a kit that would normally be subject to a Q or current registration mark will have to pass the approval scheme. Those building a kit which would legitimately be able to retain the donor registration will not have to undergo SVA but may have to undertake the 'Super MoT' (see Section 1).

Many of you reading this book may already be building a kit or may yet buy a kit prior to Single Vehicle Approval coming into

force in early 1997. SVA recognises that older kits which are still unregistered may not meet the most up-to-date regulations due to the manufacturer being unaware of them when the kit was produced. Certain dispensations will make it easier for these kits to pass SVA so long as the kit goes through the test prior to April 1999.

A kit car will have to undergo the SVA test just the once, before it can be registered, and from then, like a production car, it will be exempt from an MoT for three years before reverting back to the normal MoT tests. The cost of this initial test is going to be around £200 (with the cost of re-tests yet to be finalised) and will be carried out at specially equipped Heavy Goods Vehicle (HGV) testing stations rather than a conventional MoT approved garage. It's expected that the test will take around three hours and the owner is expected to remain present throughout in order to show the inspector certain areas and help him open bonnets etc if the catches are not immediately obvious.

As with an MoT, the onus is on the builder to ensure that the car meets SVA requirements. If lights are too low, the steering column non-collapsible or the chassis just plain dangerous, it will be up to you to sort it out prior to the SVA test or afterwards if you fail. As

such, it's is blatantly obvious that you must take precautions prior to buying any old kit just because you like the look of it. If you don't buy a kit because it has not been designed to pass SVA then the onus moves from you and onto the manufacturer in question to get his product sorted out.

Once your kit car has passed the test you will be given a Minister's Approval Certificate and can complete your kit car's registration.

Section 4
SVA tests outlined

WITH INSURANCE SORTED out, you will be able to drive your completed kit to and from your nearest SVA testing HGV station. Currently there are only around 16 of these stations in the country, so the chances are you will be driving your car some distance prior to having it tested. As such, setting up suspension, tracking and generally making sure your car works normally must be done prior to this test unless you intend to trailer the car to the testing station. Unlike an MoT, if your car fails the test you *will* be allowed to drive it to and from a place where rectification work can be carried out.

Whilst we have not looked at the obvious tests which are currently included within an MoT,

This Ginetta G32 was the last kit car to undergo Full Type Approval. Since then Low Volume Type Approval has suited the requirements of other large kit car manufacturers such as Westfield with it's ZEi model. This is the Cosworth powered 220.

Sevenesque cars such as this Sylva Striker will have to undergo the new Single Vehicle Approval tests. With some careful thought put in by the builder there should be few problems for a car such as this to easily pass the tests.

we have tried to outline below some of the tests which are specifically new to SVA and which may also require consideration by the kit car manufacturer in order to ensure his product passes. It may be worth making a note of some of these features before you visit a particular manufacturer so that you can check them during your walk about. However, this is not a comprehensive listing and it is proposed that you'll be able to buy an SVA Inspection Manual from relevant testing stations for around £25 should you want the full details.

Seats

● Seats must be securely fastened to the chassis or other load bearing part of the vehicle.

● Seats which tip forward must have some form of locking mechanism to hold them upright. Unlocking mechanism must be easily accessible.

Seat Belts

● Each seat belt anchorage point which uses a single bolt must be of at least 11mm diameter and have a fixed threaded hole or captive nut.

● Must have relevant approval markings.

● Structures around the belt must not cause abrasion or damage to it.

● Belt anchorage points will be checked for correct position for maximum efficiency (particularly on 3-point harnesses).

Interior fittings

● This largely relates to any dangerously sharp edges that any occupant may come into contact with in the event of an accident. Common sense would seem to rule out a lot of potential trouble areas here. Traditional toggle style dash mounted flick switches could possibly cause problems (check before you fit them).

Glazing

● windscreens and side window either side of the driver must display suitable markings (BS or E marks).

● all other windows must be made of a recognised safety glass or plastic (ie glass that will not shatter on impact).

Lighting

● This has often been an area for concern with kit car builders. Construction and Use Regulations have always specified positions of certain lamps but only now will they be actively checked. Three measurement are usually given – maximum distance from the side of the car, maximum height and minimum height. Maximum height will rarely be a problem but the other two are important.

Maximum distance from the outside of the car is measured from the extreme outer edge of the car, disregarding wing mirrors etc. Vertical position from the ground is measured to the lower edge of the illuminated area, except when looking at a dipped beam headlight. In the case of the latter it is where the apparent trace of the beam 'cut-off' can be seen on the lens.

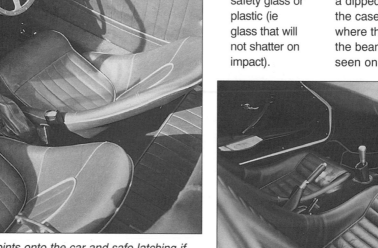

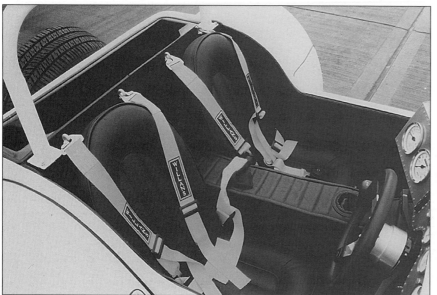

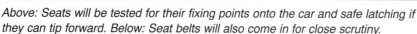
Above: Seats will be tested for their fixing points onto the car and safe latching if they can tip forward. Below: Seat belts will also come in for close scrutiny.

For the first time, kit cars will be assessed for internal protrusions that might cause injury in the case of an accident. Steering wheel and boss must be Type Approved or show evidence of Type Approved characteristics. Below: Headlight heights will be measured.

OBLIGATORY LAMPS

	Max dist. from side	Min Height
Dipped Beam	400mm	500mm
Main Beam	–	–
Front side lamps	400mm	–
Rear side lamps	400mm	350mm
Rear registration light	–	–
Stop lamps	400mm apart	350mm
Rear fog lamp	–	250mm
Indicators (front, sides & rears)	400mm	350mm
Rear retro reflectors	400mm	350mm

● There must be 'tell-tale' warning lights visible from the driving seat to let the driver know when rear fog lamps, indicators, hazard lamps etc are in use.

Mirrors
● You must have at least one interior mirror and one off-side mirror.
● If the external mirror protrudes beyond the extreme outer edge of the vehicle then it must be capable of pivoting towards the vehicle when impacted from either front or rear.
● Rearward vision from these mirrors will be checked for suitable field of view.

External projections
● Watch out with mascots.
Steering
● Both steering column and steering wheel/boss will be inspected for protection capability in the event of a front end shunt. Steering column must have some collapsible element to it and steering wheel boss must either be Type Approved or show characteristics of a Type Approved product - eg. a collapsible boss.
Vehicle design and Construction
● Position of the steering rack in relation to the front axle centreline will be inspected.

If the rack is ahead of the centreline then evidence of some energy absorbing device will be required such as a correct bumper, chassis crumplezone etc.
● In some cases the tester may drive the vehicle to confirm its roadworthiness. As such, tracking and any other suspension adjustments must be done prior to the test.
● Chassis and suspension will be inspected for its construction quality.
● Fuel and brake lines will be inspected along with all wiring in relation to moving parts and potential abrasion.
Noise
● Decibel levels will be checked. 101db at 3500rpm measured for 0.5m from the exhaust.
Emissions
● Amateur-built vehicle emissions levels will be set at the date when the engine was designed. Thus a brand new Chevy 350ci V8 will be tested on the emissions levels relevant to the date when the engine was first designed and not its current manufacture date.
Speedometer
● A speedo must be working.
● When tested on a rolling road it must not read *less* than the true speed. It may read higher, but only by a specified amount. This will be particularly important to cars where different wheel and tyre combinations have been used to the donor. Larger wheels and tyres will inevitably slow the speedo reading.

As we have already mentioned, these are not all the tests that will be carried out during the SVA, but only the ones we feel are particularly relevant to the home constructed car and which would not have been tested in the old MoT.

Below: External protrusions will be looked at during the new SVA tests. Bonnet mascots could cause a problem and wing mirrors must be able to pivot forward or backwards on impact if they stick out beyond the bodywork.

Above: If the steering column is situated ahead of the front wheel centreline, then there must be evidence of some form of crumplezone or other impact absorbing feature. Below: Watch out! Loud exhausts could prove tricky.

Chapter 11
TROUBLESHOOTING

Section 1: Road readiness
Section 2: Running in

Section 3: Heat-proofing
Section 4: Current affairs

Section 1
Road readiness

SO, YOUR CAR IS DEFINITELY on the road. There may have been MoT problems but you've sorted it all out to get the registration. End of story? Nope. In our experience, the vast majority of kit cars get an MoT test and all appropriate paperwork qualifications well before completion.

If you're on your second or third build, chances are that you will have done a more thorough job. Unless you're supremely confident, though, you'll need to instigate a good checking system and adopt a very unselfish attitude to correcting any faults found. This will probably entail taking the car off the road once again until it's fixed.

A keen home mechanic, who may have maintained the family car in the past, will have a distinct advantage. Diagnosing

problems is the key skill here. If you're not aware that certain noises, handling characteristics, vibrations and engine reactions are warning signs, then you'll carry on regardless until disaster strikes in one form or another.

You just have to be a bit clinical about it. In the first instance, obvious faults will become apparent when you drive to and from the MoT, or during early use of the car. There are various things that you can't check until the car is on the road, so be prepared to find extra faults that you couldn't predict.

Some manufacturers offer a post-build-up checking service, usually free, to give inexperienced car builders some peace of mind. Take advantage of this at all costs as it'll save you a lot of time. The manufacturer will know what to look for. Be careful to ask about any problems you're not sure of.

One of your first trips should

be to a tyre fitter to get the tracking (toe-in/out) set at the front wheels (and at the rear wheels if there is adjustment to be made there too). Some higher-tech tracking and geometry companies (such as Autoline) will also be able to set up cars to manufacturer's specifications if adjustment is required for castor and camber. The manufacturer should tell you how to temporarily set the car up in your own garage so that it can be safely driven to the experts.

Even if your car passed the MoT easily, your second trip to a specialist should end at a garage with accurate engine diagnostic machinery and the ability to tune your particular engine with whatever special equipment may have been fitted to it. Your car may well have been MoT tested before it was registered and the tester may have given it only a visual smoke test as far as emissions are concerned.

Even if you do subsequently get a Q-plate and future emissions testing promises to be only visual, you can only be sure that your engine is running properly when it has been tested with the correct equipment. It's unlikely that anyone will be able to afford accurate diagnostic gear at home and setting up a pair of Webers or SUs can be a real art.

Getting the timing and the dwell right at home is only a small part of engine tuning. Mixture setting at idle and assessing the main jet's performance are jobs which are too complex to try at home with cheap equipment. Varying compressions, worn valves, poor plug leads and plugs and a dodgy distributor shaft can all complicate things for the amateur.

Balancing and tuning multiple carburettors can be a nightmare – don't trust the 'stethoscope' balancing method

Whilst this tuned Jaguar V12 engine may look totally stunning, are you really going to try and set up six twin-choke Webers by hand? Such attempts rarely prove fruitful and could easily prove expensive if your engine runs badly for an extended period. Take the car to a specialist with the right tools and experience to do the job properly.

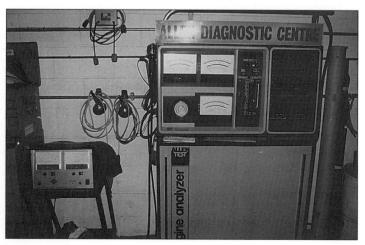

Getting hold of an MoT testing station's check sheet may help you sort any potential failure problems before the test. Construction and Use Regs are the other point to consider.

From a practical point of view, you want to make sure that things last more than five minutes. While this fuse box looks neat, the terminals are not fully insulated which might cause a short-circuit.

of simply listening to each choke in turn and adjusting for the same noise. It takes a lot of experience to do this correctly.

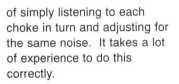

THE WHICH KIT? TIP

Odd squeaks and rattles from some hidden corner of the car can drive you potty. It's almost impossible to find them on your own whilst driving the car. Get someone else to drive or look for the mystery movement and you'll find the faults much more quickly

After 100-200 miles, you may have compiled quite a list of niggling faults which you have been easily able to identify. You should also make a systematic check of the vehicle, looking for problems in the donor equipment, the parts supplied in the kit, any special parts you got from after-market suppliers and any parts that you made up yourself.

A good start can be made if you can get hold of a copy of the MoT tester's standard 'failure' slip. This lists the points that the MoT tester has to check, although you can generally be more thorough than this as you know the vehicle much better than the MoT tester. The very fact of assembling each component by hand will give you plenty of

clues as to the source of any fault with the car.

Unfortunately, budget usually dictates that any faults you find must be listed in order of priority. Obviously safety comes right at the top of the list. Using your knowledge of the car's mechanicals, the

Whilst you may have reconditioned your braking components properly when you started the build, if you left the system without fluid in for too long the seals can fail.

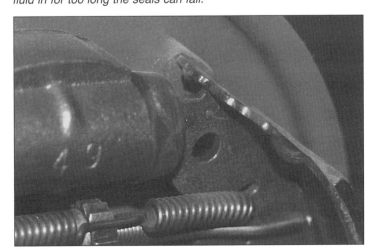

fault-finding sections of the donor's *Haynes Workshop Manual* and advice from the manufacturer and the owners club, you should be able to track down safety-related faults quite quickly.

Any steering, roadholding and braking anomalies should get priority. Fuel, brake fluid or coolant leaks are danger areas. Electrical problems can compromise safety and become a fire hazard (don't think that a mere 12 volts is incapable of getting a fire underway).

Insufficiently secured bodywork, especially the bonnet and weather gear, can cause disaster at high speed and faulty cockpit equipment

can also be a risk. A loose driver footwell carpet, a shaky rear view mirror, obscured instruments and dodgy hand controls can all be calamitous.

Section 2
Running in

WHETHER YOU HAVE OR have not discovered faults in the first few miles, you should undertake a thorough inspection of the underside of the vehicle. Support the car safely on axle stands all round. If you support the car using recommended points on the body/chassis, the suspension should be at full droop all round.

If you support the car using the suspension arms or axles, the suspension should rest at the normal ride height for the car. You might want to carry out checks at both of these suspension positions to be doubly sure.

Starting with the rear suspension, look out for any fluid leaks from shock absorbers, brake components and the differential. Are the rear wheels rotating freely or are the brakes rubbing too much (if drum brake system)? Does the handbrake adjustment need resetting (disc or drum)? Remove brake drums to check for fluid leaks

and correct assembly of all springs and retaining posts etc. Any sign of grease or oil on friction surfaces?

Is there any sign of wheel rubbing in the inner or outer wheel arches? Is there anything else, such as brake hoses/pipes threatening to rub against the wheel? If so, are the wheels/tyres really too wide?

Are the wheels too far inset? (Try to avoid using wheel spacers at all costs as they alter wheel offset). Does your live axle need a Panhard rod? (Fitting a manufacturer's Panhard rod option could well allow you to keep those wheels/tyres and avoid using spacers).

Is there any evidence of metal filings near or under moving parts such as the half-shaft or propshaft universal

joints? We have seen propshaft bearings bind up when they are required to operate through an excessive angle between the differential flange and the gearbox output shaft or flange. The manufacturer or club will tell you how to get around this dangerous situation or where to buy the correct propshaft for the job.

Half-shafts can also be damaged if there is an excessive angle between the transaxle flange and the stub axle flange. Is the transaxle/gearbox the wrong type or is it mounted too high or at an odd angle? Are the suspension springs too long or too stiff, causing the ride height to be too high? Do you have exactly the right half shafts and bearings for the job? Are they simply worn out due to age and lack of reconditioning at

the kit build stage?

Is there any evidence of components being damaged at rear suspension full bump? That includes pipes, cables, exhaust, fuel tank, fuel pump, any metal to metal contact with chassis, tyre contact with wheel arch tops, propshaft contact with transmission tunnel top or chassis cross-bracing or any similar anomalies with half-shafts, DeDion tubes, Panhard rods, radius rods and any other rear suspension linkages.

Is this being caused by bad positioning of affected components? Are the springs too short, soft or simply worn? Are the bump-stop rubbers worn or should they be replaced by larger alternatives? It's probably the cheapest option to re-position affected components but you may have to contact the

manufacturer or club to find the best specific answer. Any damaged parts should be replaced, especially fuel, wiring loom or brake parts, even if the contact appears to have been minimal.

Squeaks and groans may be caused by twisted suspension bushes. Even if you did let the car rest on its wheels before tightening the relevant suspension bolts, it may have rested down even further after a little running in. With the car sitting on its suspension (even if on axle stands) loosen the bolts and re-tighten.

Check the centre section of the car for any fluid, fuel or coolant leaks. Propshaft rubbing might be rectified by altering the transmission tunnel shape. Is the gearshift linkage (for mid or rear-engined cars) fouling anything? Is the handbrake cable clear and are

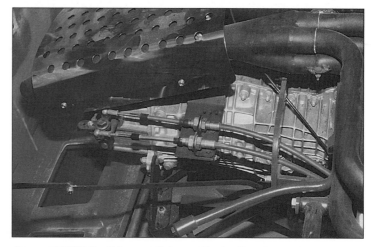

Top: Front ride height is easily adjustable when using Marina front torsion bar suspension. Below: If a modified propshaft is too long, it may end up damaging the gearbox.

Above: GTD'S flexible gear linkage. Engine/gearbox movement can affect solid rod linkages. Below: Clearance between this rear tyre and McPherson strut looks small but always stays constant.

the front to rear fuel and brake pipes unaffected by rubbing?

Is there anything obviously prone to damage from stone chip or from a sleeping policeman or other zero ground clearance situation. Obviously all components should be protected from this by the body/chassis.

Up at the front, many of the leak, clearance and suspension travel checks specified for the rear are still valid. The big exception here is that the wheels can steer as well as moving up and down on the suspension. Any

usually require removal of the calipers, disc pads or brake shoes as these can hide free play in the bearing. Be very careful not to overtighten wheel bearings and make sure that you use a new locking washer and split pin where appropriate,

Worn suspension ball-joints are a little more difficult to check. At the front end, it can be done several ways. An assistant can firmly hold the steering wheel and apply the foot brake (vehicle on axle stands) as you attempt to move the wheel in all

THE WHICH KIT? TIP

After a few hundred miles it's a good idea to check all the suspension mounting bolts. Whilst nylocs shouldn't move, components bolted together can bed in over this initial mileage, causing looseness. After checking each nut, dab it with a coloured paint. This should be done from the visible side and will quickly show you whether you've missed any nuts

rubbing caused by lock to lock movement at rest or at full droop? Any evidence of rubbing at full bump? Loosen and retighten suspension bush bolts with car at normal ride height.

Checking for loose wheel bearings at the front end will

directions. This might reveal excess movement in a track rod end, upper or lower ball-joint or rose joint. Firm sideways force applied to the suspect joints with a lever can also get free play to show.

Loose, protruding and scuffed nuts and bolts should

be dealt with by tightening and/or replacing with more appropriate items. You might find that an underbody exhaust system hangs too low or is insufficiently supported. There are various after-market sources for exhaust mounts in the kit car trade and a good exhaust centre may well be able to alter the system for you so that it improves ground clearance. Be careful to get a quote first.

Simple faults like wrong tyre pressures can leave some builders foxed. Don't presume that the donor's tyre pressures are the right ones. Get the specification for your wheels and tyres from the kit manufacturer. The pressures might have to be a lot lower than you thought.

Section 3
Heat-proofing

MOST PROBLEMS SEEM TO come from the engine fitment. The worst offenders are overheating and an inability to get smooth running in all conditions. Secondary considerations include poor clearances (especially hot exhaust parts getting too close to important components), general electrical problems, servicing access, untidiness and a host of problems associated with deviations from the standard engine specifications.

In addition to these, mid or rear-engined cars can also suffer from excessive heat in the engine bay (affecting fuel

Serious wheel and tyre combinations can put added strain on wheel bearings, especially with odd offsets. The situation is made considerably worse with the addition of wheel spacers.

Top: Household plumbing pipes can sometimes prove invaluable for solving complex twists and turns in a cooling system. Below: New bends in this bracket might cure a rubbing hose problem.

Overheating is a common complaint with privately built cars. Using an old rad is often a false economy and make sure you fit a decent fan. Positioning the rad correctly is also vital.

and carburettors), water splash problems if the inner rear arches are either insufficient or non-existent and excessive noise level for the occupants (from the rear bulkhead area).

Overheating, unfortunately, is often a result of design and specification shortcomings by the manufacturer. Many kit cars have little or no aerodynamic or air flow design concessions (quite often the opposite for traditional roadsters and jeeps) and, even if the radiator and intake aperture appear to be large enough, there is no way in

which a proper rate of air flow can be directed through the radiator at speed.

This problem might be complicated by the use of a compact radiator, small intake aperture or excessive engine horsepower. There can be extra confusion - a club member with the same radiator and engine might claim to have no cooling problems.

Where do you look first? Obviously, the manufacturer and the club are the first help lines after you have made sure that your engine is in a correct state of tune. There is a host

of other reasons why an engine might tend to overheat on tickover, at low speed or at high speed.

You should check for coolant leaks (especially those which happen only when the engine is hot), worn pressure cap seals, cylinder head gasket leak (get a compression test), coolant pipe restrictions, electric/mechanical fan effectiveness (if problem is at tickover) and thermostat operation. Water pump and fan belt wear are usually obvious through noise and water leaks.

It is important to avoid second-hand radiators unless you know that they are in good working order. Even a new-looking radiator might have a well-blocked core if someone reverse-flushed an old engine block through it. Replacing this with a new unit could be the simple answer.

Coolant loss with or without overheating, can be caused by omitting the overflow bottle. The overflow pipe from your radiator filler neck (or similar) should end up immersed in coolant in a remote reservoir.

If your reservoir does not have a pressure cap (a typical radiator cap with a spring valve and a central return valve), then the radiator should. If the radiator has a simple blanking cap, then the expansion tank should have the pressure cap. There should not be a pressure cap on both the radiator and the overflow bottle as this can over-pressurise the system.

The idea is that hot water expands and if you don't have an expansion tank, the water will simply overflow and be lost. If the overflow pipe leads into a tank, the displaced water will be 'sucked' back into the cooling system as the engine cools down after use, hence reducing the chance of an air gap and making the system pressure more consistent.

Some manufacturers have

This specially welded header tank looks terrific, but plastic donor car tanks work just as well and may be important to your kit's cooling set-up. A pressure cap on your radiator may not be correct.

On a tuned engine it's going to be very important that the oil is kept in good condition and that's where an oil-cooler comes in. This one even has its own cooling fan.

If no production radiator seems to suit your requirement, companies such as Serk Marston are more than capable of making up one-offs.

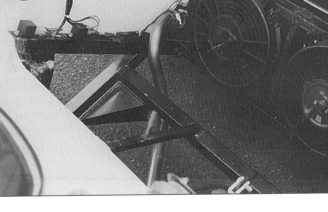

Above: Whilst a radiator should happily cool a moving car without the aid of a fan, when caught in traffic you'll be in trouble without one. Below: One of these fans operates automatically while the other can be switched on as back-up.

discovered that various new after-market radiators have fewer cores than the original equipment. That meant substantially less cooling capacity. It might be OK for the production car model involved but it often isn't for some kits which were happy with the more efficient original equipment.

If there is someone in the club with the same engine and no overheating, take a good, close look at the density of their radiator core. Remove the cap and compare the rows of visible tubes inside. Has the radiator been fitted differently? Is the central matrix thicker? Are the pressure caps the same? Are the thermostats the same? How has that person bled the air from the coolant?

There's no point having excellent air flow into the radiator core unless the air passing through it has somewhere to escape to. Production car designers have spent mega-bucks shaping car

bodies so that low pressure behind the radiator helps to 'suck' air through it while the car is moving.

Kit cars often end up with a high pressure area behind the radiator, which inhibits air flow through it. If your overheating is prevalent at higher speed, this could well be the problem. Extra engine side panel louvres or vents, 'pointing' rearwards, might help to extract air from the engine bay. Proper front wheel inner arches might also relieve the pressure build-up behind the radiator if the car has full or scalloped wings.

If your electric cooling fan is working properly (check for correct blade rotation direction) or if your mechanical fan is the right diameter and within an inch of the radiator, overheating

at tickover will probably mean that your radiator isn't up to the job. Don't just throw out the thermostat and hope for the best.

If the worst comes to the worst, you may have to do some dismantling and change the radiator. It is quite likely that other club members will already have done this if a kit specification error causes overheating with the recommended radiator. Find out the best alternative radiator used by a club member.

Kit builders have discovered that the radiators fitted to many modern

hatchbacks are compact and very efficient. Many come with an integral cowling, cooling fan and thermostatic switch. Before you pay for one of these, phone your local Serck Marston or other radiator supplier and get a quote for a tailor-made radiator capable of handling your engine's heat output (usually measured as a function of engine horsepower).

If you haven't done your build preparation as thoroughly as you should have or if you've opted for a larger than standard engine, you might

Kit car enthusiasts are great ones for fitting the most powerful engine they can find into the tightest spots. This Cosworth engine in a Dax Rush produces over 300bhp and the turbo, not surprisingly, develops a lot of heat. Note the special heat shield to protect the brake and clutch master cylinders over the pedal box.

find that there are clearance problems in the engine bay and problems accessing service parts. If you've chosen an engine that's obviously too big for the engine bay, it's your own lookout.

Various kit manufacturers have fitted V8s into their demo cars to impress the public and to show that it can be done. If you want to go the same route, take careful note of special components required for the fitment. Kit cars with a Rover V8 fitted often have such extras as a remote oil filter, special radiator, non-standard carburettors, manifolds, air filter, exhausts, modified pulleys, water pump, alternator position, shallow sump, special engine mounts etc. etc.

Don't ever believe that it's a straightforward swap across from the donor's engine bay into the kit's. If you keep your eyes open in the first place,

you won't need to fork out sums of money later.

Even though you have fitted the manufacturer's recommended engine and gearbox, exhaust and other ancillaries, there might still be clearance problems. Look carefully at the engine mounts of the demo car or others with this engine. They might have been modified or bolstered to let the engine rest at a slightly different angle.

If your engine is in a good state of tune and the engine mount rubbers look OK, they might still be ruined through fatigue. This would allow your engine to vibrate and rock as if there was something very wrong with the timing or mixture etc. New engine mount bushes can be a very quick cure for the problem.

When cutting bodywork holes for side exhausts, gearshift linkages, air filters,

coolant pipes, fuel pipes, brake servo vacuum pipes or anything that is attached to the engine, make sure you cut a sufficiently large hole. An engine will normally 'lean' one way under acceleration and the other when decelerating. Depending upon engine fitment, this could be front to rear or side to side.

This can cause associated pipes, tubes and linkages to bash against the edges of panel holes. Unfortunately, you might not know the extent to which your engine rocks until the car has been driven fairly hard. Better to err in favour of a generous clearance, something like an inch all around an exhaust downpipe or manifold, than to cut an inaccessible painted panel later. Take a look at similar cars fitted with that engine and exhaust etc.

The exhaust manifold and

downpipe (including any turbocharger) are the hottest parts of your engine bay. Heat will be conducted, radiated and convected from these parts affecting the whole engine bay. It is more likely that damage will occur when the vehicle is stationery and when there is little or no air flow through the engine bay.

Components around and above the exhaust parts will get very hot. The best way of protecting parts is, if possible, to position them away from the exhaust side of the engine bay. Not so easy if it's a V engine. Sometimes the carburettor, some fuel line, some brake line or other heat-prone material must be positioned above hot parts of the exhaust.

With foresight, you might design a steel or alloy heat shield which can be bolted in place using the exhaust manifold bolts/studs. This will redirect convected heat and will cut down on radiated heat. Other parts might need protection by coating them with aluminium/asbestos cloth.

If the style of the car permits, it's a good idea to have a vent of some kind in the bonnet. If this takes the form of a scoop, the aperture should face the windscreen. It offers better air flow through the radiator and will allow hot air to dissipate faster with the vehicle at a standstill. Beware, rain will enter through it so position it carefully.

You should always position plastic coated cables (accelerator, choke), any part of the wiring loom and the electronic ignition equipment (if fitted) well away from the exhaust. Spark plug HT leads, if adjacent to the exhaust manifold, must be tidied so that they can't rest against the

exhaust. Use the most expensive silicon leads you can afford for better heat resistance.

It is a general rule that untidy engine bays are much more prone to faults than tidy ones. They are certainly worse to work with and cause delays in fault-finding. This untidiness is often started off by using a grubby engine and gearbox and is completed by throwing in a messy wiring lash-up, straggly brake lines and cheap, rusty fasteners and add-ons.

Arm yourself with small nuts, bolts, cable ties, P-clips, Spirap, non-adhesive loom tape, alloy sheet for bracket-making, a proper brake pipe bending tool, plenty of colour-coded automotive cable of appropriate rating (see Chapter Eight) and a well matched set of after-market or donor ancillaries that will make your

engine bay look like a thoroughly thought out assembly. Fitting the engine, box, exhaust etc. was the easy bit. All these little odds and ends are the tough job.

Noise intrusion through the front and/or rear bulkheads can be offset in a couple of ways. When you trim and carpet the cockpit interior, you might go to the length of adding underlay to the bulkhead carpet or trim panels. If you're adding to this damping effect from the engine bay side, there are other materials which can be glued, screwed, bolted or riveted to the bulkhead to dull the noise.

In areas away from heat sources, waterproof and fire retardant foam or rubber mat (from upholstery suppliers), can be glued all over areas of GRP, alloy or steel sheet which might otherwise be too

transparent to noise.

In areas exposed to heat sources, several thicknesses of the heat resistant alloy/asbestos mat can be used. You might even get fire-proof sound-deadening material (exhaust silencer packing) sandwiched between bulkhead panels and specially cut alloy panels. Be careful not to make this a water trap.

For the first-time kit builder, sorting out an engine bay is a bit hit and miss. The more information you can get from those who have tackled such problems, the better. It's a task which usually isn't 100% successful first time out and will need improving as the vehicle is run in. It's one of the main reasons why kits aren't 'completed' when the last screw is tightened and the car hits the road for the first time.

This heat deflector helps protect the rear bodywork on this GT40 replica. Below: With exposed external silencers it's even more important to protect occupants as they get in/out.

These neat ball and socket sections allow more adjustment when fitting the exhaust and also take up some of the natural engine movement. Below: Alloy sheet can make excellent non-structural brackets.

Section 4
Current Affairs

ELECTRICAL PROBLEMS also rate pretty high on the list of common faults in newly finished kit cars. The advent of the purpose-made wiring loom has been a great help in reducing the number of post-build melt-downs and black-outs.

The builders who get into the worst pickles are those who set out to combine the looms from one make of donor plus the instruments from another and the switches and other electrical components from yet another. The replica builder often makes such compromises because the parts all have to look right, even if they aren't compatible.

As we have already mentioned in Chapter Eight,

your wiring work must include the correct size of wire, properly insulated automotive quality connectors and sound earthing wherever necessary. As ever, it might require some use of the car to uncover earthing faults and other electrical problems.

Sensible kit builders will have included a battery cut-out switch in the loom. This switch or key should be accessible from the driving position and should cut the current from all electrical components. It thereby doubles as a vehicle isolator and security mechanism. Any hint of burnt wiring smell can be followed by the instant precaution of isolating the battery.

Melted insulation on wiring can be caused by wire(s) of insufficient gauge or poor condition trying to cope with too much power, by wires

getting hot in an unventilated loom section (bigger wires are needed to dissipate heat build-up), by poor or dirty earth connections, by use of overrated fuses and by short-circuits (where a live positive feed connects directly to earth). Beware of using one wire to earth several components. It must be able to cope with all loads simultaneously.

If you see evidence of melting insulation in the loom and it isn't due to an outside heat source, you will have to trace the wire from one end to the other and assess the maximum power it will be conducting. It should be replaced by a heavier wire if all the contacts and related components are in order. Chapter Eight relates estimation factors for judging

wire gauges.

A heat build-up centred around a connector or connection will probably be a bad contact at that point. Remove, check, clean and try again. Many builders allow a layer of paint or primer to get between an earth connector and the chassis or other target earth point. When connecting an earth, make sure that the mating faces are filed or sanded smooth, down to the bare metal. If you need to paint over this, do so after the connection has been securely made.

A simple electronic test meter, such as a Gunsons Test Tune, will be invaluable for checking continuity and all sorts of ignition and non-ignition faults. Spend between £20 and £40 to save yourself lots of time and trouble.

Above: Machined alloy sheets can make practical cladding for an engine bay or even a dashboard. Below: Getting your donor's engine to look like this takes tremendous patience and dedication.

Top: Some of the smartest looking engine bays are also some of the simplest. Below: Alternatively, you could go completely mad and fit a neat little motor like this!

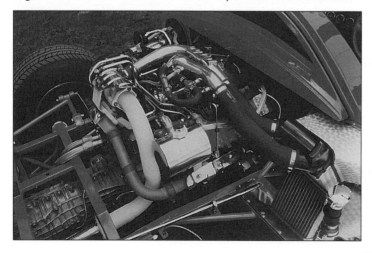

Professional auto-electricians do not come cheap and may not want to touch a car with a home-made wiring loom.

If there is a 12-volt (or other specified) supply to a malfunctioning component, a light bulb, motor, relay etc., and the necessary earths are sound, then the component itself should be suspected.

If no current, or an oddly intermittent current, reaches the component when switched on, check all the wires and connectors from the component to earth and back to the switch and power source. Insulated wires can break where you can't see it, so it's not just the connections which are to be suspected.

If the operation of one component causes another to stop or start, then there is probably an earth loop situation. This, in simple terms, means that the current passing through one component (a rear light bulb, for instance) can't take a normal route to earth. It then earths itself through another component to which it is somehow connected. When the second component is activated, the first might lose its earth intermittently or permanently and will therefore operate erratically.

Massive confusion can often be found behind the dashboard. Things that defy the ingenuity of a test meter. Wires going to oil pressure, water temperature and fuel tank senders can give very confusing read-outs on a voltmeter.

Immense quantities of short wires light up and earth switch bulbs and instruments. Big bunches of wires from the donor loom are kept instead of being carefully trimmed down. Be very aware that you might have to deal with this if the manufacturer doesn't offer an easier solution.

Don't be naive. A dashboard switch doesn't have just two wires attached to it! When you're at a scrap yard, take a look behind some of the switches of a simple car. You might be surprised to see that there are bunches of wires leading to some switches. Practically none of them will have less than three.

Confused? Take the easiest option the first time round and make sure that you buy a kit with its own recommended instruments, switches and loom or a kit which uses the instruments, switches and loom from one donor which you have dismantled and tagged personally.

Unless you are the first customer for a revolutionary new kit car, remember that you're not alone in trying to sort out any early running problems. We can't overstate the value of joining a relevant club and getting to know others who have done the build-up before. Some of them will be highly skilled mechanics or engineers, so you could get some excellent advice that you'd otherwise have to pay dearly for.

This fantastic YKC Berlinetta has been immaculately built from the ground up. It also looks very simple and uncluttered in the engine bay and interior. Combined with sensible reconditioning it provides quiet and refined touring without the rattles and shakes of some creations.

Chapter 12
STAY SHARP

Section 1: When's enough, enough?
Section 2: A day at the races
Section 3: Game over!

Section 1
When's enough, enough?

A LARGE PART OF THE popularity of kit cars is that they have the flexibility to allow for a wide range of amateur tuning and tweaking modifications that might seem a bit ridiculous on a production car.

Indeed, many kit car chassis are 'over-engineered' and can tolerate the stresses caused by higher than standard engine horsepower. (Unless a full scientific analysis has been completed and documented, the manufacturer won't know exactly what engine power is the safe long-term maximum for the chassis).

In order to get the very best value for money when uprating your kit car, it is essential to categorise all of the different types of improvement that could be considered separately.

What is the difference between what your car needs and what you want to fit? How do you identify the shortcomings and how do you rectify them?

In this section we'll be taking a look at the running gear and how you can recognise faults and improve overall road performance other than by increasing horsepower. The amateur car builder is subjected to all kinds of street-wise advice about go-faster bits. Some of it is valuable and some of it most decidedly isn't. Even so, it's amazing how many will throw good money at a problem in the hope that after-market goodies will provide a miracle cure in the end. That doesn't happen very often.

What kind of performance or general road-going anomalies might be associated with the running gear of your car? Which of these affects performance? What are you meant to do about them? It's a subject that could fill a few text

books but we'll try to cover some typical aspects.

Improving your car's road performance isn't all about increasing engine horsepower. Anyone who has driven such vehicles as the Cosworth Sierra and the Astra GTE can tell you what a dollop of excess power can do to a car when the handling and roadholding aren't up to it. The Sierra's maverick rear end reduces predictability to a bare minimum and the GTE's bhp is far in excess of the front wheels' traction capability. Both faults are exaggerated in the wet.

You should also avoid the temptation to adopt the principles used for making track-bound cars handle. Zero suspension movement, rock hard springs and shocks, tiny ground clearance, massive castor angle plus wide wheels and tyres can all make a car go well on the track but will destroy its general road-going ability.

For argument's sake, let's imagine that our checklist for good and sporty handling, roadholding and general driveability is made up of five points. These are not necessarily listed in order of importance but all contribute to the car's competence in this department.

1) **Steering.**
2) **Acceleration.**
3) **Braking.**
4) **Cornering.**
5) **Springs and Dampers.**

Before diving headlong into the realms of the esoteric, don't forget to consider the obvious. Find out the correct information about tyre pressures, tyre and wheel sizes, wheel offsets, toe in, donor brake types and possible variations, faulty or badly adjusted springs and dampers. Even if you have ordered components to precise specifications, it doesn't guarantee that you have been supplied with such. Check it all.

These storming great tyres will certainly look out of this world, but your car's handling may also have gone AWOL. It's a good idea to stick with your kit manufacturer's wheel/tyre recommendations.

Specially made double wishbone suspension is the way to go for excellent road comfort and great handling but it's going to need some careful setting up to get the best out of it.

For simplicity's sake we can define handling as the vehicle's ability to do what the driver wants it to do, predictably, safely and without hesitation. Roadholding might be described as the extent of the vehicle's ability to corner hard without sliding or spinning. This implies a certain balance of the available grip at the front and at the rear of a car. The balance is more important than the total potential grip available.

1) Steering

After you have driven your kit car for a few thousand miles, you'll start to get very used to its steering feel. It might be more helpful to note down all of your praises and criticisms of the car's steering characteristics when it's still a relatively fresh experience.

Common steering-related faults which we have experienced when test driving poorly set up and/or badly designed kit cars include such nasties as bump steer, poor self-centering, excessive self-centering, heavy steering at

manoeuvring speeds, steering wheel wobble, imprecise steering response at speed, steering rack gearing too low or high and unpredictable steering response under braking.

Bump steer is not, as the name suggests, a situation where the front wheels are pushed left or right by road bumps. More precisely, it is an unpredictable directional instability caused when the steering rack, or any related component, has been wrongly positioned.

Whether the front end of the vehicle is level, rising or dropping on the suspension, conflicting arcs of travel associated with these components might cause the front wheels to toe in or toe out excessively. (Remember that steering systems are designed so that the front

wheels increasingly toe out as they approach full lock).

This causes a slight or serious wandering which cannot always be controlled by steering. It will probably be more acute on uneven road surfaces and it wrecks the whole personality of the car, making high-speed driving even more dangerous than it inherently is.

Even if a manufacturer has used a complete front suspension subframe from the donor vehicle, bump steer can arise when the standard springs are cut down or replaced with re-rated items.

Incorrect ride height, larger wheels and tyres can exaggerate what might have been a tiny problem.

If you have built the kit using the specifications as described in the manufacturer's manual and are satisfied that all is assembled as it is meant to be, contact the manufacturer. You should have noticed this in the demo car during the test drive and if the demo car doesn't do it, how is it different from yours? Contact the manufacturer and find out.

Correcting this problem really isn't that easy. It's easiest to assume that you

Above: Your donor's springs may be less than ideal on your lighter kit car. Below: Using complete front subframe ensures steering rack is in correct position – no bump steer problems.

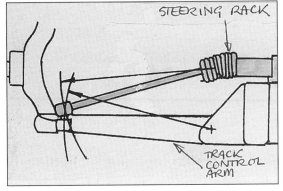

Above: Clashing arcs of track rod and track control arm cause bump steer. Below: Lowering rack position aligns the arcs and should cure the Problem.

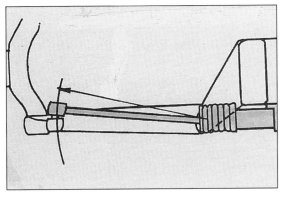

have the right rack, track rods, ends and steering arms but that the rack needs repositioning to get the best out of the vehicle. In essence, you will need to remove the front springs and evenly jack the front of the vehicle up and down, wheels on the ground, measuring how much variation in toe-in/out you get from full bump to full droop.

You may need to adjust the position of the steering rack to get the least variation in toe-in throughout that range of suspension travel most commonly used in normal road driving circumstances. It will probably be impossible to get even toe-in all the way from full bump to full droop. Most front suspension geometries are compromises due to lack of space under any bonnet.

The best advice might come from a club member who has had to undertake the same exercise. Someone might be able to tell you specifically that your rack must be shimmed up using 2mm steel spacers etc. You might even find out that you have used a slightly different steering rack by mistake.

Unfortunately, it may well be a job for a steering geometry specialist as the equipment needed to accurately measure toe-in is pretty expensive and a home-made jig, which measures the distance between the front inner wheel rims as a set point each side, can be a complex thing to make accurately.

If you're desperate, you may well be able to cut your own steering rack shims from steel and simply experiment with the rack positioned a little higher. If this exacerbates the problems, then your rack might have to go lower. This can be a real problem if it bolts right down onto chassis rails.

Don't ignore the possibility that the rack might need to go fore or aft or that the rack mounting holes on the chassis may have been punched or drilled in the wrong spot. Get detailed reference measurements from the manufacturer to see if your rack mount holes tally.

This really is a problem that you should not have to face once a kit has been correctly built as per instructions. A reputable manufacturer's demo car won't have any hidden steering modifications and your test drive should show you how your kit will steer. If you didn't get a test drive and you couldn't get the opinion of seasoned owners, then it's your own lookout.

Non-existent or savage self-centering of the steering wheel, light or heavy steering feel are usually down to something called castor angle. In general, most kit cars are steered by the front wheels and the front suspension geometries are designed so that there is always a self-centering force exerted on the front wheels/tyres, especially when the vehicle is moving forwards.

It is quite astounding just how many different donor car suspensions allow for

Above: Where suspension and steering components are located directly onto the chassis, very careful measurement is necessary to ensure correct geometry. Below: This upper wishbone on a Dax Rush can be adjusted at the end for camber.

A small castor angle generally creates a light steering feel, weaker self centring and less road surface feedback. Increase angle for the opposite effects.

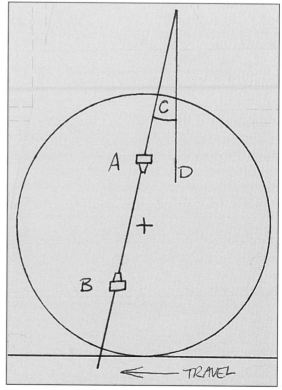

The more hi-tech your kit the more adjustable the suspension and the more important it becomes to get everything right. Here the rear suspension of a Transformer Stratos replica is being checked for its toe-in setting.

adjustable front castor angle. If you look at the front suspension from the car's side elevation, you will be able to draw an imaginary line between the top ball-joint of the upright and the bottom balljoint. (As in a Cortina or double wishbone type suspension).

Similarly, this line can be drawn between the top mount of a McPherson strut and the bottom balljoint. (As in a Mk.2 Escort and many modern car suspensions). It is very rare that the line drawn will be vertical. It is usual that the top of the McPherson strut or the top balljoint will be to the rear of the lower joint. The angle this makes with the vertical is a measure of the positive castor angle.

The bigger this angle, the more inclined the axis you will draw. In very generalised terms, a large castor angle will make for heavier steering (especially at low speed), better self-centering of the steering wheel and a more accurate feedback to the driver. You'll have a better idea of when the front wheels are about to lose grip in a corner.

A small positive castor angle could well mean light steering at all speeds, less self-centering of the steering wheel and less indication of when the front wheels are beginning to lose grip. You guessed it, lots of modern cars are aiming for the latter, leaving the sporting sector to keep alive the secret of what a car really ought to feel like.

This is why so many drivers of modern saloon cars might regard sporting kit car steering as rather vulgar, heavy and rough. It takes a while to wean yourself away from the insulated steering of the standard Cortina, Accord, Sierra or Cavalier and make full use of real feel.

Adjustments in castor angle can usually be made by altering the position of an upper or lower suspension link. For instance, the Cortina front suspension tie rods control the castor angle because they can be used to alter the fore and aft position of the lower Cortina suspension arm in relation to the upper.

Some double wishbone kits will offer castor adjustment by means of mobile upper or lower wishbone mounts or by using shims in strategic places where the wishbones pivot at the chassis. Rose-jointed wishbones might have one or two extendable legs which can be adjusted to put the outer balljoint further forwards or backwards.

Some kits or donors come with totally fixed suspension mounts, leaving no adjustment for castor or anything else except toe-in. Either way castor adjustment, if it is to be done properly, requires sophisticated measuring equipment which is sometimes available at modern tyre-fitting garages.

In some cases, a kit manufacturer can explain to the builder just how to ready-reckon the requisite castor angle without expensive equipment. Either way, a kit with adjustable castor should arrive with build manual guidelines on how to set it up initially.

If you are sending a car to be set up at a tyre centre with the appropriate equipment, make sure they can explain to you just what castor angle is and how they intend to adjust it. We have heard a catalogue

Fitting different engines will alter your car's handling and roadholding. Cobras can often be front heavy which in-turn reduces rear traction. Wheel-spin city!

On the other hand, mid-engined cars are better suited to serious acceleration thanks to better weight distribution. However, they can also feel a little jittery if not set-up perfectly.

of disaster stories relating to poor service and lack of expertise from tyre fitting companies with seemingly high-tech capabilities. You must also furnish them with your required positive castor angle measurement.

Increasing or decreasing castor angle can radically alter the roadholding ability of your car. It can improve or reduce front end grip. Treat the vehicle with care after castor adjustments have been made as it may have assumed a different personality!

If your car happens to demonstrate light steering feel when driving normally but heavy feel when manoeuvring, there may be other factors involved. Refer to Chapter Nine where we discussed wheel offset and inset.

If you have had to fit wheels with negligible positive or negative offset, steering might be heavy at low speed or at a standstill. Similarly, a large kingpin inclination might have the same effect (this axis is the same line you imagined to reveal the positive castor but this time viewed from the car's front elevation).

These won't be cured by altering castor angle but we're entering into the realms of engineering here. Normally, you won't be able to change these characteristics without altering the wheel offset/inset

or by redesigning or very accurately adjusting the front suspension.

Imprecise steering is an utter pain. It really wrecks a car's personality although it's amazing just how many production cars are designed with this inherent quality! A whole host of reasons can be put forward for this trait in some kit cars.

Crossply tyres, high profile radials, poor quality retreads and remoulds and heavy and/or large diameter spoked steel wheels can all be blamed. We have also experienced this characteristic in kits which use the Cortina front subframe and all of its rubber bushes.

The effect is nearly acceptable when using the

Cortina wheels and tyres but swap these for larger alternatives, in a kit with a different roll axis, and you can watch the whole subframe move independent of the chassis. If the mounting bushes are worn, it's terrible.

As the front wheels are turned one way or the other, the subframe shifts in that direct and the chassis follows a few moments later when the very elastic bushes have transmitted the message in their laconic way. It was a problem with our Rotrax project car. Steer your car's course well in advance to anticipate its reaction!

Luckily, many kit manufacturers recognise this problem and use the Cortina

Worn bushes or poor location of these Cortina suspension arms can cause rear-end steer. Movement of the axle when acceleration or decelerating gives the back of the car a life of its own.

subframe solid-mounted or opt out of it altogether. In other kit cars, it can be due to wear in the front suspension bush. It's difficult to check this kind of metalastic bushes as any damage might only be obvious when the thing is completely trashed.

The MoT tester should spot worn suspension bushes and the amateur might be able to spot free play in the front suspension assemblies by firmly supporting each corner off the ground and pushing or levering the suspension arms to tension the bushes. If in doubt, replace the suspect bushes, balljoints or rose joints.

If you know that all the bushes and joints are in good order, you may have been guilty of tightening some of them before the vehicle was sitting happily on its own four feet. Loosen all the mounts and re-tighten with the car at normal ride height.

Check the steering rack and all of the joints in the steering linkage right back to the steering wheel. Make sure of any related fasteners. Even a small amount of slop in universal joints can be translated into a large amount of steering vagueness. Check for perished rubber flange joints in the column assembly.

If the rack itself is suspect, there's usually little option but to get a reconditioned example.

Make sure that the track rod ends are OK before condemning the rack itself, they're a lot cheaper. Some racks are mounted on rubber or vinyl bushes. This might invite excess sideways movement if worn or underrated. You should make enquiries about quality replacements and more solid alternatives for better response.

Some lookalikes and replicas specify large diameter wheels and tyres. When you fit these to a donor suspension not specifically designed for them, vagueness can be the result. Even if a suspension assembly has been manufactured for the kit in question, it might not be ideal for the job. Again, try before you buy.

On a more pessimistic note, you should, given the unexplained occurrence of poor front end reactions, check all the relevant suspension and steering mounts, brackets, fasteners and chassis members for obvious or very subtle breaks and stress cracks.

It is possible for welded joints or steel members to crack and it is usually the highly stressed items which go first. Tie rod brackets, wishbone brackets, spring mounts etc. Some cracks are surprisingly tiny and you need to look very closely, having cleaned the assemblies thoroughly.

Rest assured that it's not as simple as all that. You can even get situations where the rear suspension components can affect the steering response. Live-axled cars are usually more guilty than front drive, IRS or DeDion cars but it is certainly relevant to make checks relating to the rear suspension joints, bushes and the effectiveness of axle location. A rear end steer effect might be just as manifest at the front end.

If, after a few thousand miles, you feel that the steering is too low or high-geared for your taste, consult the manufacturer for information about different donor steering racks that might fit. It's not simply a question of changing the diameter of the steering wheel.

If you have used a rack from a model which may have been used in track or off-road competition, there may well be a selection of steering racks available from after-market sources. It is more common for owners to be in need of a quicker or higher-geared rack, so that a smaller movement of the steering wheel has a greater steering effect.

Donors such as Mk.2 Escorts, Capris, Minis etc. will be well catered for by the after-market tuning companies. Donors that never won many notable laurels, such as the Marina, Cortina, Granada, Herald, Spitfire etc. will be more difficult to uprate. This should be a consideration when choosing a kit.

Your manufacturer might also inform you of a power steering rack if you are in need of lighter steering at slow speed and there might also be a lower-geared rack of the same dimensions if your current steering set-up is too aggressive. Don't forget the club, you won't be the first one to embark on a search for this equipment.

As ever, suspect that the use of narrow, wide, large diameter, heavy or otherwise old-fashioned wheels and tyres might produce a slow or excessively sharp steering response.

Odd steering responses under light or harsh braking can be very alarming and we have quite often driven kit and production cars which suffer

The arrows point to the locations of front suspension bushes in a standard Cortina front subframe set-up (rear top wishbone bush obscured here). Wear or inappropriate loadings can cause really erratic front suspension behaviour.

from this affliction. Your first reaction might be concern over the condition of the brakes. Front and rear brakes, if operating unevenly, can cause a steering effect when applied.

It is more probable that blame can be placed upon the drum brakes, if fitted. Most drum brakes commonly used in kit car donors (such as Beetle, Cortina, Escort Mk.2, Triumph etc.) are of an old and distinctly dubious design quality and must be in tip top condition to work anywhere near properly. Whether wear adjustment is manual or automatic, you must first check to see if operation is uniform.

Any garage set up to undertake MOT tests should be able to test all your brake assemblies for relative efficiency. If one or two assemblies are giving an unpredictable performance, then your problem may be easily solved.

Other than that, we get back to our old friends, the front suspension bushes and joints. When these get worn, braking forces can cause one or both of the front wheels to suffer from excess castor, camber or toe-in/out. Maybe a combination of these maladies. The result, apart from steering vagueness exaggerated under braking, might also be accelerated wear at the inner or outer edge of one or both front tyres. Check it all carefully.

2) Acceleration

Are there problems experienced when your car accelerates? No, we don't mean "it ain't quick enough!" A well-designed and built sporting car will be able to properly exploit the power available under foot. It will turn it into acceleration with neither drama nor crisis. Minimal wheelspin, snaking, tramping etc.

Powerful front or rear drive cars fitted with a normal differential will happily start to spin one of the powered wheels when its tyre loses grip. That loss of grip might have been caused by a poor road surface, oil, water or a small mammal getting in the way. However, it might have been triggered by wrong tyre pressures, poor springs and/or dampers, different tyre types or tread patterns on the same axle and poor suspension design etc.

Altering tyre type can help. There is a huge performance gap between the cheap and the expensive tyres available today. A high performance Yokohama A008 or AVS, Avon CR28, Pirelli P-Zero and BF Goodrich Comp T/A 2 will be a transformation compared to yer average cheapo 'Budget Plonker' radial designed for 'long life.' It's very rare for a tyre to be an excellent gripper and to last a long time. You pays yer money...

Beware of simply increasing tyre width unless those in the know claim that it is all in order. Wider tyres, if they do fit your rim width, can make for better grip and traction on the road in the dry but can also increase the tendency to aquaplane in the wet. Mud and ice are also problems for wide tyres - look at a standard Land Rover's tyres, they're pretty narrow.

If you have a few quid to spend, you might swap your differential for a limited slip version. This complex piece of kit usually costs a bomb but prevents one powered wheel from spinning away while the other one idles stationary. Both powered wheels will be forced to turn and the theory is that this shares the torque evenly between them.

There are situations in which you can do nothing to improve your vehicle's ability to accelerate smoothly. Many of the Cobra lookalikes

Below: Axle tramp in a live-axled, leaf sprung car. Axle torque reaction twists springs in acceleration and rebound causes tramp effect. Anti tramp bars are often available to counter effects.

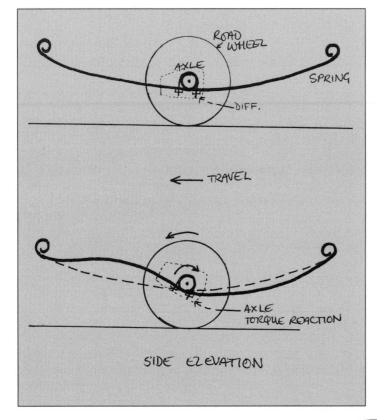

SIDE ELEVATION

Below: Transverse Watts linkage is essentially a sophisticated alternative to a Panhard rod. Very few kits use this set-up but its effectiveness is in no doubt.

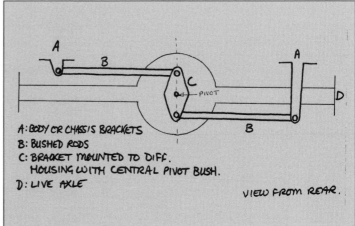

A: BODY OR CHASSIS BRACKETS
B: BUSHED RODS
C: BRACKET MOUNTED TO DIFF. HOUSING WITH CENTRAL PIVOT BUSH.
D: LIVE AXLE

VIEW FROM REAR.

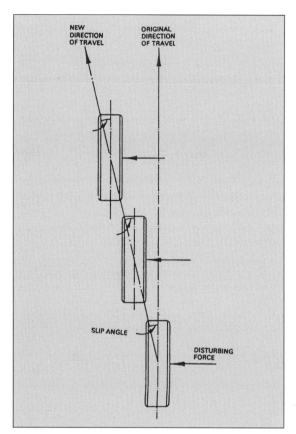

Above: A tyre, subjected to a sideways force, will deviate from its original course. Difference between actual line of travel and direction the tyre is pointing is called slip angle.

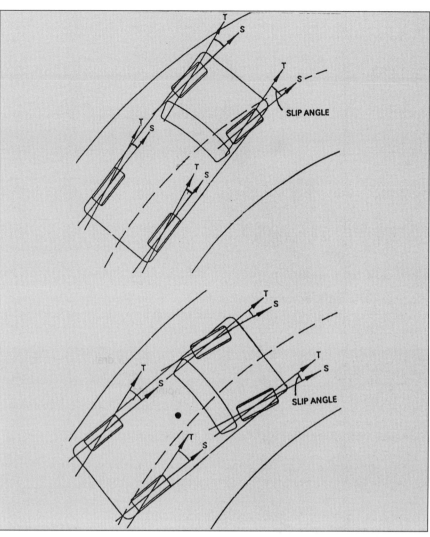

Below: Top drawing shows larger slip angle which means understeer. More 'lock' needed. Bottom picture shows larger slip angle which means oversteer. Back off steering. S is steering direction. T is actual direction of travel.

demonstrate that an excessively front-heavy weight bias will tend to permit rear wheel spin. A few slabs of concrete paving in the boot might help you to get off the mark but may well cause handling problems.

Time after time, the mid-engined format seems the best for assuring excellent traction characteristics. With the engine behind the occupants, the rearward transfer of weight during acceleration helps to keep the tyres pushed down onto the road.

Well designed front engine, rear drive cars can emulate this balance but the predominance of the mid-engined principle in all types of competition does tend to underline the system's success. Front drive generally scores the lowest marks on the traction stakes.

For rear live-axled cars with poorly located axles, acceleration can be a problem in causing tramp. A live axle is forced to rotate in a direction opposite to that of the rear wheels it is driving. If the axle locating arms or leaf springs cannot sufficiently stop the axle from reacting, it is possible to get a situation where the axle starts to twist in this opposite direction and then it twitches back into position.

This causes the vehicle to jerk backwards and forwards and to perhaps kangaroo up and down under acceleration. It will be exaggerated if the engine isn't pulling smoothly. If leaf springs are the only axle location, then you may need to fit proprietary anti-tramp bars which are quite commonly available. Stiffer or newer springs might also help.

In some cases, the manufacturer or club might offer a retro-fitted axle locating assembly with a torque tube, new radius rods, longitudinal Watts linkage(s), leading links, semi-trailing links, an A-frame or similar. It might involve some dismantling work and professional welding of brackets but it could well be worth it. A transverse Watts linkage or even a Panhard rod will also help axle location but will not prevent tramp.

3) Braking

It might not be obvious at first but one of the key factors in a car's ability to motor quickly is an ability to stop in a controlled fashion, in all weathers and in a very short distance. In mainstream magazines, the 0-60-0mph or 0-100-0mph tests are becoming more pertinent by the day.

There's no point in having a rocket of a car when you have to start braking half a mile before each corner. If you can approach a corner or obstacle at a good whack, nudge the brakes for just an instant and suddenly be down to the right speed to negotiate the turn safely, you'll spend less time braking and more time maintaining the speed you want.

Ford based kit cars are especially lucky when it comes to brake uprating. The Dax Rush, by DJ Sportscars of Harlow in Essex, uses a Cortina front upright. However, DJ offers its customers the choice of standard Cortina front discs or Granada vented front discs fitted to these uprights.

A small welding job on the

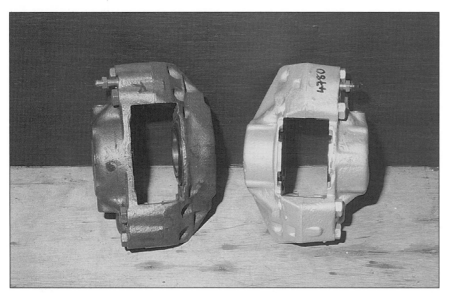

Above: Tilton pedal system with twin brake master cylinders and balance bar for adjusting front to rear brake bias. Below: Massive 4-pot caliper and vented, drilled disc.

Standard Cortina ATE front brake caliper (right) with heavy-duty alternative caliper. Below: Vacuum operated servo boosts braking power but lighter kit cars often don't need it. Follow your manufacturer's recommendations.

forged Cortina uprights and an easily explained combination of front wheel bearing components from the Cortina and Granada will allow customers to fit the Granada hub and disc, while retaining the Cortina caliper.

Kits based on the Mk.2 Escort will have a choice of after-market and Ford uprated discs and calipers which can be fitted with a minimum of fuss. Similarly, kit cars which use a donor servo might benefit from a more powerful servo from a different donor in the range.

An automatic or estate variant might yield a better servo and/or master cylinder. Vans and estates can have better braking systems all round but check with the kit manufacturer for compatibility with the kit's brake pipe and hose set. It is quite possible to go over the top on braking and end up with a nose-diving, hair-trigger monster.

When studying donor Haynes Workshop Manuals and even when working on your own cars, you may have noticed something called a brake compensator valve between the front and the rear brake circuits, usually near the rear of a production car. These are often omitted on kit cars.

In theory, they are designed to gradually reduce braking effort at the rear as the car's weight shifts forward. They usually operate in response to inertia or to the vehicle's increasingly nose-down stance. It is very important that the front wheels lock up before the rear wheels in any lock-up situation. Premature rear wheel lock-up is more likely to cause a spin.

It is more of a problem for production cars, which are generally heavier than kit cars, and are usually more front-heavy to start with and have longer suspension travel. Take advice from the kit manufacturer regarding the fitment of the brake compensator. If it is necessary, then the kit's brake pipe kit should allow for it and the kit's build manual should show how to fit it.

If you are a little more enterprising and the spare cash allows, you can fit a Tilton pendant or floor-mounted custom pedal box. This offers a choice of twin brake master cylinder sizes and adjustable front to rear brake bias. Make sure you have fully understood fitting instructions and are aware of how to adjust the front to rear brake bias. Again, a friendly MoT garage may have the brake testing equipment to help you get an exact adjustment.

Beware of high performance or competition brake parts such as drums, discs and pads. These are often designed to work well under the very high temperatures that competition engenders but they will often not work very well until they have got very hot. That means you have to drive around like Nigel Mansell before you can fully trust your brakes. The result will then be impressive but it might also be too late!

Always try to use the original equipment drums, shoes, discs and pads specified for the relevant donor parts. Some of the after-market stuff can give a very variable performance even though it looks the same. Variations in the sizes of after-market pads and shoes can make them very difficult to fit and the poorer quality items can cause perpetual brake binding when new.

Silicon brake fluid, when used in a braking system not designed specifically for it, can cause all sorts of safety compromises. Stick to the brake fluid recommended by the donor manufacturer. It may absorb water and strip paint but it is what the brake system was designed to use and, if kept in good condition, will not fade unduly.

Brake fade is usually a result of water being absorbed into normal brake fluid which has not been changed regularly or properly. The water in the fluid, adjacent to the caliper or slave pistons, boils into steam and the resultant vapour bubble

absorbs pedal pressure, preventing sufficient compression of the brake fluid to create a braking effect. It can also be caused by glazing of the brake shoe or pad friction surfaces when the material overheats and burns to a shiny finish (glazes).

If you suspect reduced braking efficiency during or after a thrash, check for fluid leaks, get the fluid changed and take a good long look at the pads and shoes. They're relatively cheap considering their importance. Remember that brake friction material often contains asbestos and the dust will be spread all over the wheels and the brake and suspension assemblies.

Wear a nose and mouth filter mask, don't get it on your skin and don't disturb the dust by brushing and blowing it all over the place. Vacuum it all up or

wash it away with a detergent solution first. Replacement pads and shoes are available without asbestos for some donor brake systems.

4) Cornering

Cornering is yet another broad-as-the-horizon subject which we don't have room to consider in too much detail here. However, there is certainly a core of common complaints about the cornering characteristics of cars. Most relevant aspects here are the much-used terms oversteer and understeer. Roll centres, pitch and polar moment of inertia are also terms which are often used to baffle others when examining a car's cornering characteristics.

We will try to explain what each of these mysteries is, how they affect your car and the general principles behind tackling such problems. We must warn you that car handling still seems to fall into a 'black art' category and that opinions vary widely on the subject.

Successful cars in many categories have shown that there is not a single 'right answer' to the problem of handling and roadholding. A car lauded by one driver for its competence could be accused by another of being a real pudding.

Most cars can be made to oversteer or understeer. These terms, however, are mostly used to describe how the car generally reacts in a normal circumstance when cornering in usual road circumstances.

Understeer happens when the slip angle of the front tyres is higher than that of the rear tyres. As the car is cornered more tightly, the front wheels will lose grip earlier than the rear wheels. This will probably mean that the car ploughs straight onwards, at a tangent to its recent course, until the driver can regain control or the car comes to a halt.

However, it will be less inclined to spin around and

modern car designers claim that an understeering car is safer as the natural 'panic' reaction to a loss of grip (foot off the accelerator pedal and maybe a shove on the brakes) is less likely to end in an out-of-control situation.

More demanding drivers tend to dislike an understeering car because when the front wheels lose grip and/or traction, there is also a loss of steering response. The driver must try to return grip to the front wheels before they can steer the car effectively again. Front drive, rear drive and four wheel drive cars can all be designed to understeer in normal circumstances.

Oversteer is when the slip angle at the rear wheels becomes greater than that at the front and the back end loses grip/traction as the car is cornered tighter or harder. This will tend to slide the back end of the car around in an arc and can end up with a spin.

The natural panic reaction of decelerating and maybe braking will increase the chances of a spin because weight is then shifted forwards and off the rear wheels, which then slide more easily.

Some drivers prefer oversteer as the front wheels tend to retain grip and allow the driver to steer if the correct techniques are followed. Careful use of the accelerator can also decide the behaviour of the rear end. Again, we find that oversteer can be invoked in all kinds of cars but it is more often associated with front-engined, rear drive cars and rear-engined cars.

Neutral steer occurs when tyre slip angle limits are reached at the front and rear at about the same time. When the limit of grip is thus reached, the car neither ploughs ahead nor does it spin. It tends to slide or skip evenly sideways, while still pointing in the right general direction. It can also be very forgiving when the driver accelerates and/or

Below: A drum brake with shoes heavily contaminated by oil or hydraulic fluid. This can be caused by a faulty pipe, joint, slave cylinder or differential oil seal. Shoes must be discarded.

brakes at the wrong moment.

If you think that your car is suffering from an early front or rear end break-away when cornering, don't necessarily jump onto the wider wheels 'n' tyres bandwagon. It might help but it might not.

Early improvements might be achieved by playing with tyre pressures in accordance with the manufacturer's instructions. Remember that high speed and long distance driving requires higher cold pressures than town driving for most (but not all) tyres.

It is possible for a car that is producing maximum grip to be a disastrous roadholder. There might be a huge imbalance between the front and rear, leading to either dramatic over or understeer on the limit. The fear of getting out of control will make you back off and the car won't be driven to the best effect.

What you need is a more neutral feel to the car, so that it becomes easier to control on the limit and won't threaten to put you in a ditch at the slightest provocation. Here's where you can see the sense in strategically increasing grip at one end of the car or losing part of the excess grip at the other end in order to balance out the remainder.

If your car normally understeers, you might want to increase grip at the front end only or even decrease grip at the rear to even things out. If the car oversteers, you might want to increase rear end grip or reduce front end grip. If the car is neutral, you might want to increase overall grip.

Improving grip at the front or rear can be done in a number of ways but remember to consult the manufacturer or other experts in the club or

race scene if you're not wholly confident in your actions. As we have said, better quality tyres on lighter wheels might help. (Alloy wheels aren't necessarily lighter than normal steel wheels so check, if you have a choice).

Wider wheels and tyres can help, if approved by the manufacturer. They may reduce grip/traction in adverse weather, creating an effect opposite to that desired. You might increase wheel diameter and use a lower profile tyre, even if the ride does become bumpier.

Reducing grip must be done with caution as you might go a bit too far and turn a slight understeerer into an awful oversteerer by mistake. Using cheaper, harder tyres (always avoid retreads, remoulds and make sure that you use new

radials with the correct speed rating for your car) can reduce grip in the dry. They might improve grip in the wet.

Narrower wheels and tyres can also strategically reduce grip at the appropriate end. It seems like an odd route to take but it can work. Look at a 911 Porsche. They are traditionally notorious oversteerers in rear-engined, rear drive format. Everyone says "look at those wide rear wheels." Not "look at those narrow front wheels!" The rears are wide for good dry weather grip but the fronts are kept narrow to improve the balance. Again, beware of speed ratings here.

Those kits with adjustable suspensions or interchangeable springs can also be tuned in the roadholding department. In general terms, stiff suspension doesn't necessarily make for

High polar moment of inertia can be desirable for a comfortable, long-distance tourer but if you want agile handling and fast line changes, concentrate vehicle weight low and towards centre.

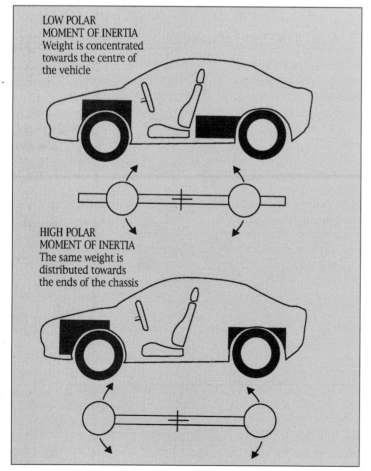

LOW POLAR MOMENT OF INERTIA
Weight is concentrated towards the centre of the vehicle

HIGH POLAR MOMENT OF INERTIA
The same weight is distributed towards the ends of the chassis

Top: Mid-engined Transformer Stratos replica – low polar moment. Below: Roll centre (D) for a McPherson strut suspension. Roll axis inclination can be altered.

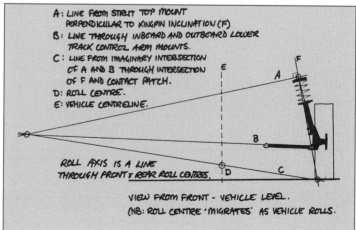

A: LINE FROM STRUT TOP MOUNT PERPENDICULAR TO KINGPIN INCLINATION (F)
B: LINE THROUGH INBOARD AND OUTBOARD LOWER TRACK CONTROL ARM MOUNTS.
C: LINE FROM IMAGINARY INTERSECTION OF A AND B THROUGH INTERSECTION OF F AND CONTACT PATCH.
D: ROLL CENTRE.
E: VEHICLE CENTRELINE.

ROLL AXIS IS A LINE THROUGH FRONT & REAR ROLL CENTRES.

VIEW FROM FRONT - VEHICLE LEVEL.
(NB: ROLL CENTRE 'MIGRATES' AS VEHICLE ROLLS.)

better roadholding on the Queen's highway. It might be OK for the circuit, where there are no bumps, but it can be a liability where there are.

If your car has adjustable spring rates, you might experiment with a slight stiffening of the rear springs and/or softening of the front springs to offset an understeer. Similarly, an oversteer might be offset by progressively softening the rear springs and/or stiffening the front.

If your car doesn't have adjustable suspension, there might be other donor springs which can be used to soften or stiffen a front or rear suspension set-up as necessary. It's a long-winded process but the parts probably won't be too expensive if they're used donor parts.

Be careful to check with the manufacturer that alternative donor parts can be fitted.

Second hand springs can be very unevenly worn, especially if they are supplied off the shelf and have come from different donors. If there's no obvious difference in the curve of leaf springs or the length/diameter of coils, it's difficult to tell if they're knackered.

If you have chosen a car with a high polar moment of inertia, you may well be wasting your time somewhat when trying to fine-tune the roadholding or cornering. This odd phrase describes the 'dumb-bell' effect of high concentrations of mass at the front and rear ends of the car.

A heavy engine mounted well up front, a heavy rear live axle, heavy wheels and tyres, a large rear fuel tank or a large rear luggage load, long bodywork overhangs beyond the front and rear axles, engine to the rear of the rear

axle, long wheelbase etc. – all of these can contribute to high polar moment.

If the mass is concentrated at the ends of the car, especially if it is uneven, it will exert a turning force on the car as the car is cornered. The front or rear end will want to swing out and this can result in wallow, slide and/or spin. Imagine a car shaped like a dumbell, with the weights at the front and rear ends.

Front engined kit cars usually have the engine and gearbox pulled well back in the chassis, sometimes creating legroom problems in a car that looks quite big. This is to help centralise the mass, especially if large and heavy engines are to be fitted. Fine weight distribution isn't the reserve of the mid-engined cars.

Chances are, there will be very little you can do to offset weight imbalance in your car.

Perhaps a lighter alloy engine, lighter wheels/tyres etc. but it probably boils down to a design fault. You might further offset the symptoms by keeping luggage in the cockpit area.

Excessive body roll (side to side) and pitch (front to rear) can be an extreme annoyance unless you like driving French cars. Body roll is intrinsically linked up with the car's front and rear roll centres and the roll axis which runs between them. The latter is the axis about which the car starts to roll when cornered.

Unfortunately, the roll centres (which tend to alter or 'migrate' as the car moves into roll) are decided by the front and rear suspension geometries and overall tyre diameters. These are generally not to be messed with apart from cases in which the manufacturer can give precise

A very generalised guide to the cures for oversteer and understeer as recommended by BF Goodrich. Adjustable suspension and springs can come in really handy. Don't increase vehicle weight to alter weight distribution.

AREA OF ADJUSTMENT		TO DECREASE UNDERSTEER	TO DECREASE OVERSTEER
TYRES	Front Inflation Pressure	Increase	Decrease*
	Rear Inflation Pressure	Decrease	Increase*
	Front Section Width	Increase	Decrease
	Rear Section Width	Decrease	Increase
WHEELS	Front Wheel Width	Wider	Narrower
	Rear Wheel Width	Narrower	Wider
ALIGNMENT SETTINGS	Front Wheel Camber	More Negative	More Positive
	Front Wheel Caster	More Positive	More Negative
	Front Wheel Toe	Toward Toe-Out	Toward Toe-In
	Rear Wheel Camber	More Positive	More Negative
	Rear Wheel Toe	Toward Toe-Out	Toward Toe-In
ANTI-ROLL BARS	Front	Soften	Stiffen
	Rear	Stiffen	Soften
SPRING RATES	Front	Soften	Stiffen
	Rear	Stiffen	Soften
WEIGHT DISTRIBUTION	Front	Decrease	Increase
	Rear	Increase	Decrease

*Never reduce below the recommended pressure, and increase in increments of 2 psi to gauge affect.

instructions. Stiffening the springs all round might help to offset the extent of the roll and you should consult the manufacturer for details of different springs.

Front to rear pitch, which can become exaggerated in a light car, can be combatted to an extent. There are complex mathematical equations relating to the polar moment etc. but bad pitching on uneven surfaces can be caused by mismatching of spring rates or settings front to rear and a low polar moment of inertia (which is helpful for handling precision). You might

experiment carefully with adjustable spring rates at front and rear.

Don't confuse normal pitch with nose dive and tail squat. Many modern production cars and some kit cars have cleverly designed suspensions which, in simple terms, use the inertia of weight shift to offset a braking nose dive or an acceleration tail squat.

If your vehicle has the correct springs and dampers, all in good order, but still nose dives too much under braking, you might be unable to alter the characteristic. Check for poor rear brakes in this

circumstance. Stiff rear springs might be exaggerating the condition.

5) Springs and dampers

At various intervals above, we have referred to the springs. They are obviously very important components in deciding your car's road manners. The most common types for kit cars are coil springs (with or without concentric hydraulic dampers), leaf springs (usually in conjunction with a rear live axle) and torsion bar springs (mounted across or along the car).

Some coil and torsion bar springs permit adjustment of the vehicle's ride height and spring stiffness. Leaf springs can be fitted with assisters and anti-tramp bars or replaced

with stiffer versions from other donors sometimes but are generally pretty user-unfriendly when it comes to alteration or adjustment.

Minis are fitted with rubber 'doughnut' springs. There is a wide selection of after-market equipment for Minis including re-rated doughnuts for a softer or harder ride. Some builders simply remove rubber to make them softer!

Dampers used in kit cars are usually the telescopic type, filed with hydraulic oil and sometimes with adjustable pressurised gas compartments as well. Some Leyland-based kits use the MG or Marina lever-arm dampers but they're quickly going out of fashion as new methods allow kit manufacturers to replace them with coil-over units or similar.

Dampers can be adjustable for bump and/or rebound resistance but those taken from donor vehicles usually are not

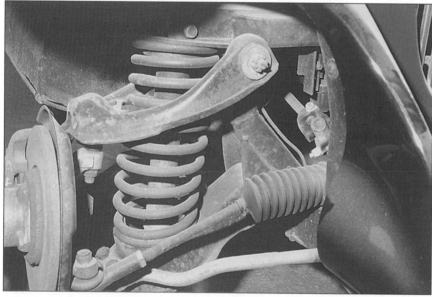

Above: Pilgrim's FT uses the Cortina rack, wishbones and tie rods but special springs and chassis mounts to replace the subframe. Below: Standard spring on Sierra McPherson strut assembly.

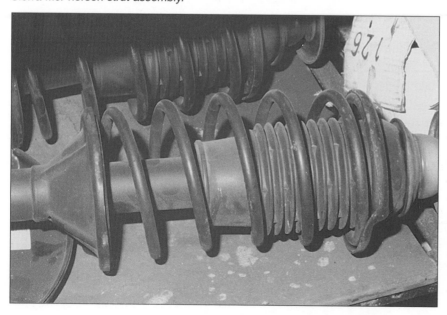

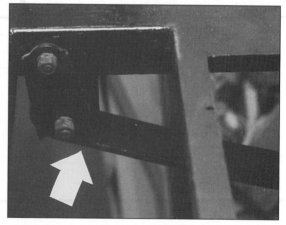

Above: Marina leaf spring mounted to Marlin Roadster chassis. Below: Marina's torsion bar and track control arm on the same kit. Some ride height adjustment here.

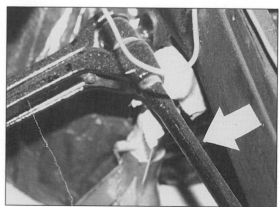

Above: Horses for courses. Dampers on this UVA Fugitive off-roader are designed to take some severe punishment. A standard road car will benefit from adjustable dampers but spring lengths are far more important to the vehicle's personality.

adjustable. If your donor vehicle has a dedicated after-market tweaking industry, then it is likely that you will be able to get a selection of whizzo springs and dampers for various purposes.

A spring is best described as a shock absorber. This is the name usually given to the hydraulic dampers but it's not quite accurate in that sense. It's the spring which absorbs the shock when a wheel is bounced upwards by a road irregularity. It turns the upwards movement back into downwards movement and returns the tyre to the ground smoothly but with as little delay as possible.

While all of this is going on, the spring is also supporting the car body/chassis up in the air. If the body is forced up or down, the spring must return it to a standard rest position

smoothly and quickly. It would be nearly true to say that the top half of a coil spring deals with the body/chassis and the lower half with the road wheel and other 'unsprung' weight which is between the spring lower mount and the road.

A damper actually resists the movement of a spring in either bump or rebound directions. If there were no dampers, the car would rock and bounce perpetually on its springs, creating a terrible nauseous effect on the occupants. Once the spring has returned the car body or wheel to the relevant position, the damper stops it from unnecessarily repeating the job. In so doing, the damper does absorb a little of the shock but only a tiny amount.

Common spring faults in kit cars more often relate to wrongly rated springs. When

donor springs are used in their entirety or in cut-down form, they can be too stiff for the lighter kit car which uses them. Some manufacturers struggled with Cortina super-tough springs before deciding to get specials made up for the job. Check carefully to see what the demo kit car is fitted with.

Leaf springs have been criticised for being too soft and for offering insufficient axle location. It is possible that you can get stiffer leaf springs by buying a brand new pair or by opting for the alternative spring from an estate, van or performance donor instead of the saloon model. The Mk.2 Escorts have shown us that a single wide leaf can be stiffer than many narrow leaves. Don't be fooled by the amount of leaves in a spring.

Torsion bar springs from a donor such as the Beetle are a

collection of thin steel bars mounted in transverse tubes at either end of the floorpan. It has been common practice for VW tuning companies to offer re-rating modifications to alter ride height and spring rate as necessary.

Round-section torsion springs, as used by the E-type and Marina front end and Renault 4/5 all round, are often splined at each end. Removing the relevant suspension arm from the splines and repositioning it can successfully alter ride height and spring rate. Threaded adjusters can also offer small variations.

Some donor models might offer narrower torsion bars than others, giving you a choice of softer or harder springing. The Marina 1300 has softer bars than the 1700 and 1800 models, for instance. If you dismantle a torsion bar donor,

Whilst hardly a common kit car, this amazing Lola T70 replica competes in the BRSCC Sports and GT Challenge against other great Cobra, GT40 and Jaguar replicas. It makes fantastic viewing even if you can't compete.

Most kit cars you can buy will be eligible for the 750 Motor Club's kit car race series. Typical entries include hordes of Sylvas. This Striker is fitted with a V8!

be sure to use the springs for the same corner of the kit as the donor. They should be 'twisted' in the same direction as they were in the donor.

If you're lucky enough to have a kit fitted with adjustable coil/over dampers, from any number of after-market producers, you will have access to a huge selection of different spring and damping rates offered by the trade - if you can afford them. The manufacturer should have supplied you the correct springs for general road use (unless you specified track or off-road) but you can negotiate different equipment if your tastes change. Few complaints come from this sector.

Springs of all types can take some time to bed into their new homes whether they are brand new or donor parts reused. If ride height seems high in a new kit car, wait for a few hundred miles before criticising the springs. If the springs do bed down, remember to loosen and retighten suspension bush bolts, with the vehicle standing unsupported on its wheels, to relieve any excess torsion that might be exerted by the new ride position.

Damping faults aren't quite so easy to pin down. Very few vehicles seem to go

bouncing up and down everywhere as the theory says they should when damping is insufficient. Pitch and roll can be exacerbated by both poor springs and dampers, let alone geometries.

Common faults are of a different nature. Simple fluid leaks are at the top of the list. When a kit has been badly designed or built, a lack of sufficient suspension bump stops or the use of the wrong donor telescopic dampers can lead to the dampers being damaged by 'bottoming out.'

The damper halves bash together at full bump or before and this causes a failure of the seals, of the damper

Autotune Gemini is another regular campaigner in the kit car race series. Its Ford base makes it cheap to maintain and light weight keeps it scrapping up the front of the grid.

mounts or a nasty cocktail of these. You usually won't spot it until a damper starts to leak or rattle loose. The opposite can happen at full droop but is much more rare. You'd probably need to get airborne a lot to bring this about.

Lever arm dampers have always been criticised for offering insufficient damping action, poor location for a suspension upright and an incredible tendency to leak prematurely. When found in kit cars, they are often supplemented or supplanted by additional telescopic dampers. They can be disabled by valve removal, filled with thick oil and used only as upright location and not as a damper.

Under-damping seems to be

more annoying than over-damping but suspension experts still argue whether suspensions should have stiff springing and light damping or soft springing and heavy damping. This is where adjustable damping comes in handy as there are many and varied handling and roadholding factors which dictate spring rates. Damping variations can be made to compensate for such alterations.

Section 2
A day at the races

APART FROM THE SHEER exhilaration of driving around in a car that you've built, knowing that it does exactly what you intended it to do, there are other ways of reaping rewards from your project. Racing of all types is very popular among kit car owners. Anything from a leisurely club Treasure Hunt, in which you could be penalised for going too fast, to full-blown track racing with the 750 Motor Club or the British Racing and Sports Car Club.

In fact, the 750 Motor Club encompasses two kit car racing series. The Kit Car Championship and the Supersports Championship.

The Kit Car Championship, encompassing various engine size classes up to 3651cc, is the cheapest to enter whereas the Supersports Championship gives you more room to modify cars and the engine size limit is higher at 4076cc. Smallest engine classes are up to 1350cc in both championships.

The various racing clubs and the RAC Motor Sports Association lay down the rules relating to driver eligibility and car specifications in terms of performance and safety. Typically, you'll need a special roll-over bar, in-car fire extinguisher, external electrical kill switch and a limited choice of tyre types and widths.

The 750 MC Kit Car Championship, for instance, also limits cars to two valves per cylinder, no injection or forced induction (turbo or supercharging), single cam per bank of cylinders, standard carbs, gearbox and

cars must be fully road legal with an MOT etc.

There are more restrictions which can be uncovered by consulting the relevant organisations at the numbers below.

Beginners will have to spend out on a medical examination and will have to pay for a competition driving test at an RACMSA approved school (about £125) which they must pass before getting a competition licence.

The 750 MC estimates that a basic car can be built for the Kit Car Championship from around £4000. Extra costs in terms of travel to each of the year's races, fuel and entry fees etc. can amount to £200 per race on average. Add to that the cost of incidental damage repairs, maintenance etc. and you could still be well within the

£10,000 barrier for the first year's racing, including the cost of the car itself.

Replica and lookalike cars can also be raced in the BRSCC's Replicar series of races, which tends to pull bigger crowds as it quite often shares a day's racing with other popular competitive series such as Thundersaloons and Formula Ford. This is predominantly the reserve of the Cobra and GT40 lookalikes, with a few D-Types and the like. Big budget, big engines and often expensive if you crash.

Contact addresses as follows:

Robin Knight,
Racing Competitions Secretary,
750 Motor Club Ltd.,
West View, New Street,
Stradbrooke,

Suffolk IP21 5JG.
Tel: 01379 384286.

RAC Motor Sports Association Ltd.,
Motor Sports House,
Riverside Park,
Colnbrook,
Slough SL3 0HG.
Tel: 01753 681736.

Julie Beard,
British Racing and Sports Car Club, Brands Hatch Circuit, Fawkham,
Longfield, Kent DA3 8NH.
Tel: 01474 874445

Section 3
Game Over!

IT SEEMS THAT MOST KIT builders take some time to perfect their creations after they have become roadworthy for the first time. You need to

So many Westfields have been produced over the years that the company started this one-make race series. It's proved extremely popular with builders, some of whom take it very seriously indeed. This car has all the spoilers to help it on its way!

cover miles to reveal any problems that you might not have been able to predict. It stands to reason that the first year of a kit car's life could be interspersed with brief off-the-road periods while the car is honed towards perfection.

Don't be disappointed if your lovingly crafted vehicle decides to shed an interior mirror or adopts an exhaust pipe rattle fairly early on. You must be prepared to sort such niggling faults as and when they make themselves known.

Improvements, as we have shown in this section, are often a lot more achievable and less ridiculous to behold in a kit car rather than a production car. Your kit car could turn into a hobby for life. Because there can be such a large DIY input in many areas, work can continue even when the budget gets a little tight.

No matter how well your first build-up goes, hardened kit car enthusiasts will often say that each subsequent build works out better than the last. Once you've finished your second car, you'll start getting pretty efficient and standards improve dramatically.

A well-built and popular kit will usually recoup your material costs if sold in good condition but some replicas and open sports kit cars can make a nice little profit.

Here at Which Kit? *we're continually surprised and pleased at the ever increasing quality we see in the industry. Driving any of the leading manufacturers' products is bound to out-do anything you've come across before.*

It's satisfying to put the effort into a car with a proper chassis, knowing that it won't rust away in the next ten years or less. No matter what happens to a non-structural body, it can be replaced time after time after time. Even easier if it's made of separate panels. A replacement chassis every decade or two won't break the bank.

In terms of ecological viability, kit cars have been criticised for re-kindling leaded petrol engines from old cars. However, as unleaded is increasingly criticised for not being as clean as we were lead to believe, this seems less pertinent.

The crucial point is that

someone who owns a car which is made from many salvaged parts, has a huge longevity and is generally not used very often, is probably a lot more environment-friendly than someone who gets a new 'recyclable lead-free' model every year or two.

It's the manufacture of new production cars which is the ecological scandal and your kit might take the place of a succession of 'second' cars which would rust to bits and get replaced every handful of years.

If you've read this manual through before embarking on a project, it may have fired your enthusiasm or it may have put you off. We aren't saying that

everyone has the ability to build a kit car. Those who do have a mechanical aptitude, though, whether they are accountants, plumbers, salespeople or retired, should find it a challenging and rewarding task.

Many of the kit builders we have talked to would probably agree that the key to success is determination fired by enthusiasm for the car. You get frustrated by some problems but a new day always brings a new perspective and there's plenty of free information to be got from fellow kit builders. If you believe that you can do it, then you probably will do it!

On a final note, we must mention that the kit car scene as a whole is particularly enjoyable and friendly, especially at the club level. Go to the club areas at the shows throughout the year and you're certain to find out something new or to help someone else by sharing ideas and workshop techniques.

There's a huge variety of people involved due to the enormous variety of kits and they will all appreciate the efforts you have put into your own creation, whatever it is. It's a rare feeling of satisfaction...

This YKC Roadster is typical of the excellent motors available today. Available with a number of different donor options, the Roadster is a top quality traditional roadster.

Many kits, such as this Tiger Super Six which was built by Which Kit?, *can offer excellent fun out on the track. This was a club organised day which proved great entertainment.*

ACCESSORY DIRECTORY

Featured here are all the accessory companies you may find of use in a typical kit car build project. There was no charge for each supplier's insertion so if anyone is missing, it's simply because we forget them or didn't know they existed! If you cannot find what you are looking for under any specific heading, please make sure you check the Miscellaneous section.

DONOR PARTS SUPPLIERS

Kit-Fit (largely Ford packages) - 01636 893453

Abbey Transmission Services (Ford axles/gearboxes) - Unit 15, Sidings Industrial Estate, Hainault Road, London E11 1HD. Tel: 0181-558 4028

Ian Harwood Ltd (Ford) - Capernhurst Lane, Whitby, Ellesmere Port, South Wirral, Cheshire L65 7AQ. Tel: 0151 339 2801

Jaguar Spares - Paxton Mill, Scaitcliffe Street, Accrington, Lancashire BB5 0RG. Tel: 01254 398476

Ford Spares - Tel: 01255 830244

Ward Engineering (Jaguar) - 23 Spencer Walk, Tilbury, Essex RM18 8EX. tel: 01375 846986

Classic Spares (Jaguar) - Unit 4, Brook Road, Brittania Road, Waltham Cross, Herts EN8 7NP. Tel: 01992 716236

ENGINE SPECIALISTS

Oselli Power (MGB & Rover V8) - Ferry Hinksey Road, Oxford OX2 0BY. Tel: 01865 791656

Repower (American V8s) - Tel: 01903 851900

Real Steel (American V8s) - Unit 9, Tomo Industrial Estate, Packet Boat Lane, Cowley, Uxbridge, Middlesex UB8 2JP. Tel: 01895 440505

RPI Engineering (Rover V8) - Wayside Garage, Holt Road, Horsford, Norwich, Norfolk NR10 3EE. Tel: 01603 891209

Vulcan Engineering (largely Ford) - 185 Uxbridge Road, Hanwell, London W7 3TH. Tel: 0181-579 3202

STAINLESS NUTS AND BOLTS

Aidpac - 38 Sabrina Road, Wightwick, Wolverhampton, West Midlands WV6 8BP. Tel: 01902 761120.

Namrick - 124 Portland Road, Hove, Sussex BN3 5QL. Tel: 011273 779864

TRIMMING SUPPLIERS (CARPET, VYNIL ETC)

DM Middleton - Rawfolds Mill, Cartwright Street, Cleckheaton BD19 5LY. Tel: 01274 871509

Woolies - Northfields Industrial Estate, Market Deeping, Peterborough PE6 8LD. Tel: 01778 347347

Creech Coachtrimming Centre - 45 Anerley Road, Crystal Palace, London SE19 2AS. Tel: 0181-659 4135

Coachtrimming Supplies - 99 Church Lane, Stechford, Birmingham B33 9EJ. Tel: 0121-784 5821

PLASTIC MOULDINGS (AIR DUCTS ETC)

Safari Supplies - 63 Rosedale Avenue, Stonehouse, Glos. GL10 2QH. Tel: 01453 825474

SHOCK ABSORBERS AND SPRINGS

Dampertech - 12 Armley Close, Long Buckby, Northants NN6 7YG. Tel: 01327 843112

PROPSHAFT MODIFICATIONS/BALANCING

Autoprop - Tel: 01342 322623

Reco-Prop - Unit 4, Newtown Trading Estate, Chase Street, Luton, Beds. Tel: 01582 412110

PLUMBING (OIL, WATER ETC)

BGC Motorsport - 23 Rork Road, Waltham Cross, Hertfordshire EN8 7HJ. Tel: 01992 787569

Pipe Lines - 27 Lon-Y-Gors, Caerphilly, Mid Glamorgan CF8 1DP. Tel: 01222 851181

WIRING

Trust Electrical - Tel: 01423 501393

Merv Plastics - 201 Station Road, Beeston, Nottingham NG9 2AB. Tel: 0115 9222783

Premier Wiring Systems - Twin-Trees Business Park, Moor Lane, Westfield, Woking GU22 9RB. Tel: 01483 715725

INSTRUMENT SPECIALISTS

ETB Instruments - The Old Forge, Watling Street East, Fosters Booth, Towcester, Northants NN12 8LB. Tel: 01327 830223

Saturn Industries - Tel: 01202 674982

EXHAUST SPECIALISTS

Mike The Pipe - 128 Stanley Park Road, Wallington, Surrey. Tel: 0181-669 1719

Custom Chrome - 17 Seymour Road, Nuneaton, Warks CV11 4JD. Tel: 01203 387808

FIBREGLASS SUPPLIERS

Glassplies - 2 Crowland Street, Southport, Lancs PR9 7RL. Tel: 01704 540626

SEAT SUPPLIERS

Cobra Seats - Unit D1 and D2, Halesfield 23, Telford TF7 4NY. Tel: 01952 684020

Corbeau Seats - Unit 17, Wainwright Close, Churchfields Industrial Estate, St Leonards-on-Sea, E. Sussex TN38 9PP. Tel: 01424 854499

WHEELS SUPPLIERS

Image Wheels - Unit 3, Fountain Industrial Estate, Fountain Lane, Tipton, West Midlands DY4 9HA. Tel: 0121-522 2442

Compomotive - Components Automotive Ltd., Units 4,5,6 Wulfrun Trading Estate, Stafford Road, Wolverhampton, West Midlands WV10 6HG. Tel: 01902 311499

Performance Wheels - Unit 1, Hatton Gardens Industrial Estate, Kington, Herefordshire HR5 3RB. Tel: 01544 231214

TSW - Tel: 01582 667788

Manx - Leisure Accessories, Brittania Works, Hurricane Way, Airport Industrial Estate, Norwich NR6 6EY. Tel: 01603 414551

Alleycat Wheels - Two Gates Precision Alloys, Parkfield Works, Two Gates, Tamworth, Staffordshire B77 1HW. Tel: 01827 286419

Cyclone Wheels - Unit 1, Davey Close, Greenstead Road, Colchester, Essex CO1 2XL. Tel: 01206 794610

MWS - 86-88 Stonebury Avenue, Off Broad Lane, Coventry CV5 7FW. Tel: 01203 463901

Davey Automotive (general supplier) - Unit 10, New Meadow Road, Lakeside, Redditch, Worcs. Tel: 01527 510483

Elite Autos (general wheel and tyre supplier) - Unit A, Suttons Business Park, 136/138 New Road, Rainham, Essex RM13 8DE. Tel: 01708 525577

Raceways (American alloys) - Museum Foyer, Donington Park Race Circuit, Castle Donington, Nr Derby DE7 5RP. Tel: 01332 812333

Racing Wheel Services - Unit L, The Enterprise Centre, 13-27 Hastings Road, Bromley, Kent BR2 8NA. Tel: 0181-462 0043

WHEEL NUTS, BOLTS & SPACERS

Select Auto Supplies - 199 Duggins Lane, Tile Hill, Coventry CV4 9GP. Tel: 01203 465845

ALLOY WHEEL REFURBISHMENT

Spit and Polish - 12B, Sovereign Way, Tonbridge, Kent TN9 IRS. Tel: 01732 367771

GENERAL SUPPLIERS WITH FULL BROCHURE

Holden Vintage & Classic Ltd - Linton Trading Estate, Bromyard, Herefordshire HR7 4QT. Tel: 01885 488000

Anthony Stafford - Unit 53, Kepler, Off Mariner, Litchfield Road Industrial Estate, Tamworth, Staffs. B79 7SF. Tel: 01827 67714

Europa Specialist Spares - Fauld Industrial Park, Tutbury, Burton-Upon-Trent, Staffordshire DE13 9HR. Tel: 01283 815609

Frost Auto Restoration Techniques - Crawford Street, Rochdale, Lancashire OL16 5NU. Tel: 01706 58619

Direct Specialist Supplies - Unit 3, 96-98 Dominion Road, Worthing, West Sussex BN14 8JP. Tel: 01903 232814

SPORTS ORIENTATED SUPPLIERS (OIL COOLERS, FANS ETC)

Merlin Motorsport - Castle Combe Circuit, Chippenham, Wilts. SN14 7EX. Tel: 01249 782101

KIT BUILD-UP SPECIALISTS

CRA Engineering - Tel: 01483 306696

Sussex Kit Cars - Chiddingly Road, Horam, East Sussex. Tel: 01435 812706.

Coventry Kit Cars - Tel: 01203 598983

MCF - Unit 8/9, Vale Park, Colomendy Industrial Estate, Denby, Clwyd LL16 5TA. Tel: 01745 822081

Westlake Engineering - Tel: 01722 73432 (Salisbury area)

Wentworth Cars - 01366 500872

INSURANCE SERVICES

Hyperformance - Garrick House, 161 High Street, Hampton Hill, Middlesex TW12 1NL. Tel: 081-979 9511

Tarnwood Insurance Services - 81 Bellegrove Road, Welling, Kent DA16 3PG. Tel: 0181-3045291

Graham Sykes Insurance - Tel: 01395 266621

Adrian Flux & Company - 124 London Road, King's Lynn, Norfolk PE30 5ES. Tel: 01553 691266

Osborne & Sons - 2 Rose Hill, Sutton, Surrey SM1 3EU. Tel: 0181 641 6633

Cheshunt Insurance - 41 High Street, Cheshunt EN8 0AQ. Tel: 01992 643225

Hill House Hammond - Tel: 01733 310899

Footman James & Co - Waterfall Lane, Cradley Heath, West Midlands B64 6PU. Tel: 0121 561 6222

Snowball Insurance - 58/60 Wetmore Road, Burton Upon Trent, Staffordshire DE14 1SN. Tel: 01283 531391

SECOND HAND KIT CAR BUYERS/SELLERS

Northwood Kitcars - 01923 823681

Terry Nightingale Autocraft (Westfield specialists) - Tel: 01799 524380

Cobalt Cars - 1 Howard Road, Reigate, Surrey RH2 7JE. Tel: 01737 222030

Fisher Sportscars - Underlyn Industrial Estate, Underlyn Lane, Marden, Kent TN12 9BQ. Tel: 01622 832977.

Hallmark Cars - Tel: 0181-597 7677

MISCELLANEOUS

Instrument refurbishement and cable modification - Speedy Cables, The Mews, St. Paul Street, Islington, London N1 7BU. Tel: 0171-226 9228

Cobra replica brightwork - Brasscraft, Farley Mount, Hogs Back, Seale, Farnham, Surrey GU10 1EU. Tel: 01252 782702

Tie wraps and general fastenings - Mr Fast'ner, Unit 6/12 Warwick House Industrial Park, Banbury Road, Southam, Warwickshire CV33 0PS. Tel: 01926 817207

General garage tools - Machine Mart. Tel: 01602 411200 for catalogue and to find nearest dealer

Rubbercoat undersealant - Carlife, Westbrook Works, 140 Thornton Road, Bradford BD1 2DX. Tel: 01943 870148

Car decals to order - Justin Pearce, 7 Hill Crest Court, Ipswitch Road, Pulham Market, Diss, Norfolk, Tel: 01379 608489 (eves)

Windscreen make-up - Triplex Replacement Services, Main Road, Queenborough, Kent ME11 5BB. Tel: 01795 663311

Appendix B
CLUB LISTING

Whilst every effort has been made to ensure that the following list is correct, secretarial positions within clubs have a habit of changing. If you cannot get hold of any club listed here then contact the *Which Kit?* offices for an updated address/telephone number.

MARQUE CLUBS

AF SPORTS OWNERS CLUB - Les Atkins, 192 Grange Road, Coventry CV6 6DA. Tel:01203 362175

ARISTOCAT REGISTER - Dave Edwards, 80 The Street, Manuden, Bishops Stortford, Herts. Tel: 01279 816536

ASHLEY REGISTER - 18 Church Road, Hilton, Blandford Forum, Dorset DT11 0DD. Tel: 01258 881051

BEAUFORD OWNERS CLUB - Mary Keeble, 11 Carey Close, Nine Elms, Swindon SN5 9XD. Tel: 01973 874684

BERKLEY ENTHUSIASTS CLUB - 27 Villa Close, Bulkington, Warks CV21 9NE.

BOND OWNERS CLUB - 42 Beaufort Avenue, Hodge Hill, Birmingham B34 6AE. Tel: 0121 784 4626

BUCKLER CAR REGISTER - John Orpin, 16 Bull Stag Green, Hatfield, Herts AL9 5DE.

BURLINGTON OWNERS CLUB - George Reed, 51 Telfer Road, Radford, Coventry, CV6 3DG. Tel: 01203 597111

CARLTON OWNERS CLUB - Mervyn Butler, 39 Moodycroft Road, Kitts Green, Birmingham B33 0AB. Tel: 0121 2438482

CALVEY MITCHEL OWNERS CLUB - Martin Scott, 7 Hazelwood, Benfleet, Essex SS7 4NW. Tel: 01268 750665

CARISMA OWNERS CLUB - Ted Legg, 11 Olden Mead, Letchworth, herts SG6 2SP. Tel: 01462 673202

CHALLENGER OWNERS CLUB - No current address

CLAN OWNERS CLUB - 48 Valley Road, Littleover, Derby DE23 6HS. Tel: 01332 767410

CLUB DUTTON - Chris Eager, 36 Wheatcroft, Wick, Littlehampton, West Sussex BN17 7NY

CLUB MARCOS INTERNATIONAL - Isobel Chivers, The Spinney, Littleworth Lane, Whitley, Melksham, Wilts SN12 8RE. Tel: 01225 707815

CLUB NOVA & AVANTE - Adrian Heath, 49 Derby Street, Burton on Trent, Staffs DE14 2LD. Tel: 01283 542097

CLUB ROTRAX - John Harding, 14 Chestnut Road, Sutton Benger, Chippenham, Wilts SN15 4RP. Tel: 01249 720494

COBRA REPLICA OWNERS CLUB - Carolyn Hobbs, 8 Ingram Close Horsham, West Sussex. Tel: 01403 255525

COBRA REPLICA OWNERS CLUB (West Midlands) - Martin Beechey, No 1 Aldersey Road, Worcester WR5 3BG. Tel: 01905 353654

COBRA REPLICA OWNERS CLUB (Northern) - Howard Holmes, Tiger Tops, Granny Wood, Hebden Bridge, West Yorks HX7 6DP Tel: 01422 844010

CONTEMPORARY COBRA & DAYTONA COUPE OWNERS CLUB - Steve Bloor Tel: 0171 723 9768

COUNTACH REPLICA OWNERS CLUB - Robert Scott, 15 Vermont Grove, Anchorsholme, Blackpool, Lancs FY5 3RL. Tel: 01253 867027

COVIN OWNERS CLUB - Glenn Kennedy, 2 Oak Farm Close, Frogmore Camberley, Surrey GU17 0JU. Tel: 01252 870766

NEW DARIAN REGISTER - 4 Browns Lane, Uckfield, East Sussex TN22 1RS. Tel: 01825 763638

DASH SPORTSCAR CLUB - P.Barnes, 22 Agincourt Street, Heywood, Lancs OL10 3EY. Tel: 01706 624504

DAVRIAN REGISTER - 11-13 Gloucester Place, Briston, Melton Constable, Norfolk NR24 2LD. Tel: 01263 860525

DAX TOJEIRO COBRA OWNERS CLUB - 40B Holland Road, London W14 8BB Tel: 0171 912 1135

DOMINO CAR CLUB - Mark West, Porch Farm Cottage, Village Road, Coleshill, Bucks HP7 0LG

DUNSMORE OWNERS CLUB - B.B.Wylam, Welcome Bank, Stratford on Avon CV37 0QE

DUTTON OWNERS CLUB - Amber Upton, 2 Rynal Street, Evesham, Worcs WR11 4QA. Tel: 01386 442100

EAGLE OWNERS CLUB - Kerry & Lex Lockyer, 83 Old Bridge Road, Whitstable, Kent CT5 1RB

ELVA OWNERS CLUB - 8 Liverpool Terrace, Worthing, West Sussex BN11 1TA. Tel: 01903 823710

FALCON DRIVERS REGISTER - Russell James, Midtown of Hatton, Aberdeen AB42 7RG. Tel: Hatton 615

FAIRTHORPE SPORTS CAR CLUB - Tony Hill, 9 Lyndhurst Crescent, Hillington, Middlesex UB10 9EF. Tel: 01895 256799

FUGITIVE OWNERS CLUB - John Dingley, 357 Classmont Road, Morriston, Swansea, West Glamorgan SA6 6BU

GARDNER DOUGLAS REGISTER - Byron Richards, Hollytree House, Main Street, Leire, Lutterworth, Leics. Tel: 01455 202659

GCS OWNERS CLUB - Julie Brown, 24 Constitution Hill, Snodland, Kent ME6 5DH. Tel: 01634 244212

GEMINI OWNERS CLUB - Richard Adams, 4 Edgehill Road, Lighthorne Heath, Leamington Spa, Warwicks. Tel: 01926 311711

GENTRY REGISTER - Frank Tuck, 1 Kinross Avenue, South Ascot, Berks SL5 9EP. Tel: 01344 24637

GINETTA OWNERS CLUB - Roger Bryson, 1 Furze Avenue, St. Albans, Herts AL4 9NQ

GILBERN OWNERS CLUB - Nick Vandervell, 18 St. Georges Road, Twickenham, Middlesex TW11 1QR. Tel: 0181 892 4810

GRIFFON REGISTER - 37 Woodside Crescent, Cottingley, Bingley, West Yorks BD16 1RE

GT40 REPLICA CLUB - Tim Martin, 39 Church Meadow, Long Ditton, Surrey KT6 5EP. Tel: 0181 398 3567

GTD 40 OWNERS CAR CLUB - Alan Barlow, 123 Stoneleigh Park Road, Ewell, Surrey KT19 0RF. Tel: 0181 224 2955

GTM OWNERS CLUB - Liz Maddison, 43 Main Street, North Auston, Sheffield, S31 7BD. Tel: 01909 550007

HAWK 289 OWNERS CLUB - Frank Allen, End Cottage, Frampton End Road, Frampton Cotterell, Bristol BS17 2JY. Tel: 01454 774208

JAGO OWNERS CLUB - Derek Roberts, 6 Cornwall Court, Cornwall Road, Uxbridge, Middlesex UB8 1BD. Tel: 01895 265102

JBA OWNERS CLUB - Les Fragle, 16 Blackthorn Close, Newton-with-Scales, Preston, Lancs PR4 3TU

JZR PILOTS ASSOCIATION - Edgar Lowe, 130 Barrows Hill Lane, Westwood, Notts NG16 5HJ. Tel: 01773 810572

KARMA OWNERS CLUB - Richard Mugeridge, 4 Dotterel Close, Chatham, Kent ME5 8NA. Tel: 01634 864809

KOUGAR OWNERS CLUB - Brian Shrimpton, 5 Wraylands Drive, Reigate, Surrey. Tel: 01737 246720

LISTAIR OWNERS CLUB - John Ravenhall, 6 Sheepy Road, Atherstone, Warks CV9 1HJ. Tel: 01827 712382

LOCUST OWNERS CLUB - Peter Lathrope, 26 Longfellow Road, Gillingham, Kent ME7 5QG. Tel: 01634 573092

LOMAX REGISTER - Peter Chitty, 8 Forest End, Courtmoor, Fleet, Hants GU13 9XE. Tel: 01252 620128

LOTUS SEVEN CLUB - Roger Swift, Lawn Bank House, Wychnor, Burton on Trent, Staffs DE13 8BY. Tel: 01283 791034

MAGIC OWNERS CLUB - Gill McKenna, 11 Ullswater Avenue, Cove, Farnborough, Hants GU14 0JR. Tel: 01252 546230

MAGENTA KIT CAR CLUB - Martin Stabler, 26 Grantham Green, Easterside, Middlesbrough TS4 3QS. Tel: 01642 815060

MARLIN OWNERS CLUB - Jan Neeld, Swedish Bungalow, School Road, Wheaton Aston, Stafford ST19 9NH. Tel: 01785 841439

MARCOS OWNERS CLUB - Colin Feyerabend, 62 Culverley Road, Catford, London SE6

McCOY OWNERS CLUB - George Hartnup, Catcune House, Gorebridge, Mid Lothian EH23 4QF

MERLIN OWNERS CLUB - Jenny Farman, Ash Grove, Wheaton Aston, Staffs ST19 9PJ. Tel: 01785 840284

MIDAS OWNERS CLUB - Peter Hills, 2 Voss Park Drive, Llantwit Major, South Glamorgan CF6 9YD. Tel: 01446 796959

MIDGE OWNERS & BUILDERS CLUB - No current address

MINI MARCOS OWNERS CLUB - Roger Garland, 28 Meadow Road, Worcester WR3 7PP. Tel: 01905 58533

MIDTEC OWNERS CLUB - Terry Morgan, 22 Grenville Court, Silverdale Road, Southampton, Hants SO15 2TD. Tel: 01703 323256

MIRAGE OWNERS CLUB - Bill Glazier, 78 Ockley Road, Croydon, Surrey CR03DQ. Tel: 0181 683 4980

MONGRELS KIT CAR CLUB - 19 Honeyholes Lane, Dunholme, Lincoln LN2 3SH. Tel: 01673 860348

MOSS OWNERS CLUB - Steve Tarbutt, 89 London Road, South Merstham, Surrey RH1 3AX. Tel: 01737 645165

M6GTR OWNERS CLUB - John Dunlevy, 18 Olde Farm Green, Blackwater, Camberley, Surrey GU17 0DU. Tel: 01252 878316

NELSON OWNERS CLUB - John Scottorn, 8 Park Corner, Nr. Nettlebed, Oxon RG9 6DT. Tel: 01491 641889

NG OWNERS CLUB - Bob Preece, 41 Gayfere Road, Stoneleigh, Epsom, Surrey KT17 2JY. Tel: 0181 393 4661

NOMAD OWNERS CLUB - Alan Barraclough, 8 Ashfield Road, hemsworth, West Yorks. Tel: 01977 616970

OGLE REGISTER - 108 Potters Lane, Burgess Hill, West Sussex RH15 9JN. Tel: 01444 248439

ONYX OWNERS CLUB - Tony Handley, 149 Wakehurst Road, London SW11 6BW. Tel: 0171 223 0135

PILGRIM OWNERS CLUB - Graham Waterworth, 21 Fieldway Close, Rodley, Leeds LS13 1EG. Tel: 01132 559848

QUANTUM OWNERS CLUB - Les Patterson, 33-35 Ashtree Road, Mixenden, Halifax HX2 8RT. Tel: 01422 249371

RICKMAN CARS OWNERS CLUB - Alan Burgess, 10 Stoney Way, Tetney, Lincs DN36 5PG. Tel: 01472 816471

ROBIN HOOD OWNERS CLUB & REGISTER - John Trickett, 2 Linden Grove, Gedling, Nottingham NG4 2QU. Tel: 0115 9526 533

ROCHDALE OWNERS CLUB - Alaric Spendlove, 7 Whitleigh Avenue, Crownhill, Plymouth PL5 3BQ. Tel: 01752 791409

RONART DRIVERS CLUB - Mike Kanter, 36 Foule Park, Basingstoke, Hants RG21 3HD. Tel: 01256 21549

ROYALE OWNERS CLUB - Paul Treloggan, 20 Windborough Road, Carshalton, Surrey SM5 4QJ

SCAMP OWNERS CLUB - Debbie Williams, 8 Bustlers Rise, Duxford, Cambridgeshire CB2 4QU. Tel: 01223 834722

SEBRING OWNERS CLUB - Terry Summers, 24 Mount Way, Chepstow, Monmouthshire NP6 5NF. Tel: 01291 625712

SPARTAN OWNERS CLUB - Steve Andrews, 28 Ashford Drive, Ravenshead, Nottingham NG15 9DE. Tel: 01623 793742

SPEEDSTER OWNERS CLUB - Vernon Mortimer, Netherdale Lodge, Bridgwater Road, Sidcot, Winscombe, Avon BS25 1NH. Tel: 01934 843007

SPIRIT OWNERS CLUB - Philip Loughlin, 142 New Road, Hethersett, Norwich, Norfolk NR9 3HG

SPYDER REPLICA CLUB - Peter Elliot, 42 Fairholme Road, Withington, Manchester M20 9SB. Tel: 0161 434 8154

STARCRAFT OWNERS CLUB - Dave James, 31 Patrick Road, West Bridgford, Nottingham NG2 7QE

STRATOS REPLICA CLUB - Bob Sharp, 31 Craigfern Driver, Blanefield, Glasgow G63 9DP. Tel: 01360 770431

SYLVA REGISTER - Jeremy Green, 115 Albert Drive, Sheerwater, Woking, Surrey. Tel: 01932 341464

TEAL OWNERS CLUB - Mike Birch, Cromer Mill, Cromer, Nr. Walkern, Stevenage, Herts SG2 7QE. Tel: 01763 281412

TEMPEST REGISTER - John Box, The Stables, Thornleigh Drive, Burton in Kendal, Carnforth, Lancs LA6 1NQ. Tel: 01524 781841

TIGER OWNERS CLUB - Colin Lloyd, 171 St. Andrews Road, Coulsdon
Surrey CR5 3HN. Tel: 0181-668 4336

TRIAD OWNERS CLUB - Alan Dee, 100 Curborough Road, Lichfield, Staffs WS13 7NR. Tel: 01543 416107

TRIUMPH SPORTS SIX CLUB - Trudi Squibbs, Main Street, Lubenham, Market Harborough, Leicester LE16 9TF. Tel: 01858 434424

ULTIMA OWNERS CLUB - Barry Edge, 12 Eastwood Avenue, Burntwood, Staffs WS7 8DX. Tel: 01543 671767

UVA FUGITIVE OWNERS CLUB - John Dingley, 357 Clasemount Road, Morriston, Swansea, West Glamorgan SA6 6BU

VINCENT REGISTER - B.R.Craft, 70 Pauls Croft, Crickdale, Wilts SN3 6AL. Tel: 01793 750529

WESTFIELD SPORTS CAR CLUB - Mark Stanton, 102 Broadmoor Avenue, Smethwick, Warley, West Midlands B67 6JU.

WILDCAT OWNERS CLUB - Stuart Barnett, Old Church House, Lower Beedings, Horsham, West Sussex RH13 6NQ. Tel: 01403 891320

AREA CLUBS

BRISTOL CLASSIC, SPORTS & KIT CAR CLUB - Graham Best, 12 Hortham Lane, Almondsbury, Bristol BS12 4JH

CLEVELAND KIT CAR & SPECIALS OWNERS CLUB - John Reece, 8 Greta Road, Redcar, Cleveland. Tel: 01642 485366

GRIMSBY KIT CAR CLUB - 89 Springfield Road, Grimsby, South Humberside DN33 3LG

HANTS & BERKS KIT CAR CLUB - Colin Jones, 3 Hillside Cottages, Frogmore, Camberley, Surrey

HERTS AND BEDS ALTERNATIVE CAR CLUB - T. Alvis, 21 Caslon Way, Letchworth, Herts SG6 4QJ. Tel: 01462 675092

KENT KIT CAR CLUB - Mac Allardyce, 9 Quested Way, Harrietsham, Maidstone, Kent ME17 1JG. Tel: 01622 859449

NORTH EAST KIT CAR CLUB - Nigel Heighton, 49 Moss Crescent, Ryton, Tyne & Wear NE40 4XL. Tel: 0191 413 5533

NORTH WEST KIT CAR CLUB - Paul Crane, 17 Yarncroft, Tyldesley, Manchester M29 7PL. Tel: 01942 875166

NOTTINGHAMSHIRE KIT CAR CLUB - Steve Marley, 20 Homefield Avenue, Arnold, Nottingham NG5 8GA. Tel: 01602 264178

SCOTTISH KIT CAR CLUB - Julie Tooley, Candleford House, Auchtertool, Fife KY2 5XH

SOUTH EAST FISHER/SYLVA REGISTER - Mac Allardyce, 9 Quested Way, Harrietsham, Maidstone, Kent ME17 1JG. Tel: 01622 859449

SOUTH WALES KIT CAR CLUB - Tom James, 39 Rutland Close, Highlight Park, Barry, South Glamorgan GF62 8AR. Tel: 01446 741985

SUFFOLK COASTAL KIT CAR CLUB - Tony Gould, 7 Harkstead Lane, Woolverstone, Ipswich, Suffolk IP9 1BB. Tel: 01473 780777

SUSSEX KIT CAR CLUB - Dave Bray, Chiddingly Road, Horam, Nr. Heathfield, East Sussex TN21 0JJ. Tel: 01435 812706

ULSTER KIT CAR CLUB - Stephen Traynor, 26 Sandyknowles Crescent, Glengormley, Co. Antrim BT36 8DJ. Tel: 01232 833686

WESSEX KIT CAR CLUB - John Hammond, 10 Redwood Drive, Ferndown, Wimborne, Dorset BH22 9UH. Tel: 01202 892328

WEST CUMBRIA KIT CAR CLUB - B.Killen, 5 Millers Walk, Cleator, Cumbria CA23 3AD

YORKSHIRE ALTERNATIVE CAR CLUB - Colin Tait, 24 Pinfold Lane, Methley, Leeds LS26 9AB. Tel: 01977 515360

GENERAL CLUBS

2CVGB - David Tilbey, 8 Pembroke Close, Sunninghill, Ascot, Berks SL5 0AB. Tel: 0860 106907

750 MOTOR CLUB - Robin Knight Tel: 01379 384268

BATTERY VEHICLE SOCIETY - 3 Blandford St Mary, Nr. Blandford Forum, Dorset DT11 9LH. Tel: 01258 455470

CITROEN SPECIALS CLUB - Carole Chitty, 8 Forest End, Courtmoor, fleet, Hants GU13 9XE. Tel: 01252 620128

CLASSIC CROSSBRED CLUB - Paul Robins, 43 Marischal Road, Lewisham, London SE13 5LE

ENTHUSIASTS KIT CAR CLUB - K.Dodd, 26 Boulsey Rise, Ottershaw, Chertsey, Surrey KT16 0JX

FEDERATION OF KIT CAR CLUBS - Dave James, 31 Patrick Road, West Bridgford, Nottingham NG2 7QE

MARCHES KIT CAR CLUB - Simon Dewe, The Black Swan, Much Dewchurch, Hereford HR2 8DJ. Tel: 01981 540295

NATIONAL BUGGY REGISTER - Mark Haynes, 26 Birkdale Drive, Alwoodley, Leeds LS17 7SZ. Tel: 01132 684310

POTTERIES KIT CAR CLUB - Jonathan Kimberley, 5 Stanfield Road, Burslem, Stoke on Trent, Staffs ST6 1AT. Tel: 01782 827593S